D0889909

Perspectives

"Light emerged from darkness in Genesis, in the creation of the heavens and the earth. Light also emerged from darkness in the life of Sandy Greenberg. This memoir reveals a triumph of the human spirit. It is the story of a man brought from blindness to richness, from darkness to light, through his passion and his accomplishments, and from a deep commitment from those who loved him. This book renews life in us all."

—RICHARD AXEL, 2004 Nobel Laureate in Physiology or Medicine

"Sandy plays the hand he got and tries to make the world a better place. He has aspirations and hope. Sandy is a role model for all of us."

—MICHAEL BLOOMBERG

"When blindness is vanquished, and it will be, we will have Sandy Greenberg and his story to thank."

—SENATOR CHRIS COONS

"There is no greater measure of character than viewing one's personal setbacks as a call to serve others. Sandy and Sue soared above their personal challenges and dedicated their lives to making a positive change in the world. We're confident that this magnificent book will be one of the most inspirational you will ever read."

—ELIZABETH AND BOB DOLE

"An inspirational story of resilience, determination, achievement and, mostly, of the power of friendship and love. I could not stop reading this extraordinary book about an extraordinary journey."

—SUSAN GOLDBERG, Editor-in-Chief, *National Geographic*

"An inspiring must-read for anyone facing challenges in life, as a guide to beating the odds and making your impact on the world."

—VICE PRESIDENT AL GORE

"A majestic book, authored by the most 'haimish' of men. This should be required reading for every young person with a dream of helping their community."

—SENATOR RON WYDEN

Hello Darkness, My Old Friend

Sanford Greenberg's allegory, Education Embraced by the Human Spirit, is the story of his perpetual heroism. —**FRANK STELLA**

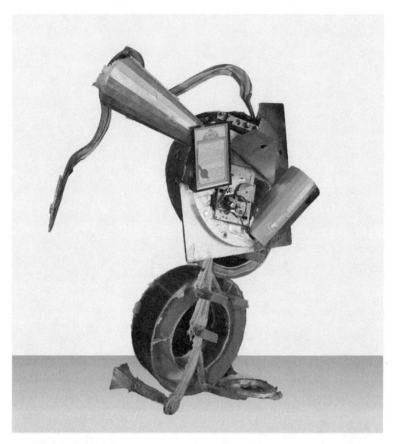

FRANK STELLA's sculpture incorporating the compressed speech machine Sandy Greenberg invented and patented in 1969. Through the use of compressed-speech technology, the human ear can now absorb as much information as the human eye has for millennia. The technology eliminates random bits of recorded information in order to speed up transmission.

Hello Darkness, My Old Friend

How Daring Dreams and Unyielding
Friendship Turned One Man's Blindness
into an Extraordinary Vision for Life

SANFORD D. GREENBERG

Post Hill Press
New York • Nashville
posthillpress.com

Published in the United States of America
Distributed by Simon and Schuster

For Sue, the one who has always been there

Contents

Had I the heavens' embroidered cloths,
Enwrought with golden and silver light,
The blue and the dim and the dark cloths
Of night and light and the half-light,
I would spread the cloths under your feet:
But I, being poor, have only my dreams;
I have spread my dreams under your feet;
Tread softly because you tread on my dreams.

—WILLIAM BUTLER YEATS

Foreword

Supreme Court of the United States
Washington, DC

A few days after the 2010–2011 Court term ended, my good neighbor at Watergate South, Sandy Greenberg, visited me in chambers. He had done so the year before, just to see how I was faring at work after the death of my husband. He is that kind of caring man. But this time he came to convey a request. Sandy had composed a volume reflecting on his life's extraordinary course. He asked if I would read the manuscript and perhaps write a brief foreword. I spent every spare hour the next week reading Sandy's remembrances. Often his memories brought smiles; other times they left me near to tears. From the first page to the last, I was captivated by his bright mind, ready wit, and indomitable spirit.

A snapshot of Sandy in 1958 at age seventeen: brainy, athletic, president of his Buffalo, New York, high-school senior class and of the school's student council, trumpet player, a tall and all-around good fellow. That year, he entered Columbia College on full scholarship. There he thrived on learning, made lasting friendships, and experienced the city's many wonders. In steady correspondence, he described his adventures to the love of his life since sixth grade, Sue Roseno, his beloved wife and soul mate now for a half century.

At age nineteen, midway through his third year at Columbia, Sandy became blind. Initial despair over his total loss of sight gave way, in small time, to a fierce determination not to be seen, or to live his life, as a blind man. He played the part well. Sandy would have no dog, or even a cane. "If you were to see me in the hallway of the Watergate," he observed, "you would not know I am blind." Quite so. I had been told, when we bought an apartment at the Watergate in 1980, two doors up from Sandy and Sue's, that his vision was poor. He could see shapes but not faces; he wore thick glasses to magnify things. I believed what I was told.

A half-dozen years passed before I learned the harsh truth. In 1986, I heard Sandy say to a throng of well-wishers: "I am blind." The occasion was his induction as a Fellow of Brandeis University at a celebration in DC.[1] Sandy could, at last, publicly acknowledge his blindness, for he had proved, time and again, that he had developed "other ways to see the world." Ideas and images generated in his mind sparked inventions—prime among them, a speech-compression machine that speeds up the reproduction of words from recordings without garbling any sounds. His agile mind also planned a succession of well-designed, impressively profitable business enterprises.

Sandy's reflections have a main theme. Though robbed of his sight (owing to the repeated misdiagnosis of an ophthalmologist in his hometown), he considers himself "the luckiest man

---

[1] In his remarks that evening, Sandy spoke of the inspiration he drew from Louis Dembitz Brandeis, whose eyesight dimmed during his student days at Harvard Law School. To cope with the problem, Brandeis enlisted fellow students to read to him. He trained his memory as he absorbed the readings. And when his sight improved, he took care to pace himself, endeavoring to "read less and think more."

in the world." How can that be, the reader, early on, is likely to ask. Sandy writes of his handholds: his family, heritage, friends, education at Columbia, Harvard, and Oxford; his White House Fellowship, which fostered collegial relationships with persons of importance in government, commerce, and the arts; his service on the National Science Board and numerous other governing bodies; his three children and now four grandchildren; and, above all else, his partnership in life with Sue, whose love and support sustain him in all things.

Yet something more, he relates, accounts for his good life, something sighted people cannot possess with the same intensity. Sandy calls it his "informed life within the mind," a mind in which thoughts proliferate and assemble "undisturbed by the constant flow of visual sense images." That special facility has helped him to experience the joys of being alive and to contribute abundantly to the well-being of others.

From a hospital bed in Detroit in February 1961, his sightless eyes moist with medication, Sanford D. Greenberg "made a deal with God." If the Lord got him "out of this hole," Sandy vowed, he would do all he could "to prevent others from going through grief like this in the future." He has carried through on that promise, directing prodigious energy to the development of technology for optic-nerve regeneration. To the same end, his steady hand is at the helm of the Johns Hopkins Wilmer Eye Institute. These endeavors and multiple other pro bono initiatives are cause for the "Big Party" Sandy hosts in a *dreamspiel* he imagines and records with élan in a chapter of this book.

Sandy will play the fine trumpet Sue gave him, and his Columbia College classmate and lifelong buddy Arthur Garfunkel will sing. An ancient Greek chorus will chant and carry on. Everybody who is anybody will be there, including saints, sinners, and lawgivers, scientists and statesmen, philosophers and artists, entertainers and captains of commerce. My husband and I, careful readers will note, are enjoying the party. In my own extension of Sandy's dream, I have my choice of people to toast: Eleanor Roosevelt, George Gershwin, Ella Fitzgerald, and other favorites by the score. Bypassing the luminaries in the huge room, I raise my glass to Sanford D. Greenberg, who chose life in all its vibrancy. *L'chaim*, Sandy, to you and to Sue. You have presented a spectacular show. May there be encores galore.

—*Justice Ruth Bader Ginsburg*

Introduction

Even this we will be pleased to recall—all God's gifts of life, shining from birth to death. *Chai*—to life! To all of it. To blindness and exaltation.

I knew him first on the steps of Hamilton Hall. We were coming out of our humanities class at Columbia College. It was 1959. I had seen him playing basketball that year—a powerful center, a bull. Now coming out of Professor Goethal's class, the powerful man was beside me, shoulder to shoulder, six feet two. I felt his duality, tender and mighty. He spoke with a gentle resonance. We had just been stirred by Achilles, star of *The Iliad*. Could such *arête*, such heroic dimension, relate to our future? He loved that I treated *all* of life as precious. I stopped to glory in the beauty of light as it lit up a patch of green, green grass. The nation wasn't funky yet. Punk had not been born. It was love of the moment to moment. We were Appreciators. Destiny sketched, character exchanged, we cast our fate as roommates.

This was our town, this friendship of ours. We are the ones who can't look at everything hard enough. What is it all but luminous? In tiniest increments, in our junior year, glaucoma set in. So I read to him. It was the natural thing to do. Follow the heart through even this. Tears blur the vision, sweet indecision to be or curl up back in the womb. We had our room, "four-o-six," we prayed at the window, your hair was shiny brown.

To slip from the shore and swim in the widening stream of our history once more starlit in the mystery of the mutual love we store against the night...

The man behind the pen who writes this book is a Man. I was so deeply touched to read Sandy's treatment of me in this magnificent book. I blush to find myself within his dimension. My friend is my gold standard of decency. I try to be his cantor, the *tallis* that embraces him.

—*Art Garfunkel*

PART 1

Day
& Night

1

Stranger on a Train

I boarded the train and put my suitcase in front of me. It was freezing in the city. I felt cold air wafting into the car like a ghostly presence and pulled my jacket tight around myself. A horn blew, and the train pulled out smoothly, as if on air. It would be an eight-hour ride from New York north to Albany, then west to Syracuse and Rochester, and finally on to Buffalo at the eastern end of Lake Erie.

My mind turned in on itself. A door had closed between my present and my future—a future that until recently had been laid out rather clearly. It was still daytime, but for me it was actually dark, my vision visited by clouds and what looked like swirling snow. This was deeply troubling: my vision still had not come back to normal, as it had done fairly promptly in the past months. I held the suitcase up in front of me like a shield. I used to scoop my little sister into that suitcase. Silently, I began to cry.

A man came up and asked if he might take the seat facing me, although the car was nearly empty. I wanted to say no, but I said yes. I had been brought up to be polite to my elders, and I could tell from his voice that he was perhaps twenty or thirty years older than I. He sat down and let out a sigh and began fiddling with his things. After a while, he asked why I was crying.

"It's nothing," I said.

"Is there anything I can do?" he asked.

"No, sir."

"I'm a doctor," he said. "Are you ill?"

"No. Well. I mean, sort of."

"I'm an orthopedic surgeon. I was in the city for a convention."

"Oh, it's just a problem with my eyes. An allergy."

"Ah. Well, I did notice they were a little runny. Teary."

Embarrassed and a little alarmed, I wiped at my eyes.

"This convention," the doctor continued, "you've never seen so many bone guys in one place. Orthopedic doctors have a bad reputation. They say we're butchers. But that's not it at all. Yes, some of it is blunt work. But with technology, it's becoming more delicate. It's not just fixing broken bones, you know."

I did not want to ask him if he knew anything about fixing broken eyes—in fact, I did not believe my eyes were broken. But they were obviously in some real peril. (In fact, they were dying.)

He went on. "My wife doesn't like it when I leave. She gets terribly worried."

I nodded. "Yeah."

"You have a girlfriend?"

"Yes."

"What's her name?"

"Sue."

"That's a nice name. Does she live in Buffalo or New York City?"

"She lives in Buffalo. With her parents."

"Is she in school?"

"Yes."

"That's nice. It must be hard, though, to be away from your sweetie."

I thought of all the letters we had written to each other. "Yes," I said, "it is hard."

"Are you sure you're all right? Your eyes look red, a little swollen." I sensed the doctor moving in closer to examine my face. I felt ugly and ashamed. Without thinking, I pushed my suitcase out with a knee to put more distance between us.

The train was now going through the countryside up along the Hudson River toward Albany. We were outside of time. The country air would have been refreshing, but the windows were closed. The land, what I could see of it, was mottled with snow and seemed to stretch forever.

The doctor took out a sandwich: peanut butter and jelly. A small carton of whole milk. A sugar cookie. I smelled all these things, and even though I was still confident that my problem would be fixed, I wondered anyway if I would become a better smeller, and a better thinker. I had just left college halfway through my junior year, without finishing my examinations. My grades would be shot, but perhaps there would be some sort of dispensation since my eye problem would certainly prove to be a legitimate medical condition. Though, of course, a treatable one. I would have to get a physician's note.

I was worried about my mother and my family, too. My father had passed away when I was such a young boy that I had had to become the head of the family. Though my mother remarried, I felt—I knew—that everyone in the family looked up to me, and I was well aware that I was supposed to be strong. But this most recent episode was a chink in my armor. I hadn't yet told my mother how bad things were, but when I got home, I would have to. Perhaps I would simply tell her straight out that I had temporarily lost my vision but that things seemed to be coming back to normal. Or so I hoped would be the case.

"I would offer you some of my lunch," the doctor said as the train rolled on, "but I'm not sure you would accept it."

"No, no thank you," I said. I did not ask the doctor why he thought I would not accept it.

"Do you have something to eat? A snack? A candy bar? I think you could buy one if you want. They sell them on the train." I was aware of that, but I did not want to get up and bang myself going through the aisles. My vision was still quite muddy. My soul was muddy as well. I found this extreme physical caution disgraceful.

"I don't like to see a young man go hungry," the doctor said.

"I'm not hungry, sir. I'm okay, actually. Thank you."

"Still …"

"Really, it's fine."

The doctor broke off half of his cookie. "Here," he said, "take half. I can't bear to see you not eat."

"No, really," I said. I felt as if there was a twig in my throat.

"Honestly," said the doctor. "I have a son. It would upset me terribly if he were hungry and not eating on a train. It's such a long ride. And I can see that you've left in haste."

"I'm fine, sir. I'm okay."

"Please," the doctor said, and in this last request there was desperation.

I did not answer, but he leaned forward, with half the cookie in his surgeon's hands. I sensed this and was unable to stop myself from leaning forward a bit, too, my long legs pressed up against my suitcase. I opened my mouth, and the doctor placed the cookie partway on my teeth. I took a bite; the sweetness seemed almost unbearable. My stomach was completely empty, and the sugar in the cookie, once I swallowed, hit me with force. I felt as if I had run a long distance and was now at home, relaxed, muscles feeling sore but good.

The doctor took my hand, opened it, placed the rest of the cookie in my palm, then closed my fingers around it. "Please finish it," he said. "If you were my son, I would very much want you to. It would kill me if you didn't. That's what I would want my boy to do."

I obeyed. I was terribly hungry and ate the rest of the cookie quickly. I began to feel euphoric. My eyes felt as if someone had put a mentholated salve on them.

"I'm glad you took it," the doctor said.

"I am, too."

"Food is a great thing. It's everything, really. I'm a doctor, I should know."

"What is happening to me?" I asked.

"I don't know," he replied, although this was clearly something of a lie. "All I know is that bones grow and then they stop. Sometimes they break. We heal them. They have in them this ability. They have a memory. The body remembers certain things."

"I feel as if I can't remember anything," I said.

The conductor came by and announced that the train was arriving at Schenectady. "This is my stop," the doctor said.

Distracted, I asked him, "Where are we?" I had no memory of the trip or how I had arrived at the place where I was.

"We're at Schenectady. I've got to go now. Are you going to be okay?"

"Yes," I said. I truly believed then that I would be. I knew, however, that things would not be easy. My heart felt as if it were wrapped with leather.

The doctor left, but what happened to me next was one of those extraordinary events that take over the mind unexpectedly. The space in front of me, where he had been sitting, was now like a vacuum—an absence. I was alone. No roommates, no comforting background noise of fellow students. Alone in simple fact, yes, but also alone with the gnawing dread about my eyesight, in a panic that suddenly mushroomed. I felt as if I were in an enormous shadowy cavern, a void empty of anything or any sensation. Struck with a sudden rush of terror, I stopped registering even the occasional small sounds coming from the idling train. My mind froze—there was nothing and no one there, or anywhere in my world. There was no world. There was no past, no future. There was only my stunned, frozen self, alone. My stomach turned to stone, and I am sure my heart stopped beating during this negative epiphany—for how long I couldn't say.

The train began to move. "Going home will be fine," I told myself again and again as the train made its way toward Rochester and…home. Just fine. The air is so clean up there on Lake Erie, and the Dutch elms on my street provide good cover.

2

Survival Skills

In my early years, I had a recurring dream.

It is a sunny late-summer weekend day at Crystal Beach, just west of Buffalo in Canada. A tall, handsome father in a bathing suit is carrying his five-year-old son on his back about twenty yards from shore out into Lake Erie. The father's face blocks his son's; a viewer from the beach would see only the boy's arms clutching his father's neck. Both are laughing as the father runs through the waves. The father playfully lowers himself and his son into the lake, and as the water slaps at the child's bathing suit, the boy begins to tremble and laugh excitedly. Danger titillates him; he has never been out in the water before. But in his father's arms, he is safe.

Suddenly, the father, still holding the child, pivots and pushes through the water toward the shore. The boy is surprised and at first amused. At the shoreline, the father hesitates for an instant—then, with board-like rigidity, slams heavily facedown on the hard, wet sand, forcing the boy's face into it. The boy rolls his father over and sees his glazed and vacant eyes, blood pouring from his mouth.

The father is dead. The boy sits and stares blankly.

The reason for this dream is clear. In 1946, I went on my first trip to the beach. Later that same year, my father died. He was a tailor who, because he struggled to keep his shop open, had trouble making time for his children.

On my father's last morning, my younger brother, Joel, and I walked him to the streetcar stop and waved goodbye as he left for work. At lunchtime, we were told later, he walked to the corner pharmacy, where he collapsed and died.

That evening, his coffin lay in the center of our living room in Buffalo, draped with a black velvet cloth embroidered with a Star of David—as if it were keeping him warm. Candles representing the divine spark in the human body burned in red glass containers. I touched the coffin with my fingers, playing on it as if it were a piano. I sat under it like a good boy. I recall fiddling with the loose stitching of the cloth that hung below the bottom of the casket. I knew it was a terrible occasion, although I did not know precisely why. I was frightened and bewildered.

And then the burial. A bleak, gray day.

Wind swept across the cemetery. We huddled together like peasants. I stood among the adults at the burial site, unable to make sense of the silent scene—as perhaps no five-year-old could. The mounds of dirt surrounded a large rectangular hole in the earth. The coffin rested to one side. Amid the anguished sobs of those gathered around me, the rabbi began chanting a prayer. We put my father in the ground. The coffin was lowered until it was nearly at the bottom. There were only a few inches between him and the cold ground, but the space, I thought, confirmed that he wasn't quite buried, and if not buried then perhaps not dead. We could open the coffin. He could come out. Climb out of the hole, come home, and shower. Have lunch, live a life. And the pain would go away.

Then the heavy, worn leather straps suspending the coffin were unhooked and whipped out. Next came something that seemed even more cruel. Those who volunteered were each handed a shovel, and they took turns throwing soil onto the coffin. I know now that this act is thought by Jewish people to be a mitzvah, a good deed. But at the time it felt the opposite. I had a strong urge to jump into the hole to rescue my father. Yet I stood immobile as each new shovelful of earth landed on top of the coffin with a thud.

My father's death devastated me. I was now the man of the family—something I recall comprehending even at that young age. I felt responsible for my mother and my little brother and sister. How could that be? My father, as a man and a breadwinner, was the indisputable head of the family. But now we were down to four, and I was the oldest male.

I also remember experiencing an uncomfortable sense of freedom. Yes, there was a wretched feeling of loss that has stayed vividly in my memory, but blessedly, there was also a counterbalance—an unfocused, frightening epiphany that I no longer had the same limits and restraints. Perhaps this was nothing more than my own way of surviving the trauma of my father's sudden death, but I recall that strange, joyless thrill to this day.

MY MOTHER'S SURVIVAL CHALLENGES were far more direct. Dad's death left her with a total of $54 to support herself, me, Joel, and Ruthie, our six-month-old sister. In desperation, she approached the Jewish Federation for assistance and was told that it would be forthcoming—but only if she agreed to place her children in three separate orphanages. The notion not only revolted her but kindled her resolve never to permit any institution or individual to compromise the integrity of her family. To support us, she took a sales position at Sattler's department store and then at the Broadway Market, both in Buffalo.

Sarah, my mother, was a quiet person, but she loved to dance. She liked coffee more than tea. She went on vacation with my father to Florida once. They sat by the pool, held hands for a moment, found the light too bright, and left. They went out to dinner. She thought about her girlfriends. She thought about her children, the neighborhood, wanting us to be safe.

Mother would hold my hand as we crossed the railroad tracks, and she would hold me back as the Erie-Lackawanna train roared past. She held my hand when we went to synagogue. She held my hand whenever we crossed the street, went on trips to see Niagara Falls, went to an apple orchard, went to Crystal Beach. Her hand had seen hard labor—a layer of tough skin covered the softer skin, mostly from her later work assembling airplane parts at the factory.

In the 1940s, until well through elementary school, we lived in a kind of *shtetl*, a bleak place on the East Side, in Buffalo's poorest section. In the early years of our childhood, following our father's death, my mother had had to shuffle us from place to place. We understood the tenuous nature of our existence. "Don't disturb the landlord" was the evening credo. By day it was the similar "Be seen, not heard." We finally rented a house, at 163 Butler Avenue on the East Side, but I continued to carry a generalized anxiety over our uncertain living situation, which somehow turned into a specific dread of blindness and cancer. The first poem I wrote spoke of the horror of each.

I remember standing hand in hand with my mother at the local ritual slaughterhouse while she ordered a kosher chicken, our Friday-night dinner staple. The *shochet* would chop its head off right in front of us. The blood squirting from its neck would run down a trough, and the chicken's head would lie on the side like nothing at all, staring up at you as if to say, "Can this be? Is this possible?" One time, the sight was more than I could take. Before I could be sick, my mother dragged me out into the fresh air, where I promptly stumbled over a blind beggar. He was sitting cross-legged on the sidewalk. He was lanky, hunched over in soiled and torn clothes, wearing oversized and disintegrating shoes, and holding a metal cup. His unfocused eyes were milky with small black spots, his teeth misshapen and decayed. Anyway, that is how I recall him, and from that moment to today that is the form in which he has been a regular visitor in my dreams.

The park near our home was dangerous. Thugs lurked there even in the daytime, and they often beat us up just for the fun of it. For amusement, we would go behind our house to play—to call the miserably small area a backyard would be misleading. My great-uncle Abraham, who owned the house, worked back there, stripping metal from bedposts over an anvil. All day long, that old white-haired man would hunch over the anvil, clanking away. His weary horse stood in its tiny stable in the rear, likely grateful for the break from hauling my uncle's heavy junk cart. Joel and I had to be careful not to get in Uncle Abraham's way.

You could hear every conversation in the upper rooms of all the homes in the neighborhood—conversations that were not always enjoyable to be privy to.

Mostly, though, our neighbors were guarded in their speech, for many of them had fled a holocaust. Although I was young then and did not know what lay behind, around, and under that silence, I sensed a bit of it. All in all, it was as if we were living in the Dark Ages. My brother and I would play football or baseball in the middle of the street until early evening. It was hot and muggy, and we loved it.

You could hear the bugs whirring up near the streetlamps. The old neighborhood women would be in their housedresses, watching us from their porches. Will Ludwig, an old blind man, would stand and "watch," too. No one knew what he did or where he came from. He just stood there in his white T-shirt and gray slacks hiked up on his hips. He was creepy but benign, like a friendly ghost. If he wasn't there, you wouldn't notice his absence. He would always stand on the same spot, arms folded, erect and intent, as though he was a referee. Somehow, his presence softened the harshness of the light from the streetlamps. There came a time when we realized that he no longer appeared in the evenings. I do not know what became of him.

Is recall being too dour? Maybe. The smell of my mother's cold cream and the scent of her perfume; the look and feel of the cloth of her worn dress; the swish of her house slippers against the wood floors; the smoothness of her voice; the sounds of her sipping tea and the clink of the saucer; her tired voice in the morning asking what I would like for breakfast; the pattern on the window drapes in her room; the joy of coming in from a frigid walk with my little brother after services during the winter, entering an envelope of warmth and calm, singing "Shalom Ale-ichem," reciting the blessings, sitting down, and beginning to eat. These were the little things that underpinned my world. But in those lean days, there was a lot to underpin.

MOTHER ALSO SUPPORTED MY BELOVED GRANDMOTHER, Pauline Fox. We called her Grandma, or Bub. Born in Poland, Grandma was a survivor of Jewish ghettos, poverty, and pogroms. When she was eight years old, she suffered a bizarre accident that resulted in the loss of her left eye. While babysitting in Poland as a young girl, a spring popped out of a crib and hit her in the eye. She never spoke of her partial blindness, but on late evenings Joel and I would see her remove her prosthetic eye and place it in her dresser. Sometimes we would secretly open the drawer, shivering at the specter of the eye staring back.

Grandma escaped pogroms in Poland by resettling in London, where she operated a candy store in a less-than-posh part of town. Shortly after arriving in Buffalo early in the twentieth century, she fell ill and continued in poor health for the remainder of her life. The only things standing between her and a sense of personal annihilation were family and the weekly Sabbath. She and my mother used to cover their eyes when they lit the candles for the Sabbath. We do the same today. It is a ritual, and it is impossible to separate one set of candles from another, even across great distances and across the many years.

Her illness may also have been an expression of relief and exhaustion, as when a marathoner crumples after the finish line. She had eluded death in Europe. She had supported herself at a marginal business in an alien and not especially welcoming land, England, with a language new to her, and had made her way to the United States across a famously cruel and capricious ocean. It was all a mammoth endeavor for this rather slight woman who had come from a tiny, insignificant place in Eastern Europe. But within her still burned the spark of life, the stability, endurance, and wisdom that had surely sustained her throughout her erratic movements across a troubled world.

It was a spark that she passed on to her grandchildren. So long as I draw breath, I will think of her with unutterable gratitude.

She lived with us, and we thought of her as a second mother. In our tribe, she was the Elder, the Matriarch. She was also like a sage. We received doses of advice and wisdom from her, more than we sought. She was mythical. It was possible to believe she had the ability to do magic. Moreover, she was dignified, which lent itself to the effect. To sit with her was good fortune. Her hands were solid—they had experienced so much. In them there was great knowledge. We would be lucky if one day our hands would know half as much. It was almost too much to be close to her, as if you might not be worthy of it. We were around her like excited pullets—always at her feet. When I grew taller than her, it was still the same way. To hug her was to be anointed; you left feeling stronger. Her age was the source of her strength; the false eye was the source of fear.

She would sit on the porch watching us play ball in the street. She never had to say anything to us, never had to shout, "Good hit" or "Good catch." It would have demeaned her. She supervised. She was beyond language, perhaps. When she did speak, it was in Yiddish. We listened to every word as if no one else in our lives would ever say something like it again, as if what she told us was how we ought to be. She was like an angel that way.

I remember the feel of her cotton housedress against my face as I hugged her. Her papery hands on my neck. Her lips on the top of my head. The layer of white sand she kept in the bottom of my old baby dresser—brought back by friends, at her request, from trips to Israel. Her black rocking chair on the left side of the porch. The solitude of listening to the radio with her on Wednesday and Thursday evenings: Paul Whiteman and the

Firestone Orchestra playing "Rhapsody in Blue"; Mr. Chameleon; Mr. Keen, Tracer of Lost Persons. Our alone time. Those times lasted past childhood, into my adulthood, and even past her death—a death that took something sacred from me but left behind something sacred, too.

3

Brighter Days

I was still in grade school when my life took two dramatic turns for the better. The first involved my Uncle Carl. Carl had been a confirmed bachelor, but in the Jewish tradition, he began courting my mother a few years after my father—Carl's brother—had died. When I was ten, they married, and my uncle became my second father.

Carl was a junk dealer. Junk was a family calling back then, and a far from glamorous or lucrative way to earn a living, but Carl was still able to buy us a home, at 182 Saranac Avenue in North Buffalo, and the home made all the difference. It had a yard, a true living room, and even a television set. The home sang with respectability; it was not a mansion, nor did it need to be. The kitchen had an eastern exposure from which we could see the sun rise. We could see the sun set, too, through the picture window in the den. I contentedly observed that shift many times in that modest house—*my* house, *our* house. I also watched it in the nearby park with my little brother, Joel, while playing basketball, as the day would wear on into evening. After our half decade of borderline survival in dark apartments, it was as if we had emerged from a tunnel into daylight. Three years into this new marriage, my baby sister Brenda came along to share the bounty with us.

In Carl Greenberg, I also found the strong male role model that my father's early death had denied me. Carl was powerful and quiet in equal measure. The quiet side of him meant that I got only sketchy details of the Greenberg family's flight from Europe.

In 1934, I learned, the family moved from Poland to Cologne, Germany, believing it would be a place of enlightenment and culture. Two years later, Carl and a handful of friends and family left in the middle of the night, crossed the Rhine, and eventually went on to England and the United States. From there he worked to save the rest of his family. My birth father, Albert, and others had endured a harrowing months-long journey in 1939, walking from place to place, knocking on doors, looking for shelter, before reaching Paris and finally migrating to the States before the Nazi invasion.

Other than that, I have only imagination to fill in the empty spaces. Carl gave out those details like a miser spends dimes. But it was enough to understand why my first father never lost the habit of looking over his shoulder and why stress finally caught up to him that day inside the pharmacy in Buffalo.

Carl's powerful physique—on a relatively short frame—was both a result of and a necessary asset in Buffalo's rough-and-tumble scrap metal and junk business. One day, for example, a disgruntled employee hurled a brick at him, catching him in one eye. As with my grandmother's eye, it, too, was replaced by a prosthetic.

As I grew into my teenage years, I began working summers for Carl in his junkyard. Handling scrap was man's work. I was not yet there, so I spent much of my time winding metal wire around several-hundred-pound bales of rags and locking it in place so the bales could be weighed and transported. The rags stank like wet dust. The metal would scrape and infect my arms, and the locking mechanisms would pinch my fingers and knuckles. We had to use a mechanical lift to get the bales onto the scale and then push them into the bed of the truck. The bales would sit on the truck bed like giant eggs in a carton. The junk shop collected and sold various metals as well as rags. Sometimes we would collect brass bed frames. Using an old hammer and a screwdriver, we would split and peel the relatively valuable brass off the supports in order to sell it. We sold the other metals, too, although for a lot less money.

Carl kept a pile of receipts on a thin metal spindle. His script was European-style—blunt and thick, as if his hands were unsuited for the act of writing. In fact, his handwriting was nearly illegible. Black ink was dug like canals into the paper. Carl did not talk much at his shop; he gave orders in quick bursts. He would tell me where to go or what to do. There was no discussion. No consideration. There were no meetings. No memos. No strategic-planning retreats.

In summer, the scrap yard was roasting hot and foul smelling; the only shade came from a large corrugated sheet-metal roof that stood over one end of the yard. The rest was open. The smell of copper and corrosive metal would get in your nose and your lungs and sting your eyes. And the heat in summertime was vicious. The sun's reflection off the metal was like a laser. I had to be careful or the sharp edges would split the skin of my shins like paper.

Two men worked for Carl at the junk shop. Arthur was a giant, though his size seemed to transcend height or weight. He could lift the shells of metal furniture all by himself and launch them into the dumpster. I thought him capable of terrible things. He wasn't violent, that I saw, but I always kept my distance. Years later, rushing through O'Hare Airport, I accidentally knocked, straight-on, into Muhammad Ali. And that is what Arthur was like—a block of a man.

The other man, Donald, was much smaller, wiry and muscular. He was really the only source of conversation I had in the junkyard. He told me once that he lived in a poor section of Buffalo, for which he paid twenty-five cents a night. At lunch break, we would sit outside the junkyard on the sidewalk curb, his glasses low on his nose, a floppy brown hat on his head. The street would be quiet in the heat. He would drink sweet muscatel wine but eat nothing. I would eat the tuna-fish sandwich that my mother usually packed for me. It was embarrassing. What must he have thought of someone whose mommy packed his lunch? I would offer him half of my sandwich, though he always declined. I suspected he was afraid it would dull the effects of the muscatel, which he needed.

For a treat, Carl would give me a nickel to go across the street to the small convenience store and buy a grape soda. It was a very big deal for me. The man who worked there, Joe Hill, knew how big a deal it was and was always happy to see me. Perhaps just happy that I was so happy.

OUR MOVE TO THE MIDDLE-CLASS RESPECTABILITY of Saranac Avenue also meant that Joel, Ruth, and I changed schools as well, and that, too, was an upgrade on many levels: teachers were better and resources more plentiful. Even as a sixth grader, I could tell the students were more eager to learn—myself among them. What's more, one of my classmates was as beautiful as a vision.

I had never seen anyone in my life as graceful as Sue. I was mesmerized by her features and her voice. I just stared. I watched Sue in class. I watched her walk down the hallway with her friends. I watched her on her bike, following her from behind. Her very existence was as if she had waved a hand in front of me, causing every one of my confusions to fall away. Like the Lady of the Lake of Arthurian legend, she rose up out of the water on a day when I was lost in the forest and said, "Now, listen."

Sue, however, wanted nothing to do with me. She was tall and had brown hair, a sloped back, and a double-jointed thumb, which fascinated me. She would not say hello to me in class or in the hallways. I would think, "Please say hello to me. I can't be the first to do it. I'm scared. But if you do it, then I can say hello back, and maybe by then I'll have thought of a question: Where do you live? What sports do you like? Do you even like sports?" But she said nothing to me, which was the most reasonable thing in the world because I never said anything to her.

Just the mere mention of her name—*Sue*—enchanted me, but that paled before the image of her walking to the front of the class to give a report on Lord knows what. Who cared? All I could remember, and it would haunt me later, was the swoop of the small of her back, her shoulders, the sweater she was wearing, as if she were a woman emerging from the body of a young girl, and though I was tall, and myself becoming a young man, I could not believe it was happening. I could not get the thought of her out of my mind. Or maybe that's why I seemed to be doing everything at once: so I wouldn't have any time left to moon over a girl who didn't seem to know I existed.

At school, I joined club after club. I can't remember anymore what the activities were, but I plunged into them with all the vigor and interest I could muster. After school, I played ice hockey, baseball, and basketball. Later, in high school, I would add cross-country and track to the sports roster. I also had to find time to rehearse with the school orchestra.

Outside school, I took trumpet lessons because I thought playing the trumpet was cool. In time, the instrument became something noble to me, like a sword at the center of a legend. I also liked the fact that it was loud—maybe too loud for my family when I practiced—but for me the sheer volume of the noise helped drown out the memory of the terrible silence of our previous life. Mostly, though, I just felt good playing it. Making music is like a prescription for a disease that cannot be cured but whose symptoms can be alleviated. Music did that for me back then, and still does.

In time, I even took a small step toward getting to know Sue. In eighth grade, we were the two finalists in the school spelling bee sponsored by the *Buffalo Evening News,* one of the two leading local newspapers. Sue, up first, was asked to spell "silhouette." She misspelled it!

Then it was my turn. I might have flubbed it on purpose, in tribute to my still well-concealed adoration of her, but I spelled it correctly and won. That potentially costly triumph amounted to a momentous breakthrough: I had come directly and forcefully to her notice as someone to be respected. The next fall, when we transferred to Bennett High School, we would have at least some sort of relationship, but it wasn't until our sophomore year that Sue began to respond as I had been hoping for so long. Encouraged, I dared to invite her to the annual Cancer Charity Ball. Almost miraculously, she said yes.

The evening of the ball, I drove to her house to pick her up, knocked nervously on the turquoise front door (my heart pounding), and was greeted by a stunning young woman. I froze. This vivacious, radiant person did not seem to be the same serious girl I knew in the classroom. Although my eyes were fixed on her, she appeared not to notice that I was staring. Instead, she took my hand and welcomed me into her home, introducing me to her parents, Helma and Marty Roseno, who greeted me warmly.

It was the beginning. Sue and I sometimes went out to an apple orchard in the countryside on fall weekends. Some of the apples would have fallen to the ground, but most were still cling-ing to the branches. We were both terribly innocent in those days. Walking between the trees, knowing that in the evening we would be busy on a date with another couple (double-dating was common in the fifties), we occasionally stopped to sit and sometimes make out a little. On date nights, we would mostly talk…and talk. I usually had a great deal to say; things needed to be sorted out, ordered—a symptom of youth, perhaps, to want to explain who belonged to what group, to understand where and how you fit in.

One warm spring evening, Sue and I went out to a small amusement park in a Buffalo suburb, the Glen Park Casino. I was in thrall to rock and roll, and we wanted to see a new duo called the Everly Brothers. They had rocketed to the top of the charts with "Bye Bye Love." We arrived early, in time to see two teenagers dressed in tightly fitted black pants, black shirts with white buttons loosely covering thin bodies, rehearsing at the front of the small stage. Recognizing the brothers immediately, I invited them to join us later for a drink. Sue was a bit taken aback when they accepted.

After the show, they came over to our table and sat down awkwardly. Phil, sitting to our left, his right leg jutting out, was more intense than his brother Don, who seemed happy to have Phil lead their side of the conversation. We talked about Elvis, James Dean (I thought Phil resembled him), and rock and roll. I was ecstatic; Sue, with her preference for 1940s rhythms, perhaps less so. Still, it was a memorable evening for two young Buffalonians.

THE CROWNING MOMENT of my growing up in Buffalo, the one etched most clearly in my memory, was my high-school graduation. When the musical introduction, Beethoven's "Ode to Joy," concluded, the audience buzzed with anticipation. I stood just outside the auditorium, nervous, my black graduation gown almost touching the floor, my mortarboard tilted slightly. My seventeen years of life seemed to culminate in that one instant. As their president, I entered the auditorium at the head of my classmates. After a few steps, I stopped. The eyes of the audience were on me. I waited, looked around the room, and smiled, catching my mother's eye. I sensed her enormous pride and knew at that moment that I had it all.

The entry for Sanford D. Greenberg in the 1958 yearbook of Bennett High School, Buffalo, New York:

> *President of the senior class; president of the student council; president of the Buffalo Inter-High School Student Council; representative of the Empire Boy's State; associate editor of the school yearbook; chief consul of the senior class; member of the Bennett*

High School Hall of Fame; member of the Legion of Honor, Key Club, French Honorary Society, cross-country team, and track team. Prom king.

My past seven years had been filled with sunlight, love, friendships, vibrancy, and (to my mind) enormous accomplishments. Those years seemed to have driven away the anxieties of the preceding years of want. I was about to enter Columbia University, and, after that, even more exciting possibilities would without a doubt open for me.

Before I left home for my freshman year at college, Sue and I agreed that to prove the strength of our relationship we should see other people, at least while I was away in the city and she was at college in Buffalo. This was supposedly to allow us to see whether our love would stand the test of time. As it would turn out, our love had to stand a much rougher test than the passage of time and a distance of four hundred miles.

4

The Seduction of the Mind

After a summer of anticipation, I found myself at last on an airplane headed to New York City to begin my college years. Late in the evening that same day, holding my one suitcase (it was green), I arrived at Broadway and 116th Street to stand before the massive iron gates leading to Columbia University's main pedestrian artery, College Walk. The gates were open inward, as if in welcome, the walkway framed by two magnificent libraries. I understood that this was one of the great moments of my life. I had made it through enough of Bunyan's *Pilgrim's Progress* to recall, "Now, just as the Gates were opened to let in the men, I looked in after them, and behold the City shone like the sun; and the streets also were paved with gold."

In a golden haze, I entered.

I had planned to enroll in a joint program administered by Columbia and the nearby Jewish Theological Seminary, the leading seminary for Conservative Judaism. But my desire to study my religion and its traditions was not to last, or maybe it's just that Columbia's secular intellectual climate quickly swallowed me in a way that I could never have anticipated.

How exciting it was to be studying with a faculty boasting such intellectual giants of the day as American historians Allan Nevins and Henry Steele Commager, Olympian polymaths Jacques Barzun (*The House of Intellect*) and Peter Gay (*The Enlightenment*), historian of the New Deal William Leuchtenburg, sociologist Daniel Bell (*The Cultural Contradictions of Capitalism* and *The End of Ideology*), literary critic Lionel Trilling (*The Liberal Imagination*), social philosopher Charles Frankel, classicist Moses Hadas, and art historian Meyer Schapiro, among other academic superstars. At seventeen, I knew a few of these names but could hardly imagine how godlike they were in their sphere and how I would soon come to worship them.

Each morning I walked from my dormitory, New Hall, through a cozy quadrangle. At its far side a large bronze of Alexander Hamilton guarded a building that became the center of my intellectual life—old Hamilton Hall. Its several stories of undistinguished architecture loomed above the quad. The building's stodgy aspect aside, it had welcomed generations of students to its classrooms, and besides, as an American history major, I was fascinated by Alexander Hamilton himself. History professor James Shenton, my faculty adviser, assigned us readings by and about Hamilton and frequently spoke at length on the great national founder, who had been a Columbia student in the mid-1770s, when the institution was known as King's College. Now, almost two centuries after Hamilton's day, I often stood before his statue in simple awe.

In the tradition of the biblical Jewish people who were "strangers in a strange land," Hamilton had arrived from the West Indies in his adopted state of New York in 1773. Despite his later preeminent role in the founding of the new nation, he always considered himself something of an outlander. He knew that the benefits of his adopted land would not be showered upon him easily; he would have to drive himself mercilessly so that, at least in the minds of others, there would be incontrovertible evidence of his superior talent. His burning desire to achieve, achieve, achieve was an inspiration for me in my early college days and in more demanding circumstances later.

As my new friends and I would sit basking in sunlight, chattering around the sundial on College Walk, I often felt uneasy, perhaps a bit disheartened. Hamilton and his colleagues at the college had fought physically and intellectually for the freedom of which we were mere passive beneficiaries. Other than the future of America itself, was there any ideal or objective to which I could harness the same zeal that Hamilton had brought to his life's ambitions? This question became everything for me. Why else had I come as far as I had, if not to pursue some great aspiration for myself, and even for my country and the world?

IN ITS OWN OFFHAND WAY, Columbia kept feeding this budding sense that I was somehow in destiny's grip. One sunny day in April 1959, I met with one of my professors, sociologist C. Wright Mills, in his Hamilton Hall office. Dressed casually in a brown tweed sport coat and an open-collared plaid shirt, and possessing a pronounced cleft chin, he sat facing me on a swivel chair. I knew that he rode a motorcycle to his office every day and that he had written, among other books, *The Power Elite*, which fascinated me because of its detailed analysis of the country's oligarchy. I dared to ask the great thinker how one could produce a great book. He instantly responded, "Write one thousand words each and every day—it's that simple."

As he went on to discuss his course subjects and his philosophy, we could hear the cheering of a crowd outside. Suddenly, he grabbed my arm, and as we flew down the stairs, he said, "You're now going to meet a great man—Fidel Castro has come to town."

Breathless, Mills introduced us to a bearded young man with bushy sideburns who was wearing a green military uniform and a crumpled, short-brimmed, baseball-type cap perched atop his black hair. Mills had somehow maneuvered us through the barricades on College Walk so that we could talk with him. When the cordial conversation ended, Mills, gripping my elbow, described the thirty-one-year-old Cuban as "a great revolutionary leader who will bring needed change to Cuba."

The next day I was back in Hamilton Hall talking to a fellow Buffalonian. He happened to be Richard Hofstadter, Pulitzer Prize–winning historian and influential commentator on American politics. He was recognized on campus for his bow tie and his friendly, unpretentious manner. I told him of meeting Castro and shared my concerns about the Cuban leader. I expressed doubt, for example, that Castro meant to hold the free elections he had promised. That led Hofstadter to a lengthy comparison of Castro to the leadership of our own revolution, and then on to an equally lengthy disquisition on American political history in general. While appropriately attentive and intrigued, I was also awaiting the moment to interject a naïve question and wondering whether I should ask it. Finally, when he had completed a thoroughgoing account of Franklin Roosevelt's administration,

I blurted out, "Professor, how do you become president of the United States?"

Hofstadter seemed taken aback by the question. He placed his elbow on his desk, then tilted his head and rested his cheek on his fist, and for the longest time said nothing. I shifted nervously in my chair, hoping that there would soon be a response of some sort—but short of ridicule. Finally, he said, "Put yourself in the stream of history."

I left his office wondering what he meant. But I was to continue to honor my intense interest in the American political tradition for the rest of my life, inspired above all by my appreciation for what the country meant to my family, including some who had barely escaped the fascist tyrannies abroad—and others who had not.

I passed by Butler Library and looked up at the names chiseled around its fascia, as I did every day. Homer—top left, most prominent—followed by the university's century-old judgment as to which of Western civilization's other intellects were the greatest: Sophocles, Plato, Aristotle, Cicero, Tacitus, Dante, Cervantes, Shakespeare, and Milton. I understood the veneration in which they were held in my new world within the university gates. It was almost as if we students, our professors, and the most supreme masters of thought of all time were mingling together at a big party within these few acres on the island of Manhattan. The Olympians became my revered guides, and they were a more diverse pantheon than I had ever expected to meet.

John Schnorrenberg, our fine-arts professor, young and intensely passionate about teaching, taught us the Parthenon for a full month. As he moved on to Rembrandt and later to Robert Rauschenberg, Jasper Johns, and Jackson Pollock, he became ever more enthusiastic. Schnorrenberg, a Princeton graduate, would often strut around the classroom, his Phi Beta Kappa key dangling from a gold chain on his belt, as he described, say, the glories of 1950s modernist art. He regularly suggested that we students purchase paintings by a fellow Princetonian, a young artist named Frank Stella. Schnorrenberg was convinced that Stella would eventually be considered a major artist. I came to share Schnorrenberg's view but could not afford even a Stella print.

Schnorrenberg also trained us to take a blank sheet with a small hole in the middle and move it so that we could follow individual lines or sections in various great drawings. Doing this line by line or section by section, we learned to be able to "reintegrate," or reconstitute, each drawing from its parts by memory—a skill we were called upon to demonstrate in Schnorrenberg's exams. (This rather arcane ability turned out to be one of the saving graces of my later life, helping me reconstitute mental images of a great many works of art.)

As I settled down for my first physics class in Pupin Hall (in the basement of which a team of scholars conducted the first nuclear fission experiment in the United States in 1939), I noticed at the front of the room a cannonball suspended from a long black chain, next to which the professor stood patiently until everyone was seated. He then grabbed the metal ball, walked it to the side of the room, climbed onto a chair, placed the ball a millimeter in front of his nose, and let it swing to the other side of the room. As the ball swung back toward him, we gasped, expecting it to smash into his face. It did not, of course. Professor Leon Lederman, having made his point, began talking with enthusiasm about the principles of physics. His dynamism and creativity entirely engaged us.

One day, however, the young professor's fervor bordered on frenzy as he discussed his own work on an oddity, a subatomic particle he called a "neutrino." The intellectual complexity of the material as well as the increasingly rapid pace of his speech caused a classmate and me to leave the lecture convinced that the professor had slipped his moorings. Many of us undergraduates were focused on the humanities and so were unaware of Lederman's international eminence. Now widely known for the discovery of the muon neutrino and the bottom quark, he was to win a Nobel Prize for physics in 1988.

Although my high-school physics teacher, John Devlin, had primed me with a love for physics, as I started my college years, my unspoken motto was: give me Aeschylus, Euripides, and Aristophanes over Newton, Einstein, and Planck. But it was because of Lederman that I not only gained an appreciation for physics theory but was also able, to a degree, to understand how Enrico Fermi and Paul Dirac and their colleagues changed our conception of reality. Even better for my future was that Professor Lederman endowed me with an intellectual platform without which it is doubtful that I would have been able to engage in the technology-related efforts of my later career.

Then there was perhaps the most renowned Columbia scholar of the time. I was present at his last class, his farewell to teaching. The great scholar, poet, and author had graced Columbia's campus for decades. On this special day, he walked without fanfare into a classroom overflowing with eager students dedicated to poetry but also to his persona. He read Milton, Dickinson, and Yeats, commenting on each of them, and then read some of his own poetry. Tall, slender, and bronze-faced, with a full head of white hair, he stood in front of us—Frostian in his demeanor—then slowly sat down on the edge of his desk.

We were charmed, as always, when he then pronounced Don Quixote as "Don Quicksote." We carefully followed each of his movements, however slight. He read and spoke with an attitude of wistfulness. "When you are old and grey and full of sleep, and nodding by the fire, take down this book, and slowly read. And dream of the soft look your eyes had once, and of their shadows deep." As he finished reciting Yeats, we knew that one day we would take down his own books and remember his aging, soulful eyes. Class ended. We arose as one and began applauding, the duration and intensity of which I have rarely experienced elsewhere. Mark Van Doren turned slowly and walked out the door.

These teachers, and the great thinkers whose work they carried forward, have been a presence for me ever since. But that bland "ever since" contains a world of significance. I could not know at the time, of course, that the impact they made on me was to be more than what we vaguely and so broadly refer to as "an education." It was not only the education those teachers imparted but also a respect and admiration for them, for their amazing, infectious passion for work and ideas, that were among the truly priceless gifts I have received. They helped set my sights high, bolstered my self-esteem, and firmed up my determination to emulate them as much as I could. Their example would later help me out of a terrible slough of despond. Without those teachers and the substantial ideas to which they led me, I do not think I would be here. (If that statement strikes you as hyperbole, I urge you to hold off judgment for a while.)

5

My Shadow Education

Not all my learning came in the classroom, nor necessarily all the most important parts of my schooling.

I had been on the Columbia campus less than a month when I happened to meet a fellow freshman sporting a trendy crew cut, beige corduroys, an argyle sweater, and the suede dress shoe known as white bucks—the regulation uniform of Ivy League college boys of the era. He introduced himself as Arthur Garfunkel. Sometime later, walking back with me after one of our classes, he stopped and asked me to look at, *really* look at, a certain patch of grass.

"Sanford, let us consider for a moment this patch of grass on the walk. It's of the utmost interest to me, this little grass square. Don't you think it's odd that it comes right up to the concrete, yet doesn't go over it? And why do you think it's green? Grass could be yellow, or even red—and yet it's green. This I find interesting, Sanford."

Then Arthur pointed to the sky, offering observations on the beauty and complexities of color in nature. I knew there were plenty of students who would have written him off on the spot as a weirdo, given him a wide berth ever after, and spread the word among their buddies. We undergrads were being prepared to conquer the world. But to ponder a patch of grass?

I was not at all put off by Arthur's personality. Quite the contrary. I had always been an amalgam of doer and dreamer. The dreamer's world was a secret hideaway for me during the lean, gray years. In the competitive school world, the doer stepped forward as needed and gradually took the helm. But the old dreamer was only dormant, biding his time. Now, as this fellow dreamer spoke of alternate colors for grass, I recognized at once that something of great importance was being granted to me. How little I grasped, at the time, just how great it was.

Thus began my shadow university education, one that sustains me still.

For a junk dealer's boy from Buffalo, Manhattan was a magnificent and magical peach, its sweet riches begging to be sampled—but never to be fully devoured. It was (and is) something of a living museum, some wings devoted to money and deal making, others to the sensibilities and the intellect. For us students, it was definitely mind over money.

With Arthur and sometimes my other favorite classmate, Jerry Speyer, I would explore Greenwich Village, Chinatown, Little Italy, Harlem, and many other neighborhoods. Each had its own distinct character: "ethnic" foods (as we say these days), cafés, clubs, music, street fairs, and a feast of distinctive architecture and streetscapes—sometimes inherited from previous ethnic groups that had moved on to the suburbs.

We were half mad with the excitement—and ultimately the bittersweet frustration—of all the plays that cried out to be seen; the great and small art and history museums and libraries to be explored; the classical, pop, and jazz concerts; the secondhand bookstores (most now long gone); the art galleries on 57th Street and along Madison Avenue.

As my freshman year moved along, I developed nothing less than a *hunger* for art. The museums were, for me, sanctuaries, holy places. My two, going on three, years in the city with my eyesight still functional provided me with a storehouse of art—images archived in my memory. I learned to *use* art to live, not just "appreciate" it in passing.

Then there were the riveting and breakthrough new films: Federico Fellini's *La Dolce Vita*, Alfred Hitchcock's *Psycho*, and Alain Resnais's *Hiroshima Mon Amour*, among others. We saw these in the movie houses on the Upper West Side, such as the New Yorker (now replaced by a supermarket and high-rise apartments) or the Thalia, or at "art houses" down in the Village.

The musical menu during those days was equally sumptuous: rock and roll or jazz some evenings, classical music other times. Imagine going to Greenwich Village in the late 1950s and early 1960s. Everybody was playing there—Bob Dylan, Joan Baez, Dave Van Ronk, Richie Havens. Jazz clubs all over town featured the likes of Miles Davis, John Coltrane, Ornette Coleman, Art Blakey, Ron Carter, and Duke Ellington. One of our haunts, not far from campus, was the world-famous Apollo Theater in Harlem. (Decades later, Jerry would be instrumental in restoring it to its former glory.)

There was no end to the city's pleasures and gifts. A single individual could not possibly attend every event, every exhibition, given even a hundred hours in a day, every day of the year. It was truly a moveable feast for us, which we dined on as we could, given the constraints of time and cash.

WHILE ARTHUR AND I DISAGREED on the comparative appeal of musical instruments (guitar for him, trumpet for me), we were in accord on the music itself. For one thing, we agreed on the beauty of the "Kol Nidre," the poignant Ashkenazic prayer sung on the eve of Yom Kippur, the Day of Atonement. Perhaps, we once brainstormed, we could take the best of Jewish music, such as the "Kol Nidre," which Max Bruch had made world famous in his variations for cello, meld it with the best of Christian music—Johann Sebastian Bach's Mass in B Minor—and produce a transcendent sound.

Certain musical experiences from those Columbia years remain especially clear in memory. In one, a young man moved to the front of a stage, bowed appreciatively, and took his seat at the harpsichord. With a flourish, he began to lead the New York Philharmonic Orchestra in Bach's Brandenburg Concerto No. 5. The sound of the brilliant and uplifting music, carrying the precision of Bach's day, seemed a parallel to our dynamic technological era. The forceful conductor, the young Leonard Bernstein, somehow captured what I thought I was in the process of becoming.

Another time, I was settled in the second-to-last row at the old Metropolitan Opera house, having purchased a ticket for fifty cents. The visual presentation of the performance covered the vast expanse of the opera house's stage in such splendor I almost felt my senses paralyzed. While the story of *Aida* was tragic, the music of the "Triumphal March" presaged a great future. My future. Or so I—an eager, somewhat arrogant young man—thought at the time.

I sometimes meditate on that moment at the opera.

So it was my first years at Columbia. One day, as Arthur and I rested on the sundial on College Walk, he hesitantly revealed that he liked to sing. I asked him to sing for me. He demurred. To reassure him, I told him that I played the trumpet. After a short pause, he sang, "Bye bye love. Bye bye happiness. Hello loneliness. I think I'm gonna cry-y."

"Arthur, that was terrific," I burst out, pleased with his singing and his selection of an Everly Brothers song. "Have you been singing long?" I asked.

"Well, mainly to myself," he said. "When I went to temple with my parents, when I was five or so, I learned some of the melodies. They stuck with me, and after school I sang them to myself on the walk home. I like to walk alone and sing. It's great when no one's around because I can let go. I love the feel of it."

"I used to sing the Hebrew melodies to myself, too," I replied. "I was too shy to sing them to others."

He sang a few notes of a different sort of melody, one that I suspect he made up on the spot. It was simple but sweet. Then I joined in and we sang the song together. Dum dum, dad a dad a dum—in just those "words." Then, once more. Even as I write this, I rerun our singing of that little tune in my mind. The moment was mystical, inexplicably so. Somehow the day...the delightful aspects of college life...the pleasures of the city...and above all our budding friendship all merged in an overwhelming exhilaration—a joy never to be forgotten by either of us.

Another occasion—this was still during our freshman year—found Arthur and me sequestered late at night in a corner booth of a dimly lit restaurant, V&T Pizzeria on Amsterdam and 110th. Tables were scattered haphazardly throughout the room, covered with red-and-white checkerboard cloths. Our conversations in the past had been mostly fleeting, tucked in between classes or during chance encounters on campus. That night we were relaxed, with seemingly endless hours at hand to share confidences.

We talked about women who attracted us—his were thin and delicate, almost fragile; mine were more full-bodied and sensual. Sports—his Phillies, my Yankees. Then we agreed on something: Lenny Bruce. "Yeah, I'm a dummy," Bruce would say, "a real dummy, me and my ten Lincoln Continentals." There were other lines and other comedians. We laughed a lot. Arthur's humor veered away from the traditional or the obvious. He enjoyed mockery and imitation. His humor lay not so much in the substance as in intonation and mannerisms.

Suddenly it was after midnight. What must the V&T employees have thought about Arthur and me sitting there, hour after hour? Two men, old, tough Italians, watching these two college kids drinking soda, their two or three slices of pizza having been consumed hours ago, their greasy napkins wadded up on paper plates. What could they talk about for so long?

In truth, just about anything. Arthur and I had known each other for only a few months, but we were already old friends. There were many such V&T nights, each exhilarating and exhausting.

Nothing about our friendship up until then excited me more than the day when, as we strolled casually toward a bookstore on Broadway, Arthur somewhat sheepishly, and with the sardonic smile I had come to know, reported that he had just joined a fraternity that was a rival of my own. I stopped walking. My eyebrows shot up. I reached out to shake his hand in an effort to mask my lack of enthusiasm, but he stepped closer to me.

"Now, Sanford," he said, "listen to me. I am going to give you five reasons why you will be my roommate next year. Here are the five reasons: Your nobility. Your devotion to pursuing a lifetime study of music, the arts, and literature. You find beauty in all of life's corners—a passion I share. We will form a pact: should either find himself *in extremis*, regardless of the cause, the other will come to his rescue, notwithstanding his life circumstances at that time. Finally, you're cool."

I thought I had heard correctly, but I was puzzled. How could he have joined a rival fraternity yet still wish to room together? Those were the days of stilted social patterns. I figured this must be another twist of his skewed humor. But the serious Arthur had shown itself. His evidently authentic feelings struck me forcefully. I knew it was a singular moment, one never to be forgotten. As my wise grandmother would have said, it was *b'shert*—destined to be. I raised my hand slowly, shook his, and responded, "Yes—of course." "Cool" was the style of the day.

ONCE WE STARTED ROOMING TOGETHER, Arthur and I would sit long hours at our desks working, or pretending to. Arthur would often act up. "Sanford, perhaps you can assist me with this proof. This is a very interesting one, don't you think? I find calculus interesting. Really, what would we do without it?" Then he would shout to Jerry Speyer, who had joined us as our third roommate. "Jerry, don't you find calculus of the utmost interest?"

Jerry would come in and shake his head. "What are you talking about, Arthur?"

"Sanford is going to help me with my homework. He's my tutor. The way Aristotle tutored Alexander. Isn't that right, Sanford?"

We took endless notes in class and at lectures. Arthur's handwriting was beautiful—he practiced it as a draftsman does. He wanted to be an architect.

Jerry's was lilting but scrunched up. We were extremely mindful of the caliber and value of the education we were receiving and paid close attention. At least I did, but when I would occasionally glance over at Arthur, I often saw his gaze slide from the page to the window. "There he goes," I would think.

"Now, Sanford, listen to me," Arthur would typically begin our conversations. Or, "Sanford, let me be clear on the matter." Or, "Sanford, it's a very interesting point you raise, but have you considered the alternatives?" Or, "I would like you to give me reasons why the sky is blue, Sanford, and they have to be convincing ones." Sometimes: "I recommend a trip to the library, Sanford, in order to answer the question at hand. Libraries are one of the best things the planet has to offer, in my opinion." Then there was the frequent, "Perhaps, Sanford, if I sing this number for you, all will be clear and nothing will be confusing, and we can begin to address the larger, more pressing questions of the day."

Other times, the assault on our study sessions was more direct. "Sanford," Arthur would chime in, "shall I play you a song? Would you like that? I think a little tune is just the thing to pick up our spirits. Reading is good for the soul, but you know, I think music is good for the soul, too. What do you think, Sanford? Try this on; tell me how it suits you."

Then he would play his guitar. People would start coming into our room. Jerry would stop work and come over. Arthur had a terrific voice. He was serious about his studies, but his music was hard to ignore. I had taken up drums and had managed to bring both my trumpet and the drums to the dorm room. Each night, while Arthur would sing and play the guitar, I would sing with him, play the drums, and deejay as well. Full of ourselves, confident of our prodigious talents, we made a record together. Rock and roll was *ours*. (Years later, on the occasion of a major birthday of his, I presented Arthur with a copy of that recording.)

FALL IN SOUTH HARLEM. (That's the location of Columbia, though it was seldom mentioned by real-estate brokers or the university's recruitment corps.) It was usually still warm and humid. We would open the windows wide so there would be nothing between the room and the sky. Sweat would start on our foreheads. Sometimes the sky would darken and we would know it was about to rain—we could smell it, as if something was issuing from the concrete. At first there would be no other sounds; then we would hear the rain hit the ground, even from our fourth-floor room. It was almost as if the city had paused. We would go to the window to watch the rain, to see people running for cover as if they were being shelled, holding newspapers or books over their heads.

In the winter, snow would bring a deep silence, as though the city was made not of iron and concrete and glass but of something soft and pliable. We often opened the window for fresh air, and heat would billow from our convection units. And then it would start to *really* snow. Giant clumps would begin piling up on the sidewalks and the window ledges. Arthur would come sit on my desk, maybe not saying anything, just looking out the window, his thin body twisted in order to see.

One day when we were studying the Parthenon, Arthur said, "Sanford, now this is something. This is something I would like to see. I think we should go. We should plan a trip." He tapped the textbook.

"Well, a trip requires money," I replied. As a scholarship student, I needed jobs to augment my funds. I worked as a waiter at my fraternity, and at home during the summer I was a truck driver, steering a long flatbed filled with bales of old clothing on the two-lane back roads between Buffalo and Jamestown, New York. I had also worked as a door-to-door salesman for the Fuller Brush Company. I was planning to work as a camp counselor during the coming summer.

"Yes, of course you would need money, Sanford. I realize that. Lots of money. But I can save over the summer. You can save, too. You won't need much money at camp. You'll eat for free. Maybe you'll need walk-around change, but otherwise they take care of everything. And then next year, we can go. What do you think?"

I thought it was unlikely, but who was I to spoil his pleasure? "I think it's a great idea. I think we should do it," I said.

"It's just strange that something could be around so long," he said, "and we still talk about it thousands of years later. There are so few things like that in the world." He sounded distant at times like this, his thoughts seeming to drift into him from far outside of himself. "If you're going to become an architect," he continued, as though talking to himself, "then you have to consider whether the work you're going to do will last. It's the same for artists. There are other professions like that, but not many. Doctors, for example, know their work won't last because all their patients will eventually die. It's a noble profession, but still—there's always that."

"Hmmm," I said. It was clear he was having trouble with the idea of what the worth of his life as an architect would be. I could not quite figure out why.

"I'm sure you'll do something memorable," I said.

"That's not it, Sanford," he said.

"What is it?"

"It's not that—it's not about vanity, necessarily. I mean, it is and it isn't. It's about having something that stops time for a bit. We'll finish this year. You'll go off to be a camp counselor. Maybe we'll really go to Europe or Greece or wherever. [We did, though not to Greece.] We'll graduate. You'll go to law school. I'll go to architecture school. We'll stay in touch, but it's hard. You'll get married. You'll have kids. This is just an example. I'm not blaming you. It's just to show how fast things go. But who's to say we'll stay in touch? Even with our friendship," he concluded.

I did not understand what he was getting at. His face was reddening. He took this subject seriously—surprisingly so, I thought. "Well, who says we won't stay in touch, Arthur? That's crazy. We'll probably even end up living here. Where else would we live? We'll hang out all the time. It'll be great."

"Do you think so?"

"Of course."

"Still," he said, tapping the page showing the Parthenon, "I can't do something like this."

"They don't make them like they used to."

"Sanford, I'm being serious. I mean, architecture school. Is that what I want to do?"

"Yeah," I said. "You can do that. There's no reason why it shouldn't be you, Arthur."

I think this lifted his spirits some. But not all the way. He was such a different kind of guy. He was genuinely agitated over that picture of the Parthenon. It was not merely a picture to him, as it probably was to many of our classmates. Something like that might have been more than just a picture to me as well, but I was never moved to the same extent as Arthur—meaning all the time, deeply, irrevocably, even painfully.

"So what if we don't know everything right this moment?" I said. "We're still young." This was a lie. It mattered a great deal to know. In fact, it was everything to us.

He said nothing to this. He looked out the window of our room, then went to his desk. Taking out a black marker, he returned to the window and started to draw on the windowpane. I walked over. He was sketching the buildings across the street. He drew the skyline in perfect detail, a schematic of the city from inside our room. Then he filled in the buildings' façades, with their windows and ledges. Next he began to draw people: office workers in the buildings, people in the shops, pedestrians on the sidewalks. Men, women, and children. He drew expressions on their faces, happy ones—he wanted people to be happy. He drew patterns on men's ties and on women's dresses. He made little lines for the sounds coming from the pigeons in the eaves of gray buildings, lines to express their motion, too, the way they flapped their wings. He drew plumes of heat rising from people who were rushing about, and he managed to show how the people who were standing still were cooler. He drew the clouds. He somehow even managed to draw the stars hiding behind the daylight, and then the shape of the Milky Way on the galactic plain. He drew it all with precision, and in so doing he made as true a rendering as I had ever seen. All that was what Arthur *saw*.

"Nice," I said.

"Thanks," he said.

"How are you going to get that off the window?"

"It's staying forever."

ONE WEEKEND, ARTHUR INVITED ME to his home in Forest Hills, in the borough of Queens, to meet his family. I was introduced to his mother, Rose, his father, Jack, and his brothers, Jules and Jerry. Rose offered me some Mallomars, which Arthur knew I loved. I was shown around their home, each brother proudly displaying his room and describing the meaning of the photographs and memorabilia. In one corner of Arthur's room stood a guitar and, hanging on the wall above it, was a photograph of him and another young man. It was inscribed "Tom and Jerry," as in the comic-book cat and mouse. I asked Arthur about it. He smiled and said, "Oh, yeah, that's my friend Paul. We sang together in high school, and we thought it was a catchy name for our duo. We love rock and roll as much as you do, and we love the Everlys, too. We try to get as close to their harmony as we can."

"How did you start singing with Paul?" I asked.

"Paul lives around the corner. He wrote this song, 'Hey Schoolgirl,' and we sang it together and somehow got it released. It did okay. We didn't make much money, but it was fun."

Arthur's boyhood friend Paul, who was going to Queens College, joined us the next day at lunch. I was struck by the contrast between the two. Paul was shorter than Arthur, his hair and complexion dark; he spoke truncated, staccato sentences in a deep, resonant voice. We chatted about college, its joys and frustrations; about women, their apparent joys and frustrations; and about what the future might hold for each of us. There was no talk of music. However, I noticed that the humor reverberating between Paul and Arthur took the same shape that Arthur had demonstrated in our own conversations—irreverent, odd, caustically imitative, bizarre, and above all, "crooked."

Paul, of course, was Paul Simon.

AS MUCH AS ARTHUR WAS MY SPIRITUAL GUIDE—and I his—Jerry Speyer was my tutor in more practical matters during our college years: dating, for example. Columbia undergraduate study was for men only back then, but there were various concentrations of college women within close range—at Sarah Lawrence and Vassar and a little farther out at Connecticut College. Barnard, across Broadway from Columbia, was a short walk away, but maybe because it was Columbia's "sister college," we tended to think of the coeds there as "the girl next door." Besides, thanks to Jerry, we had a car at our disposal. His black 1958 Buick wasn't meant to be a sports car, but Jerry often drove it that way, with a skill that allowed us to reach our destinations quickly albeit with substantial risk to our lives.

Jerry, who had joined the same fraternity I had, was warm, generous, gregarious. His intensity and powerful intellect were masked by a charming modesty. He was sturdy, both physically and as a friend. But more than most of us, he understood how to enjoy college life, a skill he generously shared with me. Fraternity parties on Saturday nights were exciting. Stunning young women swarmed around us, as I like to recall it, or perhaps it was vice versa. Ample amounts of alcohol, frenetic rock and roll, and loud laughter added to each moment. Unlike many of the partygoers, Jerry was able to drink *and* dance.

Because I did not drink, I threw every ounce of myself into dancing. We would occasionally double-date. One evening

I learned that Jerry's date was Miss Paris 1959. I don't recall how he met her or where. Nor could I believe that I was sitting with him and her. There was my date, of course, though I don't remember who she was. Drinks were served as we sat on a luxurious banquette at the Stork Club. I fumbled with my glass while trying surreptitiously to glance at Miss Paris. She was not classically beautiful, but I found her to be so attractive that before long I could not tear my eyes from her. Jerry couldn't help but notice and turned a little sour as the evening went on, but we laughed about it on our way home—all was forgiven.

As much as his girlfriends stand out in memory, Jerry's car still stands out more. He loved that black Buick the way you love a brother or a sister. He enjoyed driving around the city, fast and recklessly. He was like that in other ways as well. He would get ready in a flash, shaving and showering and putting on his clothes in no time. He dressed well, so it was always a surprise that he could pull the whole thing off so quickly. He looked clean and sharp, and everyone loved him for it.

There was one time when he and I took the car out of the city. We were going to visit friends at another college in the sticks, people we had recently met. It was an overnight drive, and he was going outrageously fast. The car was black, the night black, the trees dark. All I could hear was the sound of the tires against the road, and the engine.

"It's strange to be out here in the country," I ventured, in part to take my mind off the speedometer.

"Yeah," he said. I think he understood what I was getting at. I was feeling philosophical.

"If we were to die here, it might be a long time before someone came by."

"It could be hours," he said. I was glad he was willing to indulge. And then he was quiet for a while. We listened to the soothing sounds of a good car at high speed.

"There is a certain thing I want from life," he said at last. "You know that. It's hard to put into words. It's not…I don't know…it's like being able to live a full life. To enjoy all the things you want to enjoy and not having to compromise." I knew what he meant. Or rather, I had my own sense of what he meant.

"What about you?" he then asked.

"The same things, I suppose."

"Sometime," he went on, "I worry that nothing will happen. Like, that I'll go to school and then I'll get a job and that'll be it. And I'll have a wife and kids, maybe, only I can't think right now about them specifically, because I don't know who they will be. And that'll be it. It will just be…satisfactory. Nothing more."

"It doesn't have to be that way," I said, trying to encourage him.

"I know," he said, "but what if it *is* that way, Greens?"

"So what if it's that way?"

"I don't know. That might not be any good."

"Are you happy or sad in that life?" I asked.

"I'm nothing," he said. "I just am. It's not enough."

"What *would* be enough?"

He thought about this. It seemed as if we were traveling faster than was mechanically possible. Finally, he said, "That's the question, isn't it?"

We did not talk seriously for the rest of the night. We drove on, past fields dotted with giant bales of wheat, almost indistinguishable in the dark. Even as fast as we were going, it was comfortable in the car.

WHEN I TALK ABOUT "DATING," I have to clarify that I was going out with other girls recreationally, not for romance. Sue did not, as I had expected, drift away when I went off to college. In fact, our bond became stronger. She would come to visit me in the city, and those visits were frantic and passionate. She would stay in one of the dumpy rooms at the Hotel Paris on West End Avenue at 97th Street. The rooms were like prison cells, the beds like slabs of concrete. The neighboring guests often emitted violent noises. We made the best of it.

I would take Sue out with my college friends and introduce her around, although I always felt a nagging impulse to be alone with her. She and Arthur hit it off—he loved her because he loved me and knew she made me happy. It was the same with Jerry. We would go on double or triple dates, taking the girls out for drinks and dinner at the West End Grill, although Arthur and I could barely afford it. Sue would ask me about the girl Artie was with, what she was like, where she went to school. Often, I did not have the details; he dated, like the rest of us, but no one girl for long. Dating was not something that drove him. It did drive Jerry, however. Sue and I would marvel at the procession of women he was able to take out: beautiful women, pleasant and well educated.

When Sue was back home, my fevered thoughts and emotions would find expression in letters that ran something like this:

As I suspected, you did go out on a date with another guy. An engineering student at the U. of Buffalo. Your letter sounded like a goodbye letter, and it is only this that is sad for me. Not the idea of your going out with another man—though I can't say that pleases me. Will you be thinking of me every moment when you're with him? That is what you're saying, but can it be true? Will there be a moment when you think of him—think him nice, think him handsome, think him decent—the formulary a woman uses to find herself a good man?"

How Sue bore up under the weight of such insecurity on my part is beyond me. Her letters, by contrast, buoyed me up in a way that nothing else could match. This one, by way of example, was written after she had visited me at Columbia:

My Dearest Sweetie:

Well honey, this is the end of a wonderful two weeks; perhaps the most wonderful I have ever spent. I want to thank you for making me so happy during this time and also, and maybe more important, for being you. Sandy, I think you know what I am going to say now and I will continue to say it until I die. Sandy, I love you. The reason I love you is because you're you. Sandy, I want you to know that you are all I have ever wanted in anyone. When I think about spending the rest of my life with you, I get a warm glow within me. I think, not only in terms of sex, but as the father of our children, as a friend to whom I can always turn, as a wonderful companion, as a warm, kind and loving person, as a part of me that I never want to lose. Sandy, as I said before, and will perhaps say many times before this letter is completed, I love you...

No wonder I have saved it all these years.

Sue gave me an anchor outside the orbit of Columbia—a vantage point beyond parties and professors and the whole rich banquet that had been placed in front of me. My growing interest in politics was another extra-orbital perch, a way to understand not just America as a whole but also how I might fit into the ongoing story.

I knew from my family's table talk how important President Franklin Roosevelt had been during the war and how important the overall American effort had been for the Jewish people in Europe. Even as a boy, I sensed President Truman's steady hand as the turbulent shift to peacetime began (although it was not all smooth sailing for him). "Give 'Em Hell" Harry cared about the working guy—and Buffalo was full of working guys. Then in 1953 General Eisenhower took the helm of a country poised for ever-greater prosperity. The Eisenhower era has subsequently been disparaged as "the silent generation," as if it were a spiritless wasteland of sorts. Not for me it wasn't. Ike stood for stability and resolute leadership.

That secure world took a nosedive on October 4, 1957, when the Soviet Union launched Sputnik, the world's first manmade satellite. It's difficult for an American not of age then to comprehend the impact of that event upon the people and the leadership of the United States. The Cold War nuclear arms race was unsettling enough, but now our most bitter enemy seemed to have the capacity to wage war on us from outer space. I spent more than one sleepless night thinking about all the challenges our nation faced. Finally, I decided to get involved.

During my sophomore year, as a member of the national executive committee of the United States National Student Association (NSA), I would meet with other members representing colleges across the country. Month after month, we ardently debated policy matters deep into the night, as though our ideas about the complex and daunting issues facing the nation would be taken seriously by the decision-makers in Washington. A fellow member was Harvard sophomore Tim Zagat, a tall, athletic young man with brown hair, his voice deep and resonant. Tim was forthright and passionate about ideas, the country, and its political process, not to mention food. Despite some heated arguments on controversial issues, we forged a friendship. The NSA was later found to be working closely with the CIA, but we were innocent of such encumbrances, and under the NSA's auspices, Tim and I traveled together to other campuses around the country, working with those who shared our passion in an effort to affect the direction of our country.

I was on my way—of that I was certain.

6

Shots Across the Bow

College-level literature and history were filled with vivid warnings of the sharp turns and reverses that can happen in life. Like most of my classmates, I regarded those warnings, when I gave close attention to them at all, as merely "interesting." The fate of characters in great literature had nothing to do with me personally. Like most people, especially young ones full of themselves, I gave little thought to contingencies. Empirical reality—that was the thing. Facts and logic. Or so I thought.

The summer after my sophomore year, I was back home in Buffalo, pitching in the seventh inning of a baseball game, when my vision became cloudy. As I was winding up, the forms around me—people, trees, blades of grass, backstop, red thread on the baseball, hair on the back of my hands—became unhinged and began to vibrate. Vapor seemed to appear in front of me. It was like being in the middle of an intense, steamy shower. I didn't know what to do. After one of my pitches almost hit the batter, I stumbled to the sidelines and dropped to the ground.

I lay there, my eyes closed in an effort to control the sensation. I felt Sue elevating my head and placing it on her lap. She asked me what was wrong. I said I didn't know. Something with my eyes. They were blurry, I said. And steamy.

Within a few hours, my eyesight returned to normal. The following day, however, my eyes began to itch, so I went to see a local ophthalmologist. He told me I had allergic conjunctivitis and gave me some drops to apply—Neo-hydeltrasol. But the itching went on, and so a few days later I went to see another ophthalmologist—Dr. Mortson, I will call him—who had been recommended by a friend of the family. He prescribed Neodecadron, a corticosteroid. I was to put two drops in each eye daily. Dr. Mortson saw me regularly during the summer.

Sometime later I began having a particularly disquieting dream. I had seen a 1952 biopic about major-league pitcher Grover Cleveland Alexander (played by Ronald Reagan). In the movie, Alexander's vision blurs while he is on the mound pitching a game. My dreams replayed the emotion of shock and empathy I must have retained from seeing the film.

When I returned to Columbia in September 1960 to begin my junior year, Arthur quickly noticed that I was having difficulty seeing, and especially reading, but to me it was more nuisance than threat. Too much was going on for me to be bothered with a minor inconvenience. For one thing, the presidential campaign was in full throttle. While Richard Nixon insisted on appearing in all fifty states, John Kennedy was selective. One of my professors, Richard Neustadt, had suggested that I volunteer to campaign for Kennedy on various college campuses. So I did.

Senator George Norris of Nebraska, one of the figures in Kennedy's *Profiles in Courage*, was once introduced by Franklin D. Roosevelt with these words: "History asks, 'Did the man have integrity? Did the man have unselfishness? Did the man have courage? Did the man have consistency?'" In each speech I gave, I applied this same standard to Kennedy, and my fellow college students would roar their affirmation.

Those adrenaline-soaked days diverted my attention from my ever-increasing vision difficulties, but reality could be put off only so long. A few weeks after the start of school, I attended Yom Kippur services at the Jewish Theological Seminary, just as the High Holidays were beginning. I knew no one at the service, and no one seemed to know me. While I sat in the pew, my vision again dismantled, and I began to feel as if I were in a movie, the cantor and the angels singing the "Kol Nidre." Everything surrounding me seemed to come undone and unhinged. The lines that separated one thing from another—for instance, the pew in front of me from the altar beyond it—blurred and became steamy. Or, rather, it all blurred and became nothing. Everyone was singing and praying. I was supposed to be doing the same, but there was nothing to sing or pray about. Instead, I sat there and let the service end, feeling half of me torn away.

Despite my efforts to shake it off, the cloudiness remained. I dared not move. The fog intensified, and soon I could see almost nothing. I was terror-stricken. By now the other congregants had left; the synagogue was empty and I sat alone, my head buried in my hands. Finally, a janitor came and escorted me out of the building. His hands were like leather, his voice like breaking rocks.

What was supposed to be a beautiful, peaceful, and revelatory evening was only revelatory, and not in a good way. I was led into the street but could not see which way to go. I stumbled my way back to campus, knocking into metal trash baskets and a lamppost, the light of which looked like the halo of a launching rocket. It was as if I could hear steam filtering around my eyeballs. On the walk home, New York City was laughing at me.

Soon, I began to weep. The ten days of repentance after Rosh Hashanah, the Jewish New Year, were about to conclude. At that time, we would each be inscribed in the "Book of Life." Our futures would be determined. As I breathed in the night air, I thought of the final decrees: "Who shall live and who shall die; who will die at his predestined time and who before his time....Who will enjoy tranquility and who will suffer; who will be impoverished and who will be enriched. Who will be degraded and who will be exalted." Not until I returned to my room did my eyes finally clear.

LATE THAT NOVEMBER, I returned to Buffalo to attend my cousin Edith's wedding. As the master of ceremonies, I was expected to read the telegrams that had been sent for the occasion. Waiting behind a drape that curtained off the kitchen from the dining hall, I had to squint painfully to memorize the messages so that when I appeared to read them to the group I could do so faultlessly.

Happily, my discomfort on that occasion was barely noticed. Not only was Edy's wedding a joyous one in its own right; it was also the occasion for a special family event. For five long years during World War II, a Catholic family in the Netherlands had hidden Edy's parents, Bertha and Alfred, from the German occupiers under a windmill. Aunt Bertha never told us the exact dimensions. It was simply a sort of crevice in the earth. And there they survived.

As a surprise for Edy, her parents brought the Dutch family's patriarch, Cornelius "Pa" Deijle, to America for the wedding. He turned out to be a tall ninety-year-old man in a black suit, wearing a black hat, who spoke no English. Here before us stood a man who, if Edith's parents had been discovered, would've been shot to death, and possibly his family as well. What was his reward for the risk? Nothing material, certainly. So why did he do it? I don't really know. I can only attest that, when he was introduced, all of us at the wedding felt a swelling in our chests, and more than a few tears were shed.

A few days later, during that same visit home, Sue and I set out early in the evening, in a gentle snow, for a night on the town. We had borrowed her father's Ford Falcon. Sue was well aware by then of the uncertain condition of my eyes, but I felt invigorated by the cold air and excited about the prospect of dining alone with her and managed to persuade her I should drive, despite my eroded night vision.

Within a few blocks of starting out, I lost control of the car. Stamping furiously on the brakes, I could hear metal grinding on metal as I hit a parked car, caving in its door. Sue and I were thrust forward in our seats. Panic-stricken, I turned the steering wheel rapidly, hand over hand, the other way. Too late. The side of her father's car slid into another car door, then careened diagonally again, gliding across the snow and hammering yet another car before veering toward the center of the street, where it spun around and stopped. Sue said she would take the blame, and I let her. I didn't need any more trouble. I still had to muddle through, which was trouble enough.

I never drove again.

AFTER THAT EPISODE, I went to see Dr. Mortson once again about my continuing vision problems. Once again, he told me to keep using the eye drops he had prescribed, and I did, regularly.

As my vision continued to deteriorate, Arthur decided, in his typical smart-ass fashion, that we ought to calibrate the progression of the changes. He created a chart, which he labeled "Sanford's Decline in Vision Week by Week," and posted it on the wall of our room. I would stand at a set distance from the sign, and Arthur would ask me whether I could read the letters, which I frequently could not. Each week he saw the problems increase, as did I, but I still refused to pay serious attention to the obvious. So long as I could function, I made myself believe, either doctors or my strong constitution would resolve the issue in due course. Eventually, however, I had to stand closer than the set distance to read the letters. For a while that worked, but soon even when I stood very close, I could hardly make out the letters at all. Furthermore, I was getting headaches from my heavy course reading.

To relate these moments of decline is to describe torture. Many of the incidents took place in the presence of my family when my younger siblings inadvertently witnessed my being cut open as a person. It was embarrassing, but worse was that there was no way to hide it or make it appear less brutal than it was, and it was extremely brutal.

Sue and Arthur saw the worst of it. As my condition deteriorated, they never suggested that I was the origin of what was troubling me, nor did I think that, either. The source was always treated as if somewhere outside of our presence, on the periphery, very much like an aura, something on which we could not focus specifically. In other words, we did not speak seriously of the decline because to do so would have been to acknowledge it. I wanted none of that, and neither did they. Even after it reached its climax, there was very little talking about it. That winter, everyone, with the partial exception of Arthur, treated me gingerly, as if I were a thin-shelled egg.

Eventually, of course, the egg would have to break, but only by degrees.

THERE WAS, FOR EXAMPLE, the executive committee meeting of the National Student Association, convened that year at the University of Michigan in Ann Arbor. I went. Tim Zagat, my friend from Harvard, was there as well. Tim, who went on to found the Zagat Survey of restaurants and other venues, recalled the episode later: "We were both sitting in at these very, very long meetings, talking about all kinds of things [on] very heady subjects. Sandy and I were sitting next to each other, mainly because we liked to joke around and share our views about things we were being asked to vote on. It was around two or three…in the morning that Sandy put his hand on my left arm and said: 'Tim, I can't see.' Then he said, 'Please, if you could take me back to the dormitory' where we were staying, 'I'm sure I'll feel better in the morning.' And so I led him back to the dormitory. The next morning when he woke up, he said he still couldn't see."

My vision did return that time, at least enough of it to take a flight back to New York well before the executive committee adjourned. I could not bear to expose myself further to Tim and the others in Michigan.

There was also the visit in early December to Arthur's home in Queens. He could see my growing distress and thought a change of venue might help. We had spent many sunny spring weekends there playing basketball on a court at his old high school. He was the king of the foul shot; I was prince of the jump shot. This time, though, things were different.

Arthur's mother fed me my Mallomars, but I was uncomfortable with my condition and showed it. I gobbled up the cookies, drained the accompanying glass of milk, and stood up to escape to the bedroom. She hugged and kissed me as I stumbled off to bed. It was only around four in the afternoon, but I was soon nestled comfortably in my friend's room. The sleep I was always seeking swept me into dizzying nightmares. Final exams were quickly coming upon me in reality, but now in dreams as well. I dreamt that I was flying—first around Arthur's room, then around our room at college, and finally around the exam room. I dreamt that I feverishly wrote exam answers but failed at them all. I dreamt of crystal chandeliers, sparkling rainbows crushing my head, shards of shiny glass sticking into my body. I dreamt that my blood poured onto the floor. I awoke some twenty-two hours later.

Then there were the actual exams themselves—what cracked the egg wide open.

Not surprisingly, I couldn't sleep the night before the first of the term's final exams, even though I was exhausted from weeks of reading. At nine o'clock on the morning of the first exam, Arthur guided me into a large gymnasium and placed me in a seat in the center of the room. On my desk were a blank blue book and a list of essay questions.

The test began, and once I captured the essence of each question, I wrote furiously. I could not see well enough to make my pen follow the blue lines, so I disregarded them. I continued to write like this until an hour or so later when I glanced at my watch. I saw absolutely nothing.

I shook my head. I blinked. I rolled my eyes. I rubbed them. Nothing helped. I sat still, trying to figure out what to do. Finally, I picked up my blue book and found my way to the front of the room, where I handed it to the proctor and attempted to explain my predicament.

He took the book from me and laughed. "Son, I have heard a lot of excuses, but this tops them all. I want you to know that you will be graded on what you just handed in." I repeated that I could not see. As he obviously did not believe me, I started to leave. Watching me stumble back to my chair to get my coat, he seemed to finally comprehend the situation. He took my arm and pointed me toward the dean's office. There an associate dean, sitting sternly across the desk, asked me unsympathetically whether I would care to dictate the remainder of my exam. I told him that all I wanted to do was go back to my room, pack my bags, and return to Buffalo to see my doctor. He suggested again that I dictate the remainder of my exam to him; otherwise my grade would be adversely affected. I declined and asked whether he would please take me to my room. He grudgingly agreed.

I called my mother and told her that, as a surprise for her, I had finished my exams early so I could come home and have a longer vacation. I packed my clothes and, without thinking, gathered up my books. Arthur, quite distressed, accompanied me to Grand Central Station, which was then the terminus of the New York Central Railroad line that connected with Buffalo.

In my leaden gut, I knew I had crossed some sort of awful Rubicon. I had walked out in the middle of an important Columbia University final exam. *No one* does that! Not even, I imagined, Allen Ginsberg, howling at Moloch. He was expelled from Columbia twice—but not, I think, for walking out of final exams. An irredeemable transgression…and *I* had done it.

7

"Son, You Are Going to Be Blind Tomorrow"

The long, strange train ride I describe at the front of this book ensued, each mile taking me further from myself, further into a country I did not recognize, a place I had never sought.

And, yet, I was in fact going home. When I arrived at the Buffalo station, Sue was there, waiting to pick me up. I don't remember what we said. In a few minutes, we arrived at my house.

My mother came to the door and gave me a big hug. Before I could remove my coat, my sisters Brenda and Ruth, then six and fourteen years old, attacked me. Brenda jumped into my arms; Ruth gave me a bear hug. Even Joel got in on the action, running down the stairs to welcome me with a big embrace. Brenda had been in the middle of a piano lesson, while Ruth and Joel had happily interrupted doing their homework. On previous visits, I would scoop Brenda into my arms, open my suitcase, and place her in it, the others laughing uproariously. Not this time.

After the hugs, I was able, largely from memory, to place my luggage out of the way by the door and hang up my coat. Entering the kitchen, I quickly sat down, and my mother placed a glass of milk in front of me. When I reached for it, my hand went wide and missed. Her voice tight, she expressed concern, and I could no longer maintain the pretense. It was simply too tiring. I told her everything that had happened and said that we needed to see Dr. Mortson again as soon as possible.

Dr. Mortson was considered the best in Buffalo, so back to him we went. He had a temperate nature and spoke in an even, reassuring voice. All along he had told me to "muddle through" and continue with the corticosteroid drops. It was finally becoming clear to both of us that his therapy had been gradually poisoning my eyes. Now he decided to consult with other specialists.

As a result, I was admitted to Meyer Memorial Hospital in Buffalo, where I stayed until a different kind of doctor was sent to my room. A psychiatrist. Even in my vulnerable state, I knew this was an act of desperation by Dr. Mortson. I more or less threw the psychiatrist out of my room and left the hospital.

After further urging, Dr. Mortson consulted with a Dr. Walter King, who then examined me. It was from him that my family and I first heard my condition diagnosed as "glaucoma." We soon learned a great deal about this insidious disease, often stealthy at its onset, that causes abnormally high pressure within the eyeball. That pressure, if not properly diagnosed and treated, may lead to damage of the optic nerve.

The dangerous extent of my glaucoma was most likely caused by the very eye drops Dr. Mortson had been prescribing—corticosteroids, directly to my eyes. Corticosteroids are widely and properly used as anti-inflammatories to treat a variety of disorders, such as dermatitis, arthritis, asthma, and allergies. In people with a "predisposition," however, application of corticosteroids to the eyes may lead to glaucoma. At the very least, when corticosteroids are administered topically to the eyes, the pressure inside the eyeball should be closely monitored and the lenses examined periodically for cataracts. All this was common knowledge at the time. Yet Dr. Mortson did neither.

As a result, I now had a new and far more serious problem. I was told that, given the advanced state of my glaucoma, I had a choice of only three locations for evaluation and treatment: Boston, San Francisco, and Detroit. As the only recommended surgeon available soon was Dr. Sol Sugar, at Detroit Sinai Hospital, we arranged to see him at the earliest opportunity.

Unfortunately, my father Carl's junk business had slipped into decline, and despite my mother's remarks to the contrary, I knew that the possibility of a return to penury loomed. Moreover, my health insurance through the family's plan had expired once I turned nineteen. There was no choice but to proceed anyway.

Since the November election, I had eagerly anticipated traveling to Washington for the JFK inaugural events, but I now realized that was not going to happen, any more than I would be returning to Columbia on time to start my next semester—if I was even allowed to after skipping out on exams. In only a few short weeks, my world had been transformed from one of boundless expectations to one of frightening uncertainty.

Inauguration Day at least provided a distraction. I had enjoyed speaking on behalf of Senator Kennedy during his campaign and was thrilled at his election. Now, lying on my living-room floor in Buffalo simultaneously watching television and listening to the radio, I regained some of my enthusiasm. Then, as this promising, bright young president concluded his address, I heard words that seemed to outline the specter of my future:

"Now the trumpet summons us again—not as a call to bear arms, though arms we need—not as a call to battle, though embattled we are—but a call to bear the burden of a long twilight struggle, year in and year out, 'rejoicing in hope, patient in tribulation'—a struggle against the common enemies of man: tyranny, poverty, disease, and war itself."

I arose from the floor and heard nothing more; my mind turned inward as I stumbled upstairs in the half light to my bedroom. I was restless and exhausted, but sleep was no comfort. I had been brought low by one of those enemies President Kennedy had mentioned. In the years since, I have not forgotten those words of the president.

CERTAIN DATES IN ONE'S LIFE ARE NEVER FORGOTTEN. One for me is Monday, February 13, 1961—the day of the scheduled appointment with Dr. Sugar in Detroit.

My mother and I took the train from Buffalo to Detroit, checked into the Detroit Statler Hotel, then went directly to Dr. Sugar's office. It was late in the afternoon. The doctor's other patients had left, and we were ushered into his office immediately.

The venetian blinds were open, the sun of a cold winter day streaming in. Dr. Sugar measured my eye pressure using what he explained was an electronic tonograph machine. When he discovered that the pressure in my eyes was so high that it could not even register precisely on the machine, he was outraged. "Why did they wait so long?" he shouted. "Why did they wait so long?"

It did not occur to me until later to think about who the "they" were and what it was "they" waited so long to do. Because I couldn't see, I could not read my mother's face. But I can imagine her expression was just as confused as mine.

Dr. Sugar then guided me from the examination table to a small, round metal stool. My mother sat in a wooden chair to my right while Dr. Sugar stood above me and put his ophthalmoscope to my eyes. His brow was touching my brow. This man had the hairiest, bushiest eyebrows I'd ever seen. Though, of course, I could only feel them. And then he pulled away—I could feel him do this, like a ripping apart. Very slowly he stood upright, paused for a moment, and said flatly, not in the direction of my mother or me in particular, maybe just to himself:

"Well, son, you are going to be blind tomorrow."

It was a strange thing to hear someone say. Strange that he used the old-fashioned colloquialism "son," and without really directing the remark to me. But oddest of all was to hear a person say, in all seriousness, that someone is simply going to be blind. He did not explain *how* this person was going to be blind, just that he was. And maybe odder still was that the person—the "son"—was me.

Although I suppose Dr. Sugar continued to speak, after that sentence I heard nothing. He was the ultimate judge in my brand-new world. Any appeal beyond him would be futile. I had always assumed—as young people nowadays do— that a top specialist such as Dr. Sugar would be able to solve my problem with pills or eye drops or...something. A quick fix, then back to college. For months, with the arrogance of youth, I had leaned on that absurd rationalization and had taken no action to resolve my worsening eye condition. But in one instant, Dr. Sugar had blasted that confidence away. "You are going to be blind tomorrow." My life—all that I had been working at and was expecting to become—was ruined.

Enraged, I clenched my fists and began rising from the stool. My body twisted toward Dr. Sugar. My right arm, the arm that had once thrown the shot put, was now positioned for what might have been a blow to his face. Fortunately, probably because my mother was there, I hesitated, and then sat back down. Meanwhile, my mother sat quietly in her chair. What thoughts were racing through her mind? Her years of sacrifice must certainly have dissipated in that same terrible moment of the surgeon's statement. Her eldest son had just been consigned to life in a dark world.

I sat frozen on the stool, clasping my stomach. No one spoke for long moments. It could not be happening to me—I would not let it. As Dr. Sugar began outlining his clinical plan, my body stiffened.

"I don't like to operate on both eyes at once," he said, "but because of the severity of your condition, I must. Surgery will be scheduled for tomorrow." At that, he left the office.

We hadn't even thought to ask what operation he would be performing. At any rate, I could not have asked him in front of my mother. We gathered our belongings and went back to the hotel. Drained, I moved slowly toward my bed. As I began to sit down, I suddenly realized that I had misjudged the bed's position. I could not stop my fall. My back hit the floor, then my head.

THE NEXT DAY—VALENTINE'S DAY—I was admitted to Detroit Sinai Hospital, accompanied by my mother. Shortly before the operation was to begin, two large men strapped me onto a gurney and began wheeling me out, leaving her behind in my hospital room. As cold air rushed over my face, I heard the orderlies saying that because of my age, this was an unusual case. Glaucoma seldom occurs in people as young as nineteen, so the film that was to be made of the surgery could be "valuable." I also heard someone comment that Dr. Sugar would be submitting articles about this case to "the journals." Just as the anesthesia was about to be administered, I asked Dr. Sugar what caused glaucoma. He said, "No one knows—and they won't know in my lifetime or in yours." The doctor was not a garrulous man.

"Doctor, what operation will you be performing?" I asked.

He replied very slowly and loudly, as though I was not only blind but also deaf or mentally handicapped (a phenomenon I was to experience repeatedly in the future): "Bi-lat-er-al tre-phi-na-tions." If spoken softly, the words sound rather lyrical. In reality, they are anything but. It had been determined not only that the glaucoma, which had developed aggressively, would very soon effectively destroy my eyes but that the condition had induced an increase in pressure so severe that I would need to have my eyes surgically altered.

In the procedure, Dr. Sugar made holes in my eyes, cutting through the delicate mucous membrane covering the inside of my eyelids and then slashing through the wall of each eye to open a channel until fluid began gushing out and forming pools in the wounds. To accomplish this, he used what today's surgeons would consider crude instruments. They were like miniature pickaxes, and they mutilated my eyes.

In effect, Dr. Sugar destroyed my vision to save my eyeballs—an irony I live with still. But he had no choice: my condition was too far advanced to correct. Moreover, given what was then the standard treatment, there is some question as to whether earlier surgery would have made any difference. In any event, scar tissue began to form almost immediately on the walls of the holes in my eyes. That tissue—strong, tensile, thick, and fibrous—would eventually clog my eyes' drainage channels, causing further perilous increases in pressure and necessitating more surgeries.

There is a moment that occurs at least once in just about everyone's life, and all too commonly several times: the instant just after bad news has been given when you suddenly look back on your life and say, "My God, I did not realize how nice I had it until now." As I write this, I am trying to think whether that one day at the doctor's office in Detroit really *was* my worst day. If death outweighs everything, then the day my father died should claim that dubious honor. But I was very young then and able to get on with a life of normal hopes and dreams. The gods hadn't yet raised me up so they could bring me low.

What I do know for certain is that the kind of moment I experienced in Dr. Sugar's office subtracts something from a person. Afterward, you spend the rest of your life building yourself back up, as if the whole of your being had been cut out. And so every heartbeat of life from then on, every millisecond, every hour, every day is a matter of additions and subtractions to that moment. You work and work to get back to the feeling of wholeness, because all the good things—and one always hopes for more good things—allow your net balance of additions and subtractions to run into the black.

I save everything. Always have. Whenever I feel subtracted—just as I did that day in Detroit, completely and wholly subtracted—I can go back to the things I have saved: letters, tapes, videotapes, cards, telegrams, photographs, articles, journals, diaries, catalogues, and receipts. I look at them and feel better. These items are the precipitate of time. The longer you hold antiques, the higher their value. I am into antiquities. And tradition. And memory.

For me, memory is not casual daydreaming; it has been a life-sustaining *activity*. The process of thinking about my good moments and my bad moments, my good luck and my bad luck, functions for me something like an old-fashioned carpenter's spirit level. It has allowed me to steady myself, as though it were an extension of my limbic system (which, incidentally, is a bit handicapped for a blind person).

So to be coolly logical: that day in Detroit—Monday, February 13, 1961—was not, as I sometimes find myself thinking, the summation of a life. It does not define me. *It was not my destiny*—although it seemed definitively to be so at the time. It was just a day. On the day I found out I was going to be blind, people were going about their business as usual. I had to go ahead and discover what the rest of my life would look like.

PART 2

A Bridge Over Troubled Waters

8

Lights Out

As the effects of the anesthesia receded, I was wheeled back from post-op to my room. My hands rose to rub my eyes but instead encountered metal pads. I sank into the bed and said nothing. For a reason I still do not understand, I was unable to speak. My mother sat in a chair at the foot of the bed; she, too, was mute. Many long minutes later, after I had fallen into a deep funk, my eyes started to hurt. Had ice picks been plunged into them? The pain intensified, and I began to scream. The more I reacted, the worse it got. My hands gripped the metal bars on the sides of my bed as if that would mitigate the pain. The nurses came rushing in and quickly removed the metal pads from my eyes; as they did, tears dropped onto my cheeks. Apparently, the salt in my teardrops had caused the torment. Once the pads were removed and the tears drained, the pain subsided.

I lay exhausted on the bed, unable to express my boiling feelings. There was a great deal of pain not only in my eyes but in my heart. Surprisingly, the most significant pain was not about me but from knowing that my mother had just witnessed her son lose his eyesight. That thought made the emotional pain nearly intolerable. I realized she must have sat looking at her son's wounded eyes. I sensed her suppressing the heaving of her chest.

I remembered a moment when I was five. Shortly after my father's death, a tall, husky bearded rabbi wearing a skullcap crouched before me. He took my hand and placed it on the large, round, shiny crystal of the leather-strapped watch encircling his thick wrist. "Look at the hand as it moves past each second," he said. "Once past, each second is gone. It will never return again." Those words now returned to me with staggering force. Time lost and opportunities squandered: further emotional pain.

I had seen my widowed mother's tribulations, particularly in my youngest years—her tireless efforts to care for her ailing mother and to protect her children. She rose early to take us to school, caressed us tenderly, and went off to labor at the Curtiss-Wright aircraft factory, then performed countless household chores. But how often did I sit down, look into her eyes, and ask her how her day was, much less ask her about her deepest cares? How seldom had I, even when circumstances became brighter for us, sat down and *looked* at her? Now it was too late. The seconds had gone, never to return, just as the rabbi had warned. I had missed too many opportunities.

I still cannot explain to my own satisfaction why, at this awful juncture, it was this loss of *time* that sprang initially to my mind. But it did, and with great force. I suppose the mind, below the level of consciousness, has its own operational logic. A few months earlier, in physics class, we had discussed energy and light, mass and acceleration. Now my own light was gone. The physics formulae were all wrong: for me, light was no longer energy but had become *time*. I had no more time. It seemed to me that my problem was not about darkness or about blindness but about the loss of seconds.

Even though the metal pads had been removed, I became conscious of something like a dark-gray, impenetrable metal door on my eyes. From within I could "see" that door, because there was something on it that attracted my notice. There, dancing before me, were a multitude of patterns and configurations. Some of the ephemeral little figures and patterns were gray. Others were black or white. I shook my head in an attempt to clear them.

Those initial postoperative images did dissipate after a while, but they had pointed me toward a new way of perceiving the world. I had in effect begun the process of understanding that in my consciousness I would be able to *construct* images of the faces of the people with whom I spoke—the pigment of their skin, the shape of their eyes, noses, mouths—and the layout of a room, its depths, texture, and volume; and images of nature—the sky, the shapes of the clouds, the sunset. Thus, I vaguely sensed even in those early moments without eyesight that I might become able to view things without the contamination of the ugly.

Despite this discovery, I was not ready to be blind. Who would be? So began my slide.

THEY BROUGHT ME FOOD, but I would not eat. As a precaution, they cleaned out my medicine cabinet—took my razor and blades and left the bathroom barren. That first night, I took the sleeping pill I had been given and went to sleep. My restless dreams, more like nightmares, were punctuated by the recurring image of that blind beggar in the market in Buffalo a dozen years earlier. He was laughing at me, his head and chest thrown back, his unseeing eyes facing the sky. Dr. Sugar's words—"Well, son, you are going to be blind tomorrow"—repeated themselves over and over.

Those images and memories were soon replaced by a new one that was also to repeat itself often in my dreams during those early weeks: a large white placard with black letters reading "IT CAN'T HAPPEN HERE." Was some covert logic making connections deep in my mind? The message was a brave yet futile denial but one that was later to be transposed into a determination to be blind *on my own terms*. That imperative, while mad, turned out not to be futile.

The following day the hospital's rabbi, Rabbi Bakst—a kind, humble man—came to tell me about King Solomon's call for every jeweler in the land to bring forth the most precious ring. Despite seeing rings encrusted with rubies, emeralds, and diamonds, Solomon selected a plain gold band engraved with the Hebrew letters gimel, zayin, and yud—*Gam zeh ya'avor*—"This too shall pass." The inspirational story had little of its intended effect on me.

Unannounced, a childhood friend, Sandy Hoffman, a junior at the University of Michigan, barreled through the door of my room. Jovial and loquacious, he had driven to Detroit to visit me. His sprawling arms and large hands had often challenged me in basketball. He halted inside the door, obviously taken aback. I sensed his usually optimistic bearing quickly receding. My mother moved to greet him, and he flung his arms around her. She was extremely fond of him, often referring to him as her third son. But as I lay prone, hair disheveled, eyes moist with medication staring pointlessly upward, I extended no greeting to my friend. He moved slowly toward me, gently raised my bare right forearm, and placed it against his chest. At first he did not speak, but then, as though nothing had happened since I had seen him the previous fall, he blurted out, "How are you?" I did not respond.

"When am I going to whip you in basketball?"

Lacking animation, I said, "Anytime you want." I sat up.

"Please don't pay any attention to my jabbering," he said. "It's just my teeth chattering from the cold—reminds me of the good old days in Buffalo, when we froze our asses off." He immediately tried to withdraw those words, recognizing that "the good old days," even in the depths of Buffalo's coldest winters, had been filled with light for me. He removed his coat and threw it on my bed so that it covered my feet.

"I brought you something," he said proudly. My mother seemed genuinely excited by this rare piece of good news. "That's really thoughtful of you, Sandy," she said, and asked him to unwrap the gift. He quickly obliged. It was a record.

She read aloud the title on the record jacket—*Victory at Sea*—adding, "What a nice record."

"It's more meaningful than you can ever imagine, Hoffman," I said. "The idea of victory has been in my mind these past days—but not victory just for me. I made a deal with God. If he gets me out of this hole, I'll do everything I can to prevent others from going through grief like this in the future."

"You know, Greenberg," he said, with an intensity meant to buck me up, "I think you'll triumph over any obstacles put in your way. Do you remember when you were on the track team and you told me that you didn't mind throwing the shot put, running the mile or 440, but you could never do the hurdles? I didn't believe it then, and I don't believe it now."

I never did find out what my mother made of my "deal with God." Maybe it just passed by her. I was *in extremis*, and the young are prone to sweeping announcements. Besides, Sandy seemed to have closed the subject out with his encouraging words. But a half century later, that hospital-bed promise would blossom into the abiding passion of my life, almost my *raison d'être*.

As we sat there, my mother mentioned that another rabbi had walked in. Obviously sent to inspire me, he began lecturing. It developed that he himself was blind and had come with his guide dog. His comments were clearly expected to exert a special force on me. I put it to the rabbi—not at all in a hostile way—about how the whole thing was unfair and nobody really understood. Then I started to talk about how nothing really seemed worth it any longer. I'd had such big plans—graduate school and government and all that. Now everything was ruined. Seeing that I was not being suitably responsive, the rabbi grabbed my blanket, tore it off my bed, took my arm, and, with his guide dog in tow, dragged me up and into the corridor. He repeatedly screamed, "I will teach you how a blind man lives!"

Finally, a nurse rushed over to us, pulled him away from me, and led me back into my room. I sat on the edge of the bed with my elbows on my knees and my head in my hands, perspiring profusely. Oblivious to everything around me—Sandy seemed to have made his exit—I finally lay down and after a while closed my eyelids and fell asleep.

I seemed to wake every few moments and turned from side to side. Repetitive dreams: the placard appeared again, those black letters monopolizing my mind. The door to my room was shut, and I could hear nothing. I could see nothing. *It can't happen here.*

THOSE FOUR DAYS AND NIGHTS in the hospital were interminably long. They gave me plenty of time for reflection—too much. One afternoon I heard my mother's whispered response to a question from a hospital staff member: "We cannot pay Dr. Sugar in full at this time." My head reeled from the implications of that little exchange. Despite Dr. Sugar's blunt way of speaking, he was a compassionate man, but his horror at my previous treatment and his prompt efforts to control the damage to my eyes had left little time for conversations like this.

I would lie in bed, and my mother would be seated in the room's only chair. Every so often one of several nurses would come in to check on me, removing the bandages and gauze that covered my eyes like small pillows. She would wipe off the ointment that had been smeared over my eyes and apply a fresh coat. She would ask me how I was doing, and I would say fine, even though that reply was as perfunctory as her question, and a huge lie to boot. They would chat with my mother, sometimes talking about what was in the newspapers.

Britain was boosting its arms budget. Castro hoped to reestablish friendly relations with the United States, provided we stop arming his enemies. A mob had attacked the Soviet Embassy in Belgium. I would hear them discussing what was going on in the world, trying to make conversation, and I would think, "The world is still out there?" Then I would chastise myself for thinking such a self-centered thing—for thinking that because I could not see something, it was not happening at all.

I do not recall my mother leaving my side once during that entire week in Detroit, but there must have been times when she called home to report on my condition. One of these times she learned that her other son's stomach had started to bleed, so consumed with worry was he. A wonderfully symmetrical disaster. It was something for a philosopher to smile at, only my mother did not display humor about any of it. And yet I cannot say that she saw horror in it, either. She had lived her life with a sort of resigned sadness, as if things would always be grim. She was a woman not taken to laughing a lot, so when we did hear her laugh, it was especially nice. She was reserved, quiet, thoughtful, deliberate: as the Israelis say, *sabra*—like the prickly-pear fruit from which the term derives, tough on the outside, sweet on the inside. She had the skin to deal with grimness.

Dr. Sugar came in only once, I think. He had little to say. I suppose he just wanted to make sure my eyes had not become infected. He, too, probably asked me how I was doing, and I would have said fine. My mother would have said fine as well. God forbid we tell him the truth. He was possibly the only person in the world who knew what to do with my eyes, but he was responsible for the eyes of thousands, which probably inured him to all the pain he witnessed.

And so what did the rest of that week look like? If you eliminate everything—the bed like a skeleton, the chair my mother sat in, the pale curtains on the windows, the nozzles and intravenous tree and monitors, the little table on which they placed my food (bland and soft), the bed sheets, the safe toiletries, the towels in the bathroom, the telephone—if you take all that away, what have you got? Or what is there to be remembered? Nothing except the misery.

As terrible as that week was, though, it gave me some time to begin to figure things out—what we would now call a workout, something one does for a distressed company. Instead of being a distressed company, I was a distressed person, and I was in the earliest stirrings of setting out to turn myself around.

Much of that necessarily occurs in one's head, and by an ironically beneficial twist, a blind person is left largely with only that: the conscious life within his or her head. One then realizes how much of one's mental life had been anchored in the world one *saw*. This is something that you, the reader, must contemplate, if you are sighted, in order to understand much of what my account is about.

NOTHING WAS EVER SAID STRAIGHT-ON between my mother and me about my being blind, so nothing can be said of her thoughts on it now. We had hardly ever spoken about the Holocaust when I was growing up. Why would we speak about my blindness now?

Only once did it come up even tangentially before her passing, as hard as that may be to believe. Many years later, in Maryland, on my sister Ruth's porch, I made some kind of joke, common for me, about how I had misplaced something or knocked something over, and unbeknownst to me at the time my mother started to cry. She did not make any noise, just started shaking, I was told later, and then crying. Afterward, my sister told me that I ought not to act that way—it was too painful for Mother.

Still, nothing I write or say now can come even close to the deep emotional reality of that week in February 1961, when my mother sat with me in my hospital room. In a way, my mother and I were living in separate worlds that week; we were not, despite our physical proximity, beside each other. I do not remember what we said to each other, but it was definitely not about my blindness. Beyond any doubt, she was submerged in her own anguish that week. Anguish from seeing me in pain but also, surely, anguish because of all that I might have done with my life.

She was probably also thinking of the practical burden that had been placed on her. How was she going to take care of me? She had been living a difficult life. She had kept her family together after her first husband died, when it would have been easier to let them go to foster homes. On top of that, she had been taking care of her own mother, who at the time of the ordeal in Detroit had only recently passed away. She was now mother to four, or even five, if we count all she did for her second husband—cleaning, making dinner, doing the laundry, and all the things a woman of that era was expected to do.

Perhaps she saw my blindness as just the next in a long line of hardships. Maybe she was even comfortable with it in some way. Not comfortable that it had happened to me, but maybe it confirmed that her life was always to be an unrelenting burden. She was a pessimistic optimist, finding stability in her pessimism. Maybe, as well, there were other versions of the unsaid that hunkered down somewhere in other corners of her life, ones of which I would never know. I am certain that the horror of what had happened to friends and relatives in Europe was festering in one or another of those corners.

These days, there are support groups for every diagnosable ailment and condition, as well as for some that are not. Even if we wanted to maintain silence, it would be difficult. In all likelihood, a social worker at the Detroit hospital today would drop by to offer some kind of pamphlet, and we would have had a consultation with him or her, closely followed by our enrollment in an outpatient support group. A jumping-off point would have been provided for us. But my blindness arrived then, not now—in 1961, not in the twenty-first century—and in Detroit, in that hospital room, my mother and I spoke not a single word about it.

AFTER FOUR DISMAL DAYS AND NIGHTS, I was discharged from the Detroit hospital. It was a Saturday morning. I walked out and felt fresh air on my face; I took deep breaths. That moment remains the most glorious memory of my life—the first little push toward regaining my life—and my brain gave me a further break by not allowing itself to imagine the struggles ahead.

It was a bitterly cold day when we arrived in Buffalo. Sue was waiting for us at the station. I took hold of her and said, "Your hand is *freezing.*" We kissed and hugged, and I could tell she had lost a lot of weight since December. I had been so focused on my mother's anguish that I had almost forgotten there was another woman who loved me.

The homecoming was awkward. My siblings stumbled through the next few hours, talking from time to time, but without their usual ease. That evening I returned to the bedroom I shared with Joel, took a sleeping pill, and started to cry. From his bed, Joel reached out and touched my shoulder. Sleep came shortly.

The following days were filled with visits from relatives, neighbors, and friends. Day after day they came, and day after day we talked about everything but the obvious. They took their cues from me. My post-hospital euphoria was gone.

Sue would arrive each morning. Her *joie de vivre* was infectious; she lifted all spirits—except mine. Nevertheless, whenever I slipped into solitude, her buoyancy drew me out of myself. She even persuaded me to attend a friend's engagement party.

Horror filled me at the idea of exposing myself in my newly deformed state. It was the prelude to the rest of my new life.

As it turned out, the party was every bit as unpleasant as I had imagined. Sue stayed by my side, guiding me around the room. Her laughter filled the air, but I could feel, or imagine, that our friends were staring at me. The evening could not end soon enough.

But home and home-cooking were sources of great comfort during this time. My mother, Sue, my siblings, and my father did everything they could to make life easier for me.

Mostly I moved around the house and neighborhood by myself, slowly, tentatively, and awkwardly. Chains—black, heavy chains—seemed to rattle around my body, my every movement limited, cautious, and above all fearful. Sue, seeing me grimace, would try to alleviate the weight of the chains by holding my hand and guiding me. But I could hardly wait till evening so I could take my sleeping pill and drift away from the present. Each day seemed the same, filled with the same visits and the same chatter—all calculated to avoid recognition of the all too obvious.

Then again, actually recognizing my blindness was just as disturbing. Witness the social worker who stopped by our house to discuss my options for the future. A thin older woman with once-blonde hair turning gray, according to Sue, her face was unremarkable except that she had thin lips. She had a quiet, unaccented voice, and she used no colloquialisms. It was as if she simply appeared on our porch in Buffalo, out of nowhere.

Sue and I sat side by side in chairs like an old married couple. I did feel old—old, tired, and more than a little help-less. The social worker arranged papers and handed some to Sue. (I could hear this.) She said that Sue and I should take a drive out to the country. Some of the blind people she had helped—mainly men, for some reason—had become justices of the peace. There were other options, too, she told Sue (as if I were not there). She was matter-of-fact about my possibilities. As she saw it, I had very few of them. Aside from being a justice of the peace, she said in her flat tone, I could make screwdrivers or cane chairs. I was stupefied.

At the woman's direction, Sue drove me out to places that made Buffalo look like Midtown Manhattan—towns and villages hardly anybody knew of, mostly surrounded by farms and forest. Sue told me that the blind local justices of the peace sat in rocking chairs on their porches, looking as if they had had the life sucked out of them.

Sue pulled into a gravel driveway in front of a wooden building where we were told there was going to be a wedding. One of the blind men we had heard about would be presiding. Sue led me in, and we sat at the back. The couple being married were certainly farmers. The man, perhaps my age, was trying to stand up straight, but something in his back seemed to prevent him from doing so. He was arched at the shoulders. The bride was a heavyset woman, almost pretty. The justice of the peace, I was told, was wearing a gray suit and had on dark glasses to hide eyes that would presumably alarm people if they were to be seen. He sounded practiced but detached—possessing not a bit of joy in his voice. Members of the couple's families were present, but they were few. The building was not a church; there were no pews, just rows of chairs. Unaccountably, drawings done by schoolchildren lined the walls.

The ceremony was unremarkable. Up until a point, those two kids had been unmarried, and then, suddenly, they were married. That was it.

"They're done," Sue said.

I could hear the wedding party walking out of the building and into the dusty air. I could also hear the tapping of the justice's cane against the floor. He moved deliberately but quickly. Sue went up to him to say that she had been told we should speak with him, if he had time. Her boyfriend had just gone blind, or was blind, or, well—if he could find the time to speak to me, we would really appreciate it. He said he would, but he did not say that he would be happy to or that he was sorry to hear about my condition. He was not going to give me solace. He was going to tell—no more, no less.

We three sat on a bench outside. The justice of the peace asked us what we wanted to know, and I said I just wanted to get a sense of how he got around. He said, "I use a cane." I asked him how he got from one place to another. He said he lived in the village, but if he needed to go farther, there was a bus. I asked, foolishly, "What if you need to go into Buffalo?" He looked at me—I could feel his dark eyeglasses on me—but said nothing. I thought that was strange. Clearly, he felt the *question* was strange. Outrageous, even, as if he were on the verge of saying, "Why in the world would I go to Buffalo, young man?"

After that, I did not speak. Sue did the talking, as she always has, gracious as ever. She asked him what living in this place was like, whether he liked presiding over weddings. She talked about her schooling and mine. I could tell he liked her; I could almost see him smiling. If only he could have seen her.

Later, the social worker returned to our house to check on me. Over tea, she asked me how the visit to the justice of the peace went. I did not tell her that it was not particularly helpful. I did not explain to her that a life like that would actually be a death for me. She told me that she just wanted me to get a sense of what possibilities were available. It was odd to sit with this woman. I could hear her rise up a bit to set her teacup in the saucer. I could hear the floorboards squeak when she shifted. I could even hear her breathe—but I could not get a sense that she was actually there. It was as if there was a shell of a body pretending to be a human being in her place, like the justice of the peace.

When I asked her what else she might have for me, she told me again that I could cane chairs. I did not know what that entailed. She also told me of other blind people she knew who made screwdrivers. I did not know how a screwdriver was made. It seemed dangerous.

My mother came out to ask us whether we needed anything. I said no. The social worker said she was fine, thank you. I faced my mother when this woman spoke, as if my mother would somehow confirm what I thought: perhaps this woman was not there to begin with. Of course, my peevish attitude was an effort to deny what my life had become. I could deny it by denying the social worker's existence. She had to be a *wisp* of air, a swirl of snow left in the wake of a car. I wanted to annihilate her.

"What do you think, Sandy?" the social worker asked. I did not know what to say to her. I wanted to tell her that her rules did not apply to me—that this was not the kind of life I was going to lead. I would not be presiding over marriages in small towns. She was kind, nice, decent, and I appreciated her help. But it was not for me. I wanted to promise her that my life would not be a peaceful drive in the country or a quiet porch from which to stare at the world.

There would be no serenity. My life would be good, but it would not involve rocking chairs or slow walks down a country lane, stick tapping away. She helped me, that social worker, in ways she probably had no knowledge of. I could feel rebellion stirring in my heart.

Before my trip to Detroit, I had privately harbored notions of a future that included Harvard Law School and then, one day, the governorship. The specter of this bottommost rung of the law—a porch in some small western New York town—was unbearable. My confinement within myself seemed inevitable and without end. Yet it was unacceptable. And to be clear: For me on that day, "unacceptable" meant nothing like today's vague sense of disapproval. It meant that I *would not accept* such a life.

9

A Walk on the Wild Side

I have worked on this memoir for decades, trying to understand why I began trying to rejoin the race—both contest and human. The struggle was a long process, taking months and years. Many years. And counting.

What was it that lay between my near despair in Detroit in the winter of 1961 and the life that I cherish today, blindness and all? Hermann Hesse may have gotten close to it: "God does not send us despair in order to kill us; he sends it in order to awaken us to a new life." The awakening, though, was brutally hard.

During those dark days after Detroit, I had to decide what to do. What movement would make any sense at all? In the beginning, I saw nothing—in just about every sense of the word. My friends, family, girlfriend, classmates, and professors had all disappeared. Of course, they had not literally vanished, but how was I to know whether they would or not, at least some of them?

I knew I had some talent and some determination. But would these gifts and the support of my family be enough? My family had a tradition of nagging uneasiness about good fortune. There was always a subtle, unwelcome presence lurking. My misfortune was proof that good fortune was illusory. What then? Was my life's purpose simply to serve as a reminder that bad things can happen?

I still harbored a stubborn feeling of being unfulfilled. There were things I just wanted to learn and to know. Like pulling the proverbial loose thread from a sweater—there is always an unending more and more. Newly blind and downcast as I was, it was this hunger to know that ultimately provided the fuel for my liberation. One of my most cherished friends would apply the match.

ARTHUR VISITED ME IN THE SPRING after my operation. My family always loved it when Arthur came, and I think he liked it very much, too. Shortly after his arrival, the two of us were walking down Saranac Avenue, squirrels running across the sidewalk in front of us. We walked steadily and leisurely—a pace that seemed at odds with my condition. For the past several months my body had been tense, almost rigid; I could not move around even in my own bedroom without knocking into something. Here on the street, with Arthur, it was as if there was nothing to knock into. I lightly held his elbow as we walked along.

I was uneasy as we began our conversation. Up to this point, I had shared certain of my emerging notions only with Sue: pathetically defiant thoughts, quite possibly delusional, that had begun to percolate through to my consciousness. I was thinking I might return to Columbia and graduate and that Sue and I would marry.

Those thoughts, not quite overshadowed by doubt and pessimism, had become more insistent. Did I dare expose them to Arthur? His presence here in Buffalo was, after all, my foremost remaining link to college. My brief taste of Columbia and the city and all the great things they represented was a seed already planted, and it had the potential to grow. Seeds want to sprout and send out roots.

Putting my embarrassment aside, I related my recurrent fantasies of return to Arthur, and in one of those rare moments when he put aside the lyrical and romantic, his analytical side emerged. His speech became focused and intense as I struggled to explain my fantasy, and his voice descended to a lower octave. Sightless as I was, I could sense his blue eyes searching my face.

After a while, we turned from my predicament to discussing the university in general. It felt less awkward to focus the conversation on the subject of school itself than on my recent catastrophe and its effect on my educational career. Then, abruptly, Arthur asked me when I was going to return. *When!* It soon became clear that he was concerned merely about the great amount of coursework I had missed and would have to catch up on for the second half of junior year. As if it were that simple! I replied that, flights of fancy aside, I really did not know whether I was going to return at all. At that, he was silent for a while. Then he said that of course I was going to return, that it was his job to convince me to return: "There is no other way."

I said the opposite was true—there was no way I *could* go back. I had already missed out on so much that I would certainly not be able to graduate with our class. At bottom, however, there was always the basic underlying issue: the coursework required to graduate as a member of *any* class would be unmanageable.

That conclusion, which I stated with impressive firmness, was not in fact rock-solid for me. I needed Arthur to tell me whether or not I was dreaming the impossible. The unspoken question was: Would he be willing to room with a blind man? Neither of us knew how much that was asking.

We continued strolling along quietly for a while. It had been a few months since the surgery, and my eyes no longer hurt. I could feel the warmth of the sun when we passed between breaks in the trees. Arthur told me he would help me if I returned.

I suddenly became aware of the sound of my sneakers against the pavement, and things moving all around me—birds and squirrels perking up and bees awakening from their winter. I could even sense crocuses poking up through the earth. It was good to have Arthur there, a living reminder of a life I used to have.

"Well, I think you have to come back," Arthur said. "It just seems like the only reasonable thing to do."

"What are you talking about? You're crazy. I don't want to discuss it."

"Well, you're going to *have* to discuss it at some point. I'm going to make you discuss it."

"Well, I don't want to."

"Sanford. Stop." He repeated that he would help me if I returned.

I believed in his sincerity, but while I comprehended how much effort it would be for me to resume college, I was not sure he did. Just getting around my own house in Buffalo was a tremendous effort. The idea of going back to college, in frenetic Manhattan, seemed foolhardy. There were a few serious specific hurdles: the tight schedule of classes, the campus to navigate, and the competitive fellow students, probably scornful of a blind student. Not to mention the heavy reading load. Still,

(Top) *Sandy, at front left, with younger brother Joel, and their parents—Sarah and Albert Greenberg.*

(Left) *Sandy's Bar Mitzvah, 1953*

Sandy playing solo trumpet on his 8th-grade graduation day. He had to stop playing after his eye surgery. Blowing on the horn created too much pressure in the eye socket.

A boy and his Buick. Does life get better than this!

(Top) The Greenberg siblings in 1957: Joel at left, Brenda, Ruth, and Sandy.

(Left) With wavering vision, Sandy made this sketch of Joel in the fall of 1960. It was the last drawing he ever did.

(Right) An infant Sandy being held by his grandmother Pauline. Pauline came to America at the start of the 20th century.

(Below) Young love, first love— Sandy and Sue at the Bennett High School prom, 1958.

Sandy and Sue dancing at their wedding, 1962. Sandy insisted that the band include some numbers featuring an unknown vocalist named Arthur Garfunkel.

(Left) Sandy receiving his diploma from Columbia University Dean John Palfrey in 1962. Despite missing a full semester after he first went blind, Sandy graduated Phi Beta Kappa with his original class and as its president.

(Below) Sandy and Art Garfunkel loose on the streets of Europe, 1967.

Sandy with the compressed speech machine he invented and patented in the late 1960s. This is the same machine that lies at the center of Frank Stella's sculpture, shown in the frontispiece to this book.

Sandy with sons Jimmy on his shoulder and Paul in his arm.

Sandy and Art Garfunkel: "He's not heavy; he's my brother!"

Paul Greenberg's Bar Mitzvah, 1981.

Jimmy Greenberg's Bar Mitzvah, 1982.

Kathryn Greenberg's Bat Mitzvah, 1989.

(Left) Sandy goes up for a shot against former Sen. Bill Bradley, an all-American at Princeton and a long-time New York Knick. Sandy can sense the location of the basket by the flow of people around him.

(Below) Tables turned: This time Sandy is guarding Bill Bradley, and Bradley has nowhere to go! The inscription reads, in part: "For Sandy 'Glue' Greenberg, the toughest, roughest defender since John Havlicek."

For Sandy "Glue" Greenberg The toughest, roughest, defender since John Havlicek —
Thanks for letting me see the light a few times; my confidence needed it.

Bill Bradley

As a director of the National Committee on US-China Relations, Sandy hosted one of the earliest Chinese delegations to visit Washington. This is a gathering at Sandy and Sue's Watergate home.

Sandy with his invaluable mentor and friend David Rockefeller. The two met through the White House Fellows program, which Rockefeller helped found.

Sandy, at right, with Ted Kennedy.

Sandy with a very young Kathryn. Who's leading whom?

The Greenbergs in 1983: Sandy, Jimmy, and Paul at bottom, and Kathryn and Sue at top.

The Greenbergs, early 1990s: Kathryn, Sue, and Jimmy in front, with Sandy and Paul taking up the rear.

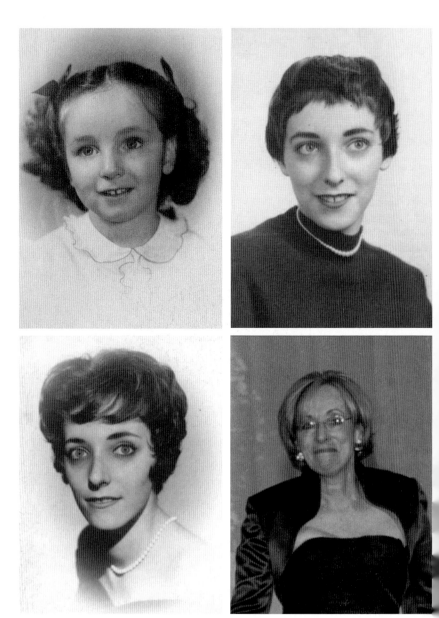

Four Sues, from the grade-school version Sandy adored for years before getting up the nerve to talk with her, through high school and college, and on to today.

I had already been considering the idea of using audiotapes. I could tape-record the classes and lectures to review later and get people to read the associated assignments to me.

"Just how are you going to help me, Arthur?"

"Well, I could get all your class notes, all your assignments. I could quiz you for your exams. I could walk you to your classes and then pick you up."

"How are you going to do that and still handle your own classes and reading?"

"We can figure something out. I think you're dodging the main question, though."

"Which is what?"

"Which is whether or not you'll return."

Arthur then laid out his underlying premise: everything else would fall into line once I made that decision. His tone of voice suddenly changed. He began to sing: "Oh Sanford, Sanford, Sanford…I made you out of clay, and now you're dry and ready. So, Sanford, we must play." With that, his intensity vanished; we both laughed and put our arms on each other's shoulders.

With his simple nonsense, he had succeeded in dispelling my uneasiness, which enabled us to continue our discussion in the same dispassionate manner in which we had discussed so many other things in the past. It felt as though we were back at Columbia, relishing our good fortune as we sauntered down College Walk. Arthur seemed comfortable, speaking as though nothing had transpired since he had seen me last. The attitude, the patter, the humor were familiar. He had made a sudden decision to help me. Was it preceded by an epiphany about the meaning of life? I don't know.

For a moment, my tension eased. I told him about that first poem I had ever written, on the horror of cancer and blindness, and the fear that either might afflict me. In 1945, cancer meant certain death, and since I had for some reason linked it with blindness back then, I told him that I now felt a nearness to death—at the "bottom of life's barrel," as I phrased it.

"Sanford, let's recite together," he said abruptly: "'Oh, to be in England / Now that April's there, / And whoever wakes in England / Sees, some morning, unaware…' Buffalo is not exactly England, but it is nice here. I love this place. As I've said many times before, it has soul."

This time, Arthur's characteristic attempt to change the subject to uncoil my melancholy failed. I stopped walking. I dropped my hands, clenched my fists, turned my ruined eyes upward, and shouted, "Arthur, look at me. I'm finished. Look at my eyes. I can't see. What has God done to me?" Yes, it was blatant self-pity, but I now like to think of it as a way of firing myself up, of creating the momentum of emotion in order to move on. It was the standard tactic of backing up to get a running start.

In any case, Arthur was having none of it. He gently put his hand on my shoulder. "You know, Sanford, when we studied the words the Greeks spoke, they were just that to us, mere words. Those words—about tragedy, glory, heroism, greatness— they were all just concepts. I couldn't really comprehend what they were talking about. But now, as I see you standing here, blind—I still can't believe it—but now I understand the words of the Greeks. They weren't just words. Seeing you as you are now shows me the *real* meaning of tragedy."

I said nothing. Here I was, battling for my life, and Arthur was talking philosophy. He quickly broke into my silence. "We read about a man dropping from the heights, and his fall to the bottom so precipitous that they called it a tragedy. But what about heroism rising? What if you're not on top when you fall?

What if you're just an ordinary guy who gets devastated? Do you remember Professor Goethals?"

"Yep," I responded. We had both taken his humanities course. Now, Arthur proceeded to mimic his resonant bass voice. "'Was Achilles a heroic or tragic figure?' It was Achilles, remember? 'A spear came out of nowhere.' Not only did Achilles survive, he triumphed." Arthur went on in his mock-Goethals bass register: "'Gentleman, Achilles was a great man, a hero.' Sanford, those words mean something to me today."

"But, Arthur, do you remember what Achilles said?" Then I put in rapidly, so as not to give Arthur time to respond, "The question was, 'Achilles, were you to relive your life, would you, knowing what you know now, select the short and glorious life you lived, or would you choose to live a long and dull one?'"

"I don't remember that. What was his response?"

"'Just give me one more day in the sunshine.'" I repeated it with emphasis, "Just give me one more day in the sunshine, Arthur. That's all I ask."

"But, Sanford, you have already lived a fine life, and I think yours will be a long life. No, you won't see the sun, but the fire in you will lead you to achievements that others can only dream about." That flowery rhetoric was pure Arthur, right out of late nights at the V&T Pizzeria.

"I don't know where I'll come out," I replied, "but wherever it is, it will sure as hell be better than sitting like a lump in my living room."

"Sanford, listen to me carefully," he said. "You will be a great man, a hero—greatness will be yours." That is the grandiose manner in which we spoke to each other in those days, yet meaning every word. "Anyway, what would you do here?"

"I don't know. Work with my father, I guess."

"You're going to work in a scrap yard?"

"Yeah, I guess. Why? Is something wrong with that?"

"No, not necessarily. It just seems a little off from what you wanted to do."

"Well, Arthur, I can't do that any longer. You don't get it, do you."

"Yes, I do get it. You're the one who doesn't get it."

"What don't I get?"

"Nothing," he said dismissively.

"No, tell me."

"Well, then, here it is. *I* need you to come back. Me. Okay? It's not that you need to come back for yourself, though you do—but *I* need you there. You're my best friend. What am I going to do for the rest of the time if you're not there?" His voice was tight. I didn't say anything. He added, "I mean, we're best friends, right?"

"Yeah," I said.

"Then you have to come back. You agreed, remember? We made a promise to each other. It was when we said we'd live together."

"Well, I don't know if this new thing counts."

"Yes, it does," he said. "Of course, it does."

"This is different," I said.

"No, it's not. This is it. This is *exactly* what I'm talking about. It's the perfect time. I need you to come back. And if you come back, then you'll need me. This is what we promised each other. This was the whole point."

ARTHUR WAS RIGHT. It was a stipulation: one would be there for the other in times of crisis. This was a chip, I would discover throughout my later life, that I would need to cash in on occasion. I would cash in one of Arthur's chips when I went back to school. I would cash in a chip when my father, Carl, died and Arthur came rushing to Buffalo to be there with me—to sit outside on the porch with me in silence for hours, days; no words, just understanding. I would cash in his chips over the decades whenever I needed to hear his voice: frank, light, resonating with truthfulness. I would take him up on his promise at the birth of my children, for he would be godfather to each—a promise that extended even beyond that.

My children would themselves call him at times about matters they could not discuss with me, or if they felt he would be a better ear, less judgmental. I called in Arthur's promise when I asked him to sing at my wedding and then, years later, without my calling him, he came to sing at the weddings of my siblings, my sons, and my daughter. There were thousands of other times when he would be there for me. Because of this commitment made to me as a young man on our way to a bookstore near Columbia, he would forgo substantial income time and again to honor it. That was in his character.

But that commitment was not one-sided. Arthur cashed in one chip right there on Saranac Avenue for my return to Columbia with him. He would have other chips of mine to cash in later. He cashed in one with me when he needed money for his early career in music. He used to send me every record he made, asking for my opinion. He needed my opinion, too, about every breakup with a girlfriend and later about many of his family concerns.

I had always thought that Arthur would be recognized as one of the greatest architects in the world. At Columbia, I had listened to his concepts about how we ought to live as human beings, both spiritually and physically. He knew precisely what environments he would create to achieve this. I had seen him examine the Seagram Building inch by inch, seen him enthralled with Ayn Rand's monomaniac architect hero Howard Roark, seen him spend endless hours making sketches and drawing plans.

Arthur and I often quoted these lines from *Our Town*:

> *Do any human beings ever realize life while they live it—every, every minute?*
>
> *Stage Manager: "No."*
>
> *Pause. "The saints and poets, maybe—they do some."*

It occurred to me then, and has been confirmed ever since, that Arthur is a genuine poet—someone who realizes life "every, every minute." I believed that, unlike in anyone I had ever met up to that time, his sensibilities had led him to an immediate appreciation of life.

I COULD HEAR BIRDS SCRAMBLING in the trees as we walked, cars going by. For some reason, there were no other pedestrians out. It was as if this conversation were taking place in the middle of the night, or in the very early morning. I felt myself slipping into an oddly calm frame of mind—the warm feeling when you are about to open a gift from someone you love.

"Sanford, do you remember Sophocles? Do you remember Philoctetes? Here was a guy stranded on an island for years, with an infected leg, a horrific festering sore. The gods had given him a special armamentarium, arrows that could pierce any object, but he didn't use them, except for survival. He suffered until Odysseus, through an intermediary, asked him to use his enormous talent and skills to help conquer Troy by vanquishing Paris. The request compelled Philoctetes to confront himself.

The question tore at his being. His decision, however, was affirmative. So come back with me and conquer Columbia."

These last simple words, following unexpectedly from that little academic recitation, struck home with such force that I could not speak. I knew he was right. I knew that, at this moment in my confusion, it was this that I needed to hear more than anything else. I could have gone to Rebbe Menachem Mendel Schneerson, the revered Orthodox spiritual leader, or I could have gone to the pope, or even, dare I say it, to the Almighty himself, but none of their words would have mattered to me so much then as these words spoken along Saranac Avenue in Buffalo. This was Arthur speaking to my heart.

So it was that, during that visit to Buffalo, Arthur tore the cover off the subterranean thoughts about returning to Columbia that were struggling to reach the light in my mind. The idea of my returning was, in Buffalo terms, terribly foolish. Arthur, artist and poet, could afford the luxury of crazy ideas. As for me, I did not know *what* I was any longer. Blind, I had the luxury of...nothing. I could hunker down in Buffalo and be safe. But safe from what? And for what? Arthur seemed to think that the sky was my limit.

We did not speak for many minutes as we continued side by side along the avenue, me stumbling occasionally on cracks in the sidewalk (a hallmark of Buffalo winters and springs). Then, we came to a large open area without tree cover. I recall the sun warming my body.

Since freshman year, Arthur had been my teacher. Now, once again, he was bringing light into my life. How could I not believe him this time? I moved so that I faced him directly and put my hands around his upper arms. "Arthur," I said hesitantly,

"I get it." Three positive yet noncommittal words. But this is what was in my head: *Now I have to go back to school.*

For a long time afterward, I wanted to think it was Arthur who made my return possible, and in a sense that is true—but the door swings both ways. I was going back because of him, yes, but also *for* him; the meaning of that took me years to fully grasp. In taking, the receiver offers an opportunity for the giver to give. The giver is a receiver, and the receiver a giver. I owe my life to that balance.

We said a lot more on that walk down Saranac Avenue. Though it was quiet out, it was noisy inside my head. I started to think about everything I would have to do to return to Columbia. One thing I knew for certain: my decision would outrage just about everyone. I liked that—not outraging my family but shocking the people back at school.

But the walk with Arthur was for me the beginning of the end of gray hopelessness. It lifted me out of the grave. I felt as if I had been reborn. I now had a clearly defined goal—a thrilling one. I knew there would be risks, but the possible reward was redemption. What I did not know then, of course, were the terrifying and amazing experiences ahead of me. How could I? But that was for later. For now, I could still move. I could go forth. And this time I had a clear direction. This was a gift to me that welled up from far deeper than mere friendship, and soared far beyond it.

MY MOTHER SAT WITH ME at the kitchen table thumbing through a stack of mimeographed pages and a fat textbook titled *Constitutional Law*. Everyone at home seemed to accept that my days at Columbia were over, and I had yet to announce my decision. In the meantime, my mother accepted my stubbornness to continue with my coursework.

"You'll have to be patient with me, Sandy," she said. "I really want to do this right for you."

"Take your time," I told her. "This material is as hard for me as it is for you."

"For a girl who didn't finish high school," she replied, "this is quite a challenge. I remember studying the Constitution in school. It always had a special meaning for me. Your grandparents could not imagine it—they had all they could do to survive." She began to cry and could not continue reading. There was complete silence in the house—my father was at work and my siblings were in school. I heard only the crickets and an occasional car passing by.

"Marbury v. Madison ..." she began.

Not that old chestnut again. I interrupted her: "Can't we pick another case?"

"Will you excuse me? I have a headache. I need to lie down for a few minutes. Then we can start again."

Her gentle hands closed the book and the folder, and she left the room. I remained in the same kitchen chair on which I always sat during the dinners that had so often been filled with talk and laughter. As I lowered my head onto the table, I could not help but think that, until I returned to college, she would have to juggle her love and responsibilities for my father and my siblings with the need to read to her blind son for hours each day. It was an appalling agenda, but as she had done in the past, she was prepared to sacrifice her very existence to help her family. Constitutional law cases—arcane theory and Latin legal terms—and concepts of physics are heavy going for almost anyone. For my mother, it meant reading dense, unfamiliar material for hours on end; for me, it meant comprehending and sorting out words and phrases that seemed to float in the effluvium of my mind. They were equally exhausting tasks.

Sue, facing her own college finals, had also been reading to me during those long days and evenings after my return to Buffalo. She knew about my decision to go back to Columbia, and her support gave me courage. But I needed my family to get behind this as well. The courage to tell them would have to come from me.

IT ALL CAME DOWN TO ONE INEVITABLE, dramatic moment at the dinner table. The scene lives in my memory with exceptional clarity. I quietly informed my family that I had decided to make a full return to the university. There was a mind-shattering silence. I heard Carl's fork fall to his plate. Joel, Ruth, and Brenda stirred nervously in their chairs.

"You can't go back," my mother snapped.

"*Duvid* [David, my middle name, in Yiddish]," Carl began as he pushed back his chair, its legs screeching on the floor. "No, no, no. You must stay here. I will not allow it. You will not go back. You're blind, you're blind."

"Carl, stop it," my mother interjected. The more I remained calm, the more upset she became. But she knew that rationality would have to prevail if she wanted to prevent my return. She needed reasons. Anger was palpable in her voice as she said, "Sandy, it will be impossible for you to go back. Do you understand what it will mean?" She paused, then continued, "Why don't you stay here in Buffalo? You could teach, you could get a good job, you could go to work for your father—he could train you."

I slowly lifted the mashed potatoes to my mouth and chewed them automatically, quivering silently, toes tapping the floor as I waited for the next volley from my father, who was now standing at the head of the table. Afraid of what might happen, I suddenly felt that I had to fill the air with words. But first I tried to deflect the tension by turning toward my siblings, hoping to obtain their sympathy and support.

"I *must* go back, don't you see? If I don't graduate with my class, I'll be set back for the rest of my life. I will never recover. And I can't stay in Buffalo. There's no future for me here." They wisely remained mute.

In the context of the moment, that last statement was a bad lapse of judgment, but not nearly as bad as what I then inexplicably shouted as I jumped up: "Look at what your God did to me!" I pounded the table with my fist, shattering a plate, and ran toward my bedroom. Carl managed to grab my arm, almost ripping it from my shoulder as he dragged me into the adjacent room. My mother followed.

Having removed me from the presence of the other children, he bent my arm behind my back and flung me onto a sofa. Pouncing upon me, he unwittingly pushed my face into the coarse fabric. My mother, shocked, did not speak. Although I was strong, I was so startled by Carl's swiftness that for a moment I did not resist. But the pain grew in my arm, neck, and head, and I started to struggle. As I began to suffocate, my head buried into the sofa, Carl screamed, "You will not go! You will not go! You will not go!"

My mother pleaded. "Sanford, you can't go back alone. You can't cross the streets of New York. You'll get killed."

Despite my own strength, I could not escape. Then I felt Carl's ambivalence as he released his grip. Uncomfortable about what he had done, he was nevertheless still angry at me. I had never encountered such intensity from my mother or so much ferocity from my father. Concern for me had moved him to this violent act. There could be no other reason; he had always been gentle. My parents were united in their determination to keep me from returning to New York City. But they were also terrified because they realized that the eventual outcome might not be to anyone's liking.

THE TAXI TOOK MY MOTHER AND ME on the familiar route from La Guardia Airport through Harlem and then on to Columbia. It was a warm day in the early fall of 1961. As we approached the campus, my mother described the crowded streets and those old, stolid buildings. The day I had hoped and fought for had arrived—and I no longer wanted it. The decaying odors and heavy air of the neighborhood screamed at me, telling me that the day was all too real. I slouched down, my heart sinking. I thought of the unsettled nights since that scene at the dinner table.

My mother came with me only as far as my old dormitory hallway, where I knew my way around. There was no one else in the hall. The pale concrete blocks were all there was—them and me. We said a quick goodbye. A kiss on the cheek, and she was gone. I didn't want to picture what was in her heart just then; I had my own immediate problems.

I felt my way down the hall. Then I was standing at an old wooden doorframe that I could feel was gouged and dented from the comings and goings of generations of students. A threshold. There was nothing behind the door except my old room. The doorway's lintel seemed small—I could feel the top as I reached up, hesitating to enter. All I had to do was open the door and walk through.

I could still turn around, I thought, make it down the hall and outside to the street with my old green suitcase, hail a cab, pick up my mother at her hotel, and return to the airport. We'd be in Buffalo by nightfall. A known life was waiting for me there—its jaws wide open, dripping safety. Although it was not the life I had imagined for myself, it was still a life, and I could try to make it a good life.

Before me, on the other hand, there was only the *possibility* of a life, a possibility so tenuous it seemed improbable. If I opened that door, I would have to go into the room. If I walked into the room, I would have to put my suitcase down. I would stand there alone. The room would smell musty, from the dust burning off the old heaters. I would have to unpack, feel my way around to the dresser, open the drawers, and put away my clothing. I would painstakingly struggle to separate my underwear from my socks, from the T-shirts, and from the slacks so I could get dressed with a minimum of fumbling. I would immediately begin to cut my fingers along the edges of the fraying wood drawers.

I thought about my old Buffalo neighborhood and how I knew it by heart. I knew the neighbors' faces and the positions of the trees, the lawns, the stores, and the junkyard. Everything was in its proper place. What did I know of New York City after two years? Proportionally very little. The city was of gargantuan scale and ever changing. If I stayed, I would have to conjure an image of everything I would ever confront: every building, everything I touched, every book I read (correction: that was read to me), every face, every hand I shook. I would have to marry voices with my own constructs of images of people I had never seen. Was my imagination capable of that? Would my mind be able to retain and process it all?

And Sue would probably *not* wait for me, I thought. Things would simply intervene for her, the way life intervenes. She might get an opportunity to pursue her education elsewhere, far from Buffalo. There might be a boy she would meet who, she would decide in her practical way, was a better choice. What woman would want to wait for me to take her elbow so that *she* could open doors for *me*, lead me around rooms, lead me to tables at dinner, make sure I did not eat the garnish, make sure my clothing matched? The list of difficulties rolled on and on in my thoughts. My stomach hurt, as did my head.

If I stayed, my downfall would just be a matter of time. I would be doomed. Not in some metaphoric sense but literally: walking out into traffic at the wrong time; stumbling down stairs; slipping in the shower; getting out of a chair and falling, hitting my head on the desk next to mine. To live this new life of mine outside the safety of home would be to thread the needle.

There was still no one else in the hallway. The other students were not back from vacation, and the campus had a hollow, desolate feel. The boys from good families would still be in their large stone houses in fine neighborhoods. Drivers would bring them back when classes resumed, or they would travel into the city on their own, not a care in the world, just eager to get back into the swing of things. Maybe not eager for the academic work but certainly for hanging out with the guys, goofing around, going to the football games or basketball games or crew meets. Going to fraternity parties and exploring the city and getting into trouble.

That part of my life was over, and I knew it. There would be no free time. I would have to work on my studies during all my waking hours—and almost all of my hours would be waking ones. If there was any time left over, say at two or three in the morning, I would use that time to write to my family and Sue.

Standing alone in that hallway, I was scared. I doubt that I had been that scared before, or had really known what it meant to be scared—to have an acrid taste in your mouth, to feel your bowels loosen, your gut turning over on itself. My hands and legs were shaking. I was thinking, "I cannot do this. I…can…not…do…this." My fingers ached in anticipation of all the hurt they would encounter, which would be extensive. I could hardly breathe. I opened the door.

I stood for a while in the open doorway, my arms resting on the doorposts, my face turned toward the room. I was deluged by the memories of those dark, sleepless nights during the past school year, with pain in my eyes so sharp I thought they would burst from their sockets. The cold packs on my eyes, the pacing of bare feet on the cold floor, the futile squeezing of the temples. Somewhere in the recesses of my mind, I had known I was going blind, but I refused to accept the fact, choosing instead to prolong my denial and—foolishly, arrogantly—trying to force myself to live a normal life in the face of impending crisis. A tour de force of my will, my determination—and one hundred percent misplaced, leading inexorably to this day, this door.

Yet something embedded somewhere within my skull told me that the *possibility* for success was still there. Not just ordinary success, either, such as safety. But material success, which would involve being able to take care of myself and my family, to read and enjoy all the things one never has the time to enjoy fully—art, literature, music, whatever. The *possibility* of that greater safety— which I can assure you is of very special importance to blind people—was there. I could feel it, and it was an affirmation of my decision to return to Columbia. But it was hardly a guarantee.

I walked in, my heart pumping with fear and excitement, and set my suitcase down. The room smelled musty. I touched each thing in the room, slowly, carefully, deliberately. Oddly, everything seemed to be exactly as it had been when I had left in a panic. How could that be? I sank into the large, soft leather chair, which was just where it had been before. I sighed, the burden of the world on my shoulders. There was no relief in that sigh; I had no idea whether I'd made the right decision.

10

The Blind Senior

The first weeks of classes as a senior were nerve-racking. I was so intent on concentrating during the lectures that, in a sort of reverse Zen exercise, absorbing what was said became ever more difficult. I walked away from classes each day with my mind tied in confusing knots of sound and in mounting dread that I wouldn't be up to the challenges in front of me. The senior year at Columbia was generally considered to be easier than the junior year. But I was already many credits behind, and it was going to take enormous amounts of concentrated effort just to keep up with a normal workload.

Gradually, though, I began to open up my brain the way a fish opens its gills—it does this or it dies. I memorized virtually every sentence read to me that year, something of which I did not know I was capable. Instead of cramming before an exam and then dumping the information and forgetting about

111

it, I had to absorb material in a way I never had before. I still remember much of what I learned then. And I discovered that acquiring knowledge at such an insane pace would be a continuous wonder and joy for my life within the mind.

In order not to waste a single moment preparing for classes, I saddled myself with anything and everything I thought might be useful. I purchased all the required books and then some, as well as dozens of blank recording tapes. I prospected for readers among my friends and acquaintances. Professors selected students they thought would be able to help me. I called up all the institutions for the blind to request volunteer readers. (I will forever be deeply grateful to those readers at Columbia and in my later studies. They made possible the life I was trying to build back for myself. Many became dear friends for life as well.)

Through all these people, I was able to set up a most intricate and complex web of meetings. My planned schedule of readers began at eight o'clock in the morning and, except for classes, would end at midnight. I set aside no time for breakfast but reserved ten minutes for lunch and a half hour for dinner. Weekdays from midnight until 2:00 a.m. as well as Saturday nights were reserved for listening to tapes. I wanted to feel secure, so I clutched at everything.

My elaborate scheduling did not work quite as planned. Many of my readers, with the best of intent, were nonetheless human and did not show up as promised. Others came late. Some came at the right time but on the wrong day. Still others came on the right day but at the wrong time. There could be four-hour stretches with no readers, and then several would show up for the same one-hour period. To make matters worse, some of the friends with whom I made arrangements to travel around campus to difficult locations would fail to appear, leaving me stranded somewhere. To the last, however, and in spite of his own demanding schedule, Arthur remained my strongest and most reliable source of support. Staying true to our pact, he always came to my rescue. Sue helped as well, regularly sending me readings on tape.

My volunteer readers recited *The Aeneid* to me that first semester. They read to me about Renaissance art and abstract expressionism, the Schrödinger equation, quantum mechanics, the Battle of Stalingrad, Shantideva, Gregorian chant and twelve-tone music, Thermopylae, and cultural variations. The voices of the readers became one voice.

Aside from the need for readers and some study notes I could make in very large, thick black letters using the shred of sight left to me (which would be lost all too soon), I began to rely on my tape recorder—one of my new survival tools. Since the time my mother and Sue began reading books aloud to me, I had had only their voices as sources of information. By the beginning of summer, that process frustrated me. It was an enormous imposition on them and served as well to make my dependence virtually complete. Those feelings gnawed at me. I had resisted asking for a tape recorder because of the financial burden it would place on my parents, but I finally summoned up the courage to ask, and they responded by purchasing a reel-to-reel machine.

In those days, there were no cassette or microcassette tape recorders to slip into the side of a book bag, let alone digital recorders the size of one's little finger. The model I got was typical: two feet in length, one and a half feet in depth, and one foot in height. When its top was opened, another two feet by one and one-half feet was added to any surface. The thing was so heavy and cumbersome that I had to use both hands to move it, and of course when I got back to college for my senior year, I had to haul it around campus to lectures and classes. The recorder was, nevertheless, a crucial step in advancing my education. It provided me with a degree of intellectual independence for the first time since the onset of blindness.

Like the voices of my readers, the voices on the tapes I made all sounded the same to me. I heard those voices in my sleep—when I did sleep, which was only four hours a night. In my dreams, there was now the hum and winding noise of the tape recorder, the tape rolling between the magnetic heads, sometimes getting caught, and the snap of the auto-off switch, each snap sounding like a gunshot, my auditory system having become so highly sensitized.

I set outrageously ambitious deadlines for myself. All senior year I worked like that—early morning to past midnight, single-mindedly attacking my work schedule for that day until full completion—and all year there were those bad dreams. Even while awake, I would hear the crack of a door, the pop of a bottle cap, and think that I had fallen asleep while listening to the tape recorder. Then there was the accompanying panic that the very minutes I might have missed were going to set me back, and lead to…what? To downfall and doom. Determination does not rule out waves of self-doubt and pessimism. When you are blind and in the Big City, things can go south in a New York second.

One Saturday in the fall, I went to a football game with a bunch of my friends. It was probably one of those good old Ivy League games—maybe Columbia-Princeton. Everything was fine for the first quarter. We were all having a grand time. Then someone had to go get a hot dog or use the restroom, so we all had to stand up. At that point, a person behind us accidentally (I have to believe it was accidental) knocked into me, and I got pushed forward a little bit. I reached out to steady myself on the back of the person sitting in front of me. But the person who had been there was gone. I toppled over the bleachers for a row or two. No broken bones, but I did need stitches—the first of many, many such times—and I felt like such a fool.

Amid the chaos of my early efforts to adjust, I had already begun thinking about the future beyond my senior year. The prospects looked unpromising. I assumed that the better graduate schools, especially the law schools, would not readily accept anyone who might appear in the slightest way unable to deal with their bloated reading lists. I traveled up to Harvard to talk with the dean of the law school—a humorless giant of a man with a wide mouth and fat cheeks, I was told—about my prospects for law school. That he even took my appointment was surprising. I asked him, given my presumed limitation, what advice he might have for me. He replied that I should continue on my course of study but that it would not lead directly to the law at this time. At least he softened the blow with "at this time." I accepted his advice.

Back at Columbia, I began to apply instead to PhD programs in government studies and international affairs. Graduate study at Harvard was still on my mind. I crossed the esplanade to meet with Samuel P. Huntington, my international-relations professor, who would soon be leaving Columbia to join the Harvard faculty.

After our meeting, I descended the campus steps and, upon reaching the edge of the famous statue of Alma Mater, placed my foot too far in front of a step. Alma Mater, her imposing bronze body couched on a square of concrete, presumably continued staring into the distance as I crashed down the steps in front of her. My pants were torn, my sport coat and shirt covered in blood, my head bruised. I got up, happy that at least no one seemed to have seen me and rushed over to help, and hobbled back to my room.

I decided to hedge my bets and apply to as many graduate schools as I could manage: Harvard, Columbia, Princeton, Yale, Wisconsin, Chicago, and Cornell. Arthur helped me with the application process, as did Sue. We worked feverishly to meet the deadlines, and we decided to inform the schools straight out that I was blind.

Arthur's writing hand almost melted filling out those applications. It was not just the application forms, either, which were many. There were also the essays. Why did I want to study government? Why did I feel I was suited to do so? Why did I want to study at "our" school? What was my background? What were my interests? Well, my overriding interest was to be able to see again, but that did not seem to be in the cards. I also used to like to sleep a few hours a night, but that was clearly out as well. I used to enjoy going to parties, but I had to forget about the partying that all my friends were doing. My interests had boiled down to me and that damned tape recorder.

Anyway, no Harvard law degree. But graduate study in anything was hardly a fallback to some dismal second choice. Issues of governance had long been of interest to me. Having fled the horrors of a once-civilized Germany, my family had imbued in me a sense of patriotism and pride in our country. The promise of the righteous land that had rescued their own lives was being fulfilled each day I attended the university. That realization was never far from my thoughts. It fed my resolve and helped motivate my ant-like discipline. Still does.

To CALL THE WIDE ARRAY OF THINGS Arthur did for me after I returned to the university "kind" or "thoughtful" or "gracious" would be an insult to him. Those words convey far too little. He divorced himself from the life he had been living, altering his own ways to conform better to mine. He fixed the tape recorder when it was broken. He read to me every day all that was not read by others, which was a great deal—and for hours at a time. He also read to me when others failed to show up or when I needed someone close by for whatever reason. He not only filled out my graduate-school applications, he also kept audiotapes of them (so I could refer to them if necessary).

Arthur would sit beside me on the bed, or he would pull a chair up to my desk. He arranged papers spread out on the floor. Like spies, we would also map out my work in the basement of his home in Forest Hills. There was nothing he would not do for me: He walked me to classes; he picked me up from classes. He escorted me across the city. He bandaged my shins when I bloodied them, which was often. He also bandaged my forehead and my knuckles, getting my blood on his hands and under his fingernails. In this way, we were like brothers. He did not say anything about his help, though I knew he did not like the sight of blood.

What my roommate and friend did, he did without having to be asked, and with vigor. He did it quietly, too; after the walk down Saranac Avenue, we never once discussed his decision to help me in the ways he did.

I certainly needed his help beyond the support I received from my readers. The help I required most urgently was to have

117

study material read to me every night. He would say, "Darkness is going to help you today." Or, "Darkness is going to read to you from *The Iliad.*" I suppose he meant that for me his voice was emerging from the darkness. The voice was smooth and light. He would read with expression and intensity, as if he had written the words he was reading.

When he walked me to classes, we walked as if nothing was wrong and talked en route. Anyone who happened to notice us must have thought it odd to see one young college student holding on to another—unless they had heard of my situation, as many people on campus had.

It was not as if Arthur did not have much to do. He was a motivated student of architecture, and he took the extensive coursework quite seriously. There was a clear formula for students back then: do the work, go to the best graduate school, get the best job, earn a lot of money, spend your life around the best people—whatever those things may mean to each student.

I do not know to what hope my dear friend most ardently clung at the time. He was an artist, a poet, a singer, and a guitar player. He mostly wanted to be an architect, however, and that demanded diligence. Left-handed, he wrote and drew with such care and precision that it was a minor miracle when he finished any graphic piece at all. While I studied, I could frequently hear the slow drag of his pencil against paper. Sometimes he would sing to himself while he worked.

What was the cost to Arthur of all the help he gave me? Reading for countless hours. Holding my elbow while taking me to meet my social worker. Holding my elbow on the subway. Holding my elbow to cross campus. Turning me away from oncoming buses, from potholes, from misfortune and tragedy. Helping me not to experience confusion or terror. Helping me with the tape recorder—that iron maiden I was wedded to. Collecting my mail and reading it to me (including all the small print). Reading my teachers' nearly indecipherable handwritten comments. Helping me plan my future and work for it.

Sometimes just his being there was the biggest help of all. We were roommates, after all. When you are blind, you are unable at times to distinguish night from day, to separate when to be awake from when to sleep. The sound of Arthur's breathing—the one deep breath before he got set to sleep at night, as he made himself comfortable in his bed, maybe reading by the light of a small lamp or finishing a drawing—was important for me, even necessary. It was part of being a normal human being living with other human beings. As a blind person, you have to pretend that everything is okay when it is not. Arthur understood this very well. Last but not least, there were his words of encouragement, the expressions of faith, the expressions of knowing something that was impossible for him to know but sounding as if he did.

Businesspeople and policymakers would refer to the hours and hours of help Arthur gave me freely in terms of the "opportunity cost" to him. What, then, was the "opportunity" for which he was willing to sacrifice hours of devotion to his own expected career in architecture? What he did for me stands outside of scale or measure.

ONE DAY, ARTHUR DASHED INTO OUR ROOM, a copy of the *New York Times* tucked under his arm. "Sanford," he said, "let me read you this article…" It was about me and how I was managing at Columbia, despite my disability.

I had known this was coming, of course—I'd talked at length with the reporter—but with all I had to do just to get through each day, the article had been low on my priority list. Arthur, though, insisted on reading it aloud. Thus I learned that at six foot two and 180 pounds, I "looked like a blocking back with glasses" and dashed around the campus like one, too. The dashing, my faculty adviser explained, was "pride....He had to prove to himself that he could manage as well—and better, if possible—than the others."

The reporter noted that I was now earning higher grades than in my days as a sighted student despite a heavier work-load than most upperclassmen. "It's a grind," I explained. "It has to be. Simple things like turning back textbook pages become painfully intricate tasks when those pages are on a tape recorder. But it's worth it. I'm fighting total frustration, and I feel I am winning."

Nights, I confided, were the worst time for the blind, "and when they awaken, the reality of their darkness is heartbreak-ing." That, in fact, is how the article ended.

"Well, what do you think?" Arthur asked as soon as he had finished.

"Arthur," I answered, "let's start with the last sentence first: 'And when they awaken, the reality of their darkness is heart-breaking.' It's not exactly what I meant. It was a glib statement. When I was reborn as a blind man, when the metal pads came off, it wasn't the reality of my darkness that was heartbreaking. When I had my eyesight, I didn't really use it, and I didn't use time. I didn't stop and really see all that was around me. That's the heartbreaking part. It concerns the loss of *time*."

Uncharacteristically, Arthur did not speak for a minute or so. Finally, he said, "I think we all squander our lives away—and we don't even know we're doing it."

"So what's the use of it all, then?"

"Maybe not much," he replied.

We both needed relief. We always thought we had the answers, but now we clearly had none. "I think the article is terrific," Arthur said, "don't you?"

"It's terrible," I said.

"What do you mean?"

"Now I have no place to hide. Everyone will think I'm a blind man."

"Sanford, you're dead wrong. It's a terrific article—highly complimentary of you."

"That's not the point. It's that I am *not* a blind student. I will not allow myself to be blind, or to be thought of that way. In any event, I don't deserve the acclaim."

"What do you mean?"

"A blind man rises from his chair—applause. He walks across the room—a standing ovation. That's what I mean. If over the years I achieve something significant by everybody's standards, then I might deserve some praise."

"I disagree," Arthur insisted. "What you've accomplished the past year has been incredible."

In my heart, I agreed with him, but doing well "for a blind person" wasn't enough. "I guess the article is okay in its way," I allowed. Anyway, the *Times* was right about one thing: I had come to believe I was winning, and, perhaps foolishly, I was confident I could pass the tests ahead.

11

Tough Love

At the end of October of my senior year, I decided I had to do something about the everyday-living side of my dilemma. I spoke with my doctor, who immediately arranged an appointment for me at what I will call the Institute for Blind Persons. Two days later, Arthur and I worked our way there through Midtown Manhattan crowds.

I was introduced to a Miss Borlak (not her real name), who was to work on my "case." She had a high-pitched voice, and her perfume seemed vaguely reminiscent of dry grass. Arthur told me later that she was probably in her early thirties, wearing glasses and purple lipstick. As she led me to her office, leaving Arthur in the waiting room, I noticed that her hands were soft. After the routine biographical information had been taken, she wanted to know whether I had any particular problem. I mentioned that things were not proceeding perfectly but that I hoped they would shortly arrange themselves.

After more of what I assumed were the standard preliminaries, Miss Borlak suddenly sprang an abrupt change of pace on me: "How do you like being blind?" I was taken aback. The question was blunt, if not crude. However, since I was asking her for help, I felt compelled to answer.

"To be frank, I don't like it. The fact is, I dislike it very, very much. The past couple of weeks, especially, have been extremely disturbing, and I really don't know that I'm going to be able to graduate this year."

"Let me be a little more specific," she responded. "Do you consider yourself to be a blind boy?"

That seemed an odd question, but I answered, "Well, in the sense that I can't read or move around by myself, I guess you might say that I'm blind. I don't think it's all that important whether or not I consider myself blind."

"It *is* important," she replied, "particularly because it affects your attitude toward life, and now you have a whole new life ahead of you. A different kind of life, not the normal, regular life you've been used to leading."

She was toying with me, in a way. I seemed to be defiant, and I made a guess that she hated defiance, particularly when she was in a position to help. It angered her to think that I wasn't going to appreciate her help, although she understood my attitude. It made sense to her—the issue of denial.

Some of that made sense to me, too, but I was not totally in step with it. She had thrown her sallies at me so rapidly that I had no time to digest them fully. When the half-hour introductory session was over, I left in a somewhat uneasy state of mind.

She walked around her desk and opened the door. Arthur ran up from the waiting room to get my elbow.

On the way back to our room, we discussed the meeting. I told him some of the things Miss Borlak had said. As I was speaking, I suddenly realized I had been naïve in the interview. I had a vague feeling that she was grasping for something. I had not helped her out but was not sure I wanted to. We returned to our dorm room to find three of my friends outside the door discussing which of them had come to read at the wrong time.

How I had gotten to that moment—that blurted-out assertion that "I don't think it's all that important whether or not I consider myself blind"—had not been easy. Just a few months earlier, I had been plagued by my own insecurities, by my desperate efforts to keep up with my studies, by my almost pathologically demanding determination to lead a "normal" life—the "life" the *New York Times* reporter took note of—and by what seemed to be the impossibility of obtaining the logistical support necessary to do so. In fact, my encounters with Miss Borlak were shortly to prove one of the critical factors in my turnaround from insecurity toward self-confidence, but not in the way she probably expected.

AT OUR SUBSEQUENT MEETINGS, Miss Borlak wasted no time with social amenities. Taking command from the moment I stepped into her office, she continued the same line of questioning. "Now, tell me, do you consider yourself to be blind?" It was as if no time had elapsed between our previous conversations and this one. At our penultimate meeting, for instance, she asked, "Do you think it's important that you evaluate your situation in the context of blindness? Or are you still trying to confront your present problems with the attitude that you're a sighted person with some visual difficulty that can be overcome by slight changes in your daily routine?"

I was surprised by her aggressive tone. I thought these sessions were supposed to deal with practical problems of daily living and were not intended to be psychotherapeutic. I did not know how to respond.

"I feel that I'm making a great effort to cope with the problem," I replied. "Because I can't read, I use readers and tape recorders. And because I can't easily travel about by myself, I often travel with someone. I don't think this is an unusual way to handle the problem. I haven't begun to perfect all the techniques that I'm sure would be useful, and that's one of the reasons I'm here."

I sensed her impatience. "That's precisely my point," she said. "You won't admit you're blind. You do everything you can to avoid being a blind person. You are fortunate in that your blindness is not as obvious as it is with most others. You are able to focus your eyes on objects, or at least appear to be able to. This is fortunate for you socially, but the plain fact is that you are blind."

I winced. The words came across as harsh, but they did not disturb me as much as Miss Borlak probably thought they would. She continued, "You're trying to do everything you used to do, as though nothing happened. If there are some inconveniences, you merely drag people in to help you face the problems. A perfect example is the fact that since you can't travel alone, you travel with someone else. Every week you come here with your friend, and you think nothing of it. Certainly, he is a devoted friend, but can you call him constantly to aid you? Is he or someone like him going to travel around with you for the rest of your life? You take about two hours out of his life each time you come here, and I can't even begin to think of the many other hours you demand of him."

I was now annoyed, and I was sure she knew it. I was about to respond angrily but thought better of it. She must have believed that her prodding would provide me with important insights. "Miss Borlak, I'm not convinced that this is your concern. My relationship with Arthur is a personal matter."

Miss Borlak was not at a loss for words. "Don't you think," she said, "it would be easier for those around you if you could travel independently? Wouldn't that restore your pride?" I was unhappy about that suggestion but nevertheless thought about its merits as she continued. "You may not like this idea, but I think it will enable you to adjust and lead a more normal life. As you probably know, there are various other means of traveling for blind persons. One of the most popular, of course, is the use of a dog. They are wonderful companions, as good as humans, perhaps even more loyal. I believe that if you would agree to use one, the institute could make arrangements to procure one for you. A dog can become a best friend."

"I already have a best friend," I said. I thought about relying on a dog and how degrading that would be. A dog would proclaim my blindness and my dependence to the world. Moreover, it would not only proclaim it; it would in itself *be* a dependence. No, I would not use one—I would remain independent. FDR, the great president, had always been a model of how one handles a disability—you carry on as if it doesn't exist.

"Or, if you would prefer, there are canes available," Miss Borlak added. "Canes are better than dogs as guides in some ways because they don't require upkeep and generally cannot be damaged. The institute can arrange to procure the most modern, lightweight collapsible model for you." I was still reeling from her comments about a dog, so the idea of a cane made me suddenly deeply sad. Politely, I asked her if we might discuss this again next week. "Well," she asked again, "how do you feel about being blind? It can be a big change in a person's life."

I looked up at her as if she were saying something very foolish, which she was. For a moment, she probably wondered whether my being blind was an elaborate scheme, for I looked directly at her. "I don't know," I said. "I don't enjoy it, obviously. Right now, I'm trying to adjust to things." I was being forthright, and yet I had the feeling that my responses came across to her as somehow rehearsed.

She concluded with, "I hope you will give these ideas serious consideration."

As Arthur and I stepped into the warmth of the sun, he must have seen my fixed expression because he remained silent. Miss Borlak had touched upon one of the painful truths of my situation. It was indeed inappropriate, even unfair, to burden my friends, and in particular Arthur. I could not easily travel alone. In many situations I did require assistance, which was at times seriously inconvenient for my friends. Since I could not bear the thought of a dog or a cane, I remained perpetually torn about asking friends for help. This was a monumental dilemma—one that, if not resolved one way or the other, promised to extend throughout the rest of my life, as Miss Borlak had bluntly pointed out. That would not be acceptable. There had to be a resolution, and before long.

AT WHAT TURNED OUT TO BE OUR LAST MEETING, in the spring of 1962, I came into Miss Borlak's office the same as I always had. Arthur brought me in and sat me down gently. I had an obvious scrape on my head from having bumped into something. She asked me whether I had changed my mind and accepted the fact that I was blind and was going to have to change my life. I said that I could not see—she was right about that. "No," she said, "you're blind. You're a blind man. You need to understand that."

"That's not really why I'm here."

"Why are you here?"

I was almost too angry to speak. She wanted me to reveal all. "I'm here because I thought this might be of some use to me. I did. But I can see that it's not. I don't want a dog or a cane."

"You don't even want to admit that you're blind, do you?"

"Well, I'm not," I said.

"What do you mean you're not? Of course, you are." Her voice rose. "You're blind. And you need help. This is the Institute for Blind Persons. You came here for our help. Do you think it's fair to drag poor Arthur here all the time? Are you going to have people walk you around your whole life? What kind of way to live is that? You can't rely on other people. You have to do it yourself."

"I don't think," I said, trying to sound calm, "that whether or not someone helps me is any of your business."

"You just don't want to look at reality, that's all. I guess I understand it, but listen, it's not going to work out for you if you don't accept reality. You just need to know that. You do know that, don't you?"

I didn't say anything for a time. I just sat quietly. She had said what needed to be said, but at the same time I'm sure she still felt a deep absence, the lack of something—a lack of recognition.

Suddenly, however, something soft and heavy brushed against me. It was a dog. The door had opened, and a man, a dog at his side, had entered the room. I began to perspire. The dog was breathing heavily. Miss Borlak said, "I thought you would like to see how a blind man travels independently." I tried to remain calm but began to panic.

As I pushed my chair awkwardly back toward the wall, the blind man moved toward me. He groped for my hand and placed it on the dog. "You're blind, young man!" he shouted, echoing that rabbi in the Detroit hospital days after I actually was blinded. "You must use a seeing eye dog. That's the only way to travel alone and maintain your dignity. This is your first lesson. Get up!"

I jerked backward, striking my head against the wall. "Miss Borlak, it's not worth the price. I have to go. Where's Arthur?"

Arthur and I rushed out of the building. I told him that the meetings were becoming intolerable. "What's going on?" he asked.

"They want me to use a damn dog! They might as well give me a tin cup and sunglasses and sit me on a street corner." I clung lightly to Arthur's elbow in an effort to be inconspicuous.

THE EPISODE THAT HAS COME TO DEFINE ME began that same day, outside the institute offices at 3:30 p.m.

Arthur suddenly remembered that he had to turn in a sketch of the famous Seagram Building, also in Midtown, at nine o'clock the next morning. He asked me what we should do. I told him that I expected a reader back uptown at the university in an hour and that we had better start back right away because I would like to be on time. He replied that wasn't an option: he had to stay in Midtown and complete the sketch, as it would count heavily toward his final grade. For the next few minutes we discussed the alternatives and concluded that there weren't any.

By this time, our attitudes had become polarized: Arthur stuck to his position while I insisted that I not miss my reader appointment. The discussion turned into a debate as to the merits of the other person's "giving in." This made Arthur an even more stubborn proponent of his proposal that I stay in Midtown with him, while I dug in on the other side, claiming that were I to miss this reader, I would be finished at Columbia. We wasted half an hour in this way.

"Well, if that's the way you want it, so be it," I said. "I've got to get back."

"Are you sure?"

"Yes, I'm sure." I felt that I was being abandoned but shrugged it off and began to move forward as though I was part of the crowd. And so I was.

Arthur had now left me. I could feel that; his smell, his voice, his presence—all had disappeared. I would have to take the subway back up to the campus by myself. So why did I not just get into a taxi? The mentality of scholarship students figures here. We did not even *think* of taking taxis—a blatant waste of precious funds. My stubbornness was a factor, too. I didn't realize that the ordeal ahead of me would take on an almost mythic cast.

I began to walk in the direction of what I thought was the subway entrance. As I walked, I held my arms out in front. That must have looked silly to the people around me, now on their way home from work. My hands and forearms came up against suited elbows and women's backs although most of the people must have known to give me a wide berth.

There is always a spark of kindness in this world. A woman asked me where I was going. I said that I was trying to reach the subway. She asked what was wrong. I told her nothing was wrong.

"Clearly, something is wrong."

"No. I'm just having a little difficulty seeing. If you could point me in the direction of the subway, that would be a big help."

"I can, but if you're having trouble seeing, how would you know how to even walk there?"

The woman seemed young, but she had a throaty voice. As she walked along with me, she touched me here and there to make sure I did not step too widely out onto the street. "I'll find it," I said.

"If you're sure you'll be okay, then I'll tell you," she said. "But you have to promise me that you'll be okay. That you're up for it. It's not an easy thing."

"I am. I will be." She gave me the directions. She explained how many steps this way and then how many steps that way. I did not know how she knew how many steps would lead me to the stairway down to the track, but she seemed to know.

"I'm going to walk on," she said.

"Okay," I said, but I did not want her to leave.

I felt my way along the edge of a building until it disappeared and the street became quieter. It was a smaller side street, and no one was on it even though it was a busy time of day. As I walked farther along, I felt as if the street were sloping downward, but at least it was easier to navigate. I placed my arm against flat brick walls and continued. My foot went into the breast of a pigeon; it chuckled and moved out of the way. A rush of sadness came over me, not for myself but for this lowly creature. My hands now felt gritty from pressing them against buildings.

I came to an intersection I needed to cross. I walked into a man's chest, bounced off, and fell to my knees. "I'm sorry," I said.

He reached down with one hand and lifted me quick as a jump. "No, it was me," he said. "It happens all the time."

"What happens?"

"I take up too much space," he said. "It's hard for me to get around. Not that I can't move—I can, but other people seem to fall into me."

I didn't know what this man was talking about. I knew only that he was a giant, well formed.

"I'm a fighter," he said. "So I guess in some regards, it's good."

"A fighter? You mean, a boxer?"

"Yeah."

"That must be hard."

"It's hard to get beaten on every day. That's no fun. But winning is fun." He had a light voice. I would never have guessed that he was a fighter.

"You seem to be having some difficulty," he said.

"No," I replied.

"Are you sure?"

"Maybe a little. It's just that I can't see. That was why I knocked into you. It wasn't your fault."

"Really," he said. "Perhaps it *was* my fault. Though, sometimes no one is at fault."

I didn't know what he was saying. It was like talking to a ghost. "I'm sorry," I said. "It's just that I'm not myself. Can you tell me where I am?"

"New York," the man said.

"Am I close to Grand Central Station?"

"Very close. Right across the way there."

"Can you point me in the right direction?"

Then the man did something amazing. He took me by the shoulders and turned me right in the direction of the station. It was such a gentle movement that it was hard to believe he was a fighter. I could hear the noise of a crowd coming from over there.

"Thank you," I said.

I left him and walked across the street and into the station. I found a railing and hung on to it as I made my way down. The railing was rock-steady, and the anger and desperation I had been feeling in my stomach were gone for a few moments because I knew the railing would always be there. It had been there for a long time, providing support for countless people. This random thought gave me an inordinate amount of comfort.

I made it down into the cavernous main area of the station, which I knew was both broad and complex. I was aware from my sighted experience that I would have to find my way to the crosstown shuttle train to Times Square. The shuttle would take me west to a change to the uptown Broadway train, which would then take me some seventy blocks north to Columbia. It gave me a sinking feeling. I asked someone how to get through the central hall to the shuttle area. He probably thought I was drunk, but he told me anyway. I still had my arms out, as if sleepwalking.

Being told directions is one thing; following them when you are blind is another. I knocked into benches, suitcases, briefcases; into people who had their backs to me. I stumbled on coffee cups that people had placed at their feet. Somehow, the skin on my shins got split open; I felt blood wetting my socks. My knees seemed to be swelling, probably because I had banged them so many times. I wanted to be both dead and alive, but alive only if I could get out of that pit.

Fortunately, I recalled some landmarks from my days with vision, and travelers around me answered my questions and turned me in the right directions. By this method, bumping into people and asking questions, I made it to the general area where I could take the shuttle train crosstown to Times Square. When I hit a turnstile, I reached into my pocket for a token, felt around the turnstile for the token slot, and paid my fare. A small thing, but it was huge to me.

I was walking toward the track when I bumped head-on into an iron column. My arms, which had been held out like a zombie's, had missed it completely and it was my face, instead, that met it. Blood came down my forehead. I swiped at it with my forearm. It hurt, but worse than the hurt was the idea that everyone would see me bleeding. I wished that because I could not see people, they could not see me.

I swung around to get away from the column. My forehead was still bleeding, but I think it had stopped a little. The smell down in the subway was greasy and oily. It made me feel dirty. I started to shuffle, little by little, toward the platform area. I again had my hands out. I dipped my toe into empty space and was suddenly greeted by a terrifying sound—to my left a train roared toward my probing leg.

I lunged backward, changed direction slightly, raised my arms once more as I pushed onward. They hit something soft. It was a woman's breast.

"Pardon me!" this woman said.

"Oh God," I said. "God, I'm sorry, I can't—I didn't see you."

"That's a first," she said.

"I'm terribly sorry."

"It's all right. In my line of work, it happens, though never like that."

"Oh," I said.

"But you're not bad," she said. "You look like a nice boy."

"Oh."

"Are you?"

"What?"

"Nice."

I thought about what to tell her, what version of myself I should reveal. I didn't know, actually, if I was a nice boy or not, good or not, decent or not. I thought I was all those things, but it was as if this affliction was somehow bringing me down, was spoiling all the goodness in me into darker things. I thought again of the market in Buffalo and the blind beggar I had seen there with my mother. The entire scene repeated itself to me now. He was a sickly looking man, with peeling scabs on his hands. He wore ragged clothes that seemed to fall off him, and his eyes were not covered—they were marked with black specks, as if they'd seen fragments of a grenade. When he held out his hand to me, my mother drew me close. Now, battered and lost in the subway, I was becoming that man.

"Well, you seem nice," the woman said. "A nice young man. There's a cut on your head." She put her hand to my forehead.

"It's nothing."

"Are you sure?"

"No."

"Hmm."

"I have to get going," I said.

"Good luck. It's always the hardest, at first," she said cryptically, "but then it gets easier, I think."

She continued on her way.

Rocked by my frustration, I nonetheless was still feeling lucky that my encounter with the woman had not turned out as badly as it might have. That feeling lasted only until, walking a bit more quickly, I slammed into a baby carriage. I fell onto the concrete and felt as if the ground would not let me up. I think the mother caught the baby. She said something very quickly, which I could not understand. It sounded angry. I couldn't blame her.

When I got to my feet, I apologized. I said I was sorry for knocking into her, for knocking her baby down, for not being able to understand what she was saying, for not being able to see where I was going. I apologized for my poor condition, for being stuck down here. It was my fault.

Well, it *was* my fault. I had been trying to make it back up to Columbia, but it was becoming more than clear that that wouldn't happen. And it seemed as good a time as any to apologize to everyone for my general failure. To my family, who, though they didn't like the idea of my going back to the city, suffered it because, at least partly, they must have believed that I could make it. That was all done now. I had tried and failed— it happens. The image of my admired senator from New York, Herbert Lehman, and the image of John F. Kennedy—they were being washed away. They had for so long fooled me into thinking that anything was possible. I'd been a very young man then. But I was no longer.

I walked until I stumbled, and when I stumbled it was forward. My hand reached over a ledge, beyond which was the space where the train would arrive. I did not know whether one was arriving at that exact moment, but if it had, my head and shoulders were exposed so completely that I would have been severed in half. It would have been a reasonable way to go— quick and painless. I would be missed, of course, but I would no longer have to fake being a regular guy. And perhaps, lying there on the subway platform, I was already receiving the punishment for what I had done, for not accepting the reality of my situation.

This was Dante's Eighth Circle, the circle of the fraudulent: those who failed to carve out their own salvation. I wouldn't have to fake it any longer in front of Sue or my friends, who I knew relied on me for the posturing, for pretending that everything was fine. It gave them comfort to see me behave as if nothing had changed. They expected me to persevere. They had put their money on me and spun the wheel. They didn't know my burden—or perhaps they did, but appreciated that I didn't share it with them. Which made me, lying there on the subway platform, suddenly realize that if they relied on me for some sense of stability in their world, then it would be selfish of me to let myself go.

That was followed by a second flash of insight. Sue, Arthur, and the others not only relied on me; they *cared* for me, cared so much that I had a reciprocal responsibility to them—not to wallow in self-pity or throw myself on the sword of my own self-esteem but to stop trying to camouflage my blindness from those closest to me.

The train was coming. I got up and righted myself. I boarded with the others and gasped a sigh of relief. When my knees pressed against a seat, I sat. I was halfway home. My legs were bleeding, but the bleeding from my head, I think, had stopped. People must have been looking at me very much the way I looked at the ruined man I had seen many years ago near the butcher. The train echoed under the city.

The issue of making it back in time for my appointment had by now fallen completely out of mind. I was simply trying to make it back, which seemed highly unlikely. Then I smelled a familiar odor—something light, pleasant, something that had no place down here. I didn't know what it was.

Where and when to exit was no challenge. The westbound shuttle made only one stop. Recalling a large gap between the train and the platform, I made sure that I took a giant step out onto the platform at the Times Square station. As I was feeling my way out of the car and onto the platform, I bumped into another man. There was again that sense of something familiar. It was nearer to me this time, like a ghost. I asked him where I could find the platform to catch the train heading north up to Columbia, and he told me. I heard some people snicker at my exaggerated movements, and I felt shamefully conspicuous. Still, I moved along with those leaving the train and managed to get down the stairs to the uptown track.

By my now customary query method, I came to an area that I thought was the right platform for the uptown local. I wasn't sure, though. The express left from the same platform, but it didn't stop at Columbia. I turned to ask anyone near me whether this was the uptown local to Columbia at Broadway and 116th. A man's voice—muffled, as if he were trying not to be heard—responded: "Yes, it's the right platform." He added that the local was the track to my left.

The train pulled in and stopped, and the doors opened right in front of me.

I worried, very briefly, that after all this I might get a shoe-lace caught in the narrow gap between the car and the concrete. It would be a fitting ending. That did not happen. Instead, I got on the train and found a seat. The train pulled out.

I was almost completely exhausted. I felt as though I had lost several quarts of blood. And I was semi-delirious. Was this madness? Why had I engaged in this absurd enterprise? I might instead have foregone the appointment with the reader—recognizing that the importance of that particular meeting was largely a creation of my own imagination. Why had I not simply waited with Arthur while he made his sketch of the Seagram Building? None of this nightmare trip would have happened.

As the train made its way north station by station, the thought of my grandmother and my parents forced itself on me. Nothing—neither poverty nor fear of the unknown future, neither disease nor war—had deterred them from their emigration across Europe and the Atlantic Ocean. They would not compromise their hopes or their dignity, whatever the price. So how trivial was my little excursion?

After quite a few stops, the PA system announced mine, and then my weary feet got me to the top of the subway steps at 116th Street. I do not think I was ever happier to find myself back at the university. I felt my way to the iron gates and went through onto College Walk. As I began to make my way, I was stopped by a young man I recognized by smell as Arthur.

"Oops, excuse me, sir," he said, a slight sardonic emphasis on the last word. Then, in his normal voice, he said abruptly, "*I* knew you could do it...but I wanted to be sure *you* knew you could do it." He had been shadowing me all along. He later admitted that he had in fact not been assigned to sketch the Seagram Building at all.

We were silent for a moment as we stood near the university gates. I wanted to kill him. Then I became euphoric. I grabbed his hands, exultantly raised them, and swung him around me. In sweeping circular motions, we waltzed out onto College Walk.

Jerry Speyer, who was a witness to that subway trial aftermath, recounted it in a speech he gave adjacent to College Walk at the 2008 commencement of the Columbia Business School: "You or I cannot even imagine how Sandy felt at that moment, but he summoned something inside of himself, some untapped courage.... I tell you this story because it has remained with me for forty-six years."

It has remained with me as well. That moment at the gates of the university, the moment of my triumphant survival of that subway odyssey, was the moment when fear—fear of risk, fear of movement, fear of change—was vanquished within me forever. I don't know if Arthur had a cathartic moment of his own then. I can say only that I realized something profound—my friends and family had become angels who would be with me and never leave. I was strong because of the strength we gave each other.

12

Moving Forward

Spring of senior year was coming up fast, and I was not look-ing forward to it. Every day Arthur would go to the mailbox, looking for letters from the graduate schools, and come back empty-handed. I began getting a daily stomachache. Waiting for those responses was like being on death row. I was fairly certain I was not going to be accepted by any of the schools. Yes, I had very good grades, what with all my grinding work, but, well… Greenberg is blind. Nevertheless, I held on to the notion that *something* was possible. Something like an appeal or a pardon or the arrival of the cavalry in the nick of time. In a word: hope.

The first letter I received was from Princeton—a rejection. I do not recall exactly what it said, but the wording was formal and empty. It had nothing to do with me as an individual. Its text was almost certainly the same sent to many other appli-cants. Holding the letter as if it were a dead mouse, I took it to my anthropology professor, Margaret Mead, who had written me a recommendation. She was one of my advisers, and I was working for her as a research assistant. She was unpretentious and outspoken, and she had succeeded in a world dominated by men.

As I sat in her office, she picked up the telephone to Princeton. "The dean of the graduate school, please," she said while my heart pounded ever harder. Soon she was bellowing: "What the hell gives you the right to reject Greenberg? He's met all of your requirements and then some." A dreadful pause. The man probably responded that Princeton simply did not think I could handle their reading loads because I was blind. (This was before people were able to sue for such comments.)

"Goddamn it," Mead yelled. "Your reading lists are no tougher than Harvard's or Yale's. This is outrageous behavior on your part." She slammed the phone down. I never really heard the words she then used to console me. I staggered out of her office but had no place to go. I bumped into a concrete bench and sat on it for hours. Hard work and diligence would yield success, wouldn't they?

The worst part was that I thought the dean at Princeton might be right. I probably could not keep on this way, spending another four or five years earning a master's degree and then a PhD, all the while listening to tapes and readers. I wasn't sure if the proper metaphor was Job or Sisyphus, but one of them surely fit.

MEANWHILE, I STILL HAD MY ONGOING STUDIES at Columbia to attend to, and the occasional side highlight as well. Ike's visit, for example. During a cocktail reception for seniors at his palatial residence, John Palfrey, the dean of Columbia College, told me that former president Dwight Eisenhower would soon be visiting the campus where he had served as president before resigning to campaign for the White House and asked if I would like to meet him.

When I told Arthur about the invitation, he approved. "A great opportunity," he said. "Great fun. But what will you say to him?" Before I had time to respond, he shouted, "I've got it, I've got it. You want to make a lasting impression, right? Here's what you do. When you're introduced, get real close to him, face to face, look him straight in the eye, and say 'blue mud.'" Typical Arthur.

The day of the meeting arrived. It was a small gathering, men murmuring in the room. I had just entered when a military aide took my arm and escorted me to a back corner. There stood the man who had charted perhaps the greatest victory of the century—the Allied landing at Normandy—and then had led the entire country through a period of relative peace and prosperity. The introduction was formal. "Mr. President, Sandy Greenberg." At that, his hand was obviously extended toward me. For a moment, I hesitated. Then I thought, "blue mud." I found and clasped his hand. "Mr. President, it is an honor to meet you."

"Thank you, Sandy," he answered. I did not respond, and he broke the silence. "I understand that you have excelled at this university of which I am so proud." He said he understood I was going through a rough patch at school. I do not know how he knew this. I said I was, to some extent. He then took on a firmer, stiffer tone, perhaps of the same steel he had used to command his troops. He went on to tell me that much of his life was spent fighting the odds. He had been down before, like me, he explained. At one point, he had become the object of ridicule among his friends for having stayed in the military when everyone else left to make money. He had spent sixteen years as a major, he said, before he was promoted to lieutenant general. Sixteen years! That was nearly as many years as I was old. He was no stranger to failure, no stranger to languishing.

"There were many who underestimated me," he said. "Many of my setbacks were not short-lived, either. Despite them, I never lost confidence in myself." I told him I was very much aware of his accomplishments but until now did not understand how he had personally approached the enormous challenges he had confronted. It was clear that he was aware I had been moved by his words. I believed, or wanted to believe, that he had faith in me.

The inspiration lingered as I made my way back to my room. Then it was gone. All I could think was: Princeton rejected me.

ONE DAY ARTHUR CAME BACK FROM THE MAILBOX with a whole bundle of letters from the graduate schools to which I had applied. "The results are in. Would you like me to read them to you?" he asked. Although I could hardly bear the thought of being humiliated in front of my friend, I had no choice. His dedication to the process had been unflagging.

"Is there one from Harvard?" I muttered. "Open it, please."

The sound of him undoing the envelope seemed to go on endlessly. The letter finally unsheathed, Arthur stood up and in an exaggerated British accent read, "It is with great pleasure …"

Harvard wanted me to join its graduate program in government. The letters from the other schools read more or less the same, but we both knew it would be Harvard for me. I fell back on my bed, overwhelmed, as Arthur laughed. A friend brought in a bottle of Scotch. Arthur ran into our bathroom, grabbed a large glass, and poured it full of whiskey. Jerry ran in, and they both towered over me as I drank the entire glass.

THERE WAS MORE GOOD NEWS. First, I was elected president of my class. Then one day Norman Cantor, my professor of British constitutional history and one of my most important advisers, asked me to join him in his office. Cantor, who had been at Oxford as a Rhodes Scholar, had told me early in my junior year that "you can't be an educated man without attending Oxford." To that end, he had wanted me to apply for a Rhodes Scholarship, but Detroit had intervened. Undaunted, he now said that he had another idea for me about Oxford, but first he had a more pressing item to discuss. He leaned back in his chair and said with great satisfaction, "Sandy, you'll shortly be receiving some very good news which, I might add, is well deserved. You have been elected to Phi Beta Kappa." He paused, waiting for my response.

"Professor Cantor," I stammered, "this news is overwhelming." I held back tears. We often look back on early successes as lesser things, but at the time this meant everything to me. Phi Beta Kappa membership was an honor bestowed by my own faculty. It was as if, having been held underwater, I was finally able to resurface.

Professor Cantor was more set on getting me to Oxford than I had imagined. Because I could no longer apply for a Rhodes Scholarship—it did not permit married students, and I was now planning to marry Sue—he suggested that I apply instead for a Marshall Scholarship. I told him I would have to talk about it with Sue. Also, it seemed premature to talk about Oxford at all; I first had to figure out how I was going to get a doctorate while paying rent in Cambridge, Massachusetts. Even before that, and most immediately, I had to actually graduate from Columbia.

THE PODIUM WAS STATIONED in front of the statue of Alexander Hamilton. I stood as straight as I could. It was a languid spring day, and the smell of recently cut grass was heavy. The mortarboard sat uncomfortably on my head, tilted to the right, its tassel brushing my face. The graduation gown clung to my ironed shirt. My fellow members of the Class of 1962 and their families sat on lacquered wooden chairs in front of me. Behind me sat the dean of the college.

The audience quieted, but I remained silent for a moment. This spot, sheltered from the city, had been the heart of my college life. I could not avoid thinking of how much my life and I had changed since my high-school graduation four years earlier.

The wooden chairs creaked and clattered. The click of a nearby camera caught my notice; I supposed that Sue's father was taking a picture. I began to speak …

13

Paying Back

Sue and her parents began making preparations for our wedding in Buffalo, and they asked me to make the arrangements for the music. I got on the phone to the leader of the band we had picked. "Mr. Shiron," I began, "I want you to know how excited we are about the prospect of your playing at our wedding. I have an idea I'm very excited about."

"Well, Sandy," he said, "my band and I are also very much looking forward to it. We've known Sue's parents for many, many years. We've seen them at numerous events where we've performed, and they're fine people."

"Okay, here's my idea. My college roommate, who is also my best friend, has an absolutely beautiful voice. He would be honored to sing at the wedding."

"What, are you kidding?" he shot back. "You want a kid to sing with my band? My men are pros—we don't work with amateurs."

"Mr. Shiron, he's not just any kid. He has an extraordinary voice that I'm sure you'll appreciate when you hear him."

"What's his name?"

"Arthur Garfunkel," I said.

"Look," said Shiron, "I know you think he can sing, but my experience is that whenever someone is put forward like this, he can't."

"Well, Mr. Shiron, I believe you'll feel differently once you hear him, and in any event this is extremely important to me. I've been given the task of arranging for the music. I'd really appreciate it if you would accompany him when he sings."

"What does he have in mind?"

"Well, he'll be singing a number of songs, but the most important, the one to which Sue and I will be walking down the aisle, is 'And This Is My Beloved.'"

"It's a nice song," he said. "Have the kid give me a call."

The wedding was held on an August weekend in 1962 at a Reform synagogue that Sue had selected. Her rabbi officiated with my rabbi, who was Orthodox. My brother was best man. I had a number of friends there from college as well as from growing up. My family and some neighbors were there, of course, as were Sue's family and friends.

It was warm out, but I think not hot. I cannot quite remember the weather, nor do I recall events of the wedding in any particular order. I do remember feeling wonderfully accomplished, even though we were about to embark on a difficult period of life. One of the greatest accomplishments was finally being wedded to the love of my life.

I remember that as the rabbis were reading the religious marriage contract, the *ketubah*, which they did in Aramaic, I felt anointed and sanctified. I felt that something spiritual was transpiring, something sacred and holy. I felt buoyant, transcendent, filled with color and light. I was probably somewhat worried before and after the wedding. But *during* the event, I was beyond that. I had my wife by my side.

The reception was held in a lovely garden adjacent to the synagogue. Arthur sang beautifully. There was lots of dancing. As the band played the "Horah," the guests lifted Sue and me up on chairs and bounced us up and down until we got dizzy. Then they picked up my mother and father and twirled them around, then Sue's parents. The old-timers smiled and probably wondered how they had arrived at this point.

I thought about how far we had come. Not so many years earlier, Sue was a girl I desperately wanted to know. We were still kids now, but initiated and anointed and ready to start our real lives. I was going to be in school, with a certain handicap, and she was going to be working and helping me out. We did not have firm ideas about what we were going to do in the long term, but we hoped it would be something important, something great. I knew I was going to be with the person for whom I felt an unlimited, unabashed love.

AFTER OUR WEDDING, SUE AND I moved into an apartment at 19 Wendell Street in Cambridge, a tiny fourth-floor walk-up barely large enough for the furniture we had scraped together. Sue began working at a school for special-needs kids, some of whom were children of Harvard professors.

There was a great deal of apprehension among us new grad students as classes began. They were taught by men and women of enormous accomplishment. Those in my field, government, had all consulted with the White House at various times. One, a famous figure during the Vietnam War period and now thought of by many people as a war criminal, *was* a criminal in at least one sense. He borrowed my tape recorder to use for a book he was writing—and broke it. I spent a lot of money to replace it. Eventually, after plenty of prodding on my part, he compensated me for the loss, but without an apology. Another professor—Louis Hartz, the great theorist on American politics—became so excited during his lecture one day that at its conclusion he slumped over the lectern in exhaustion.

The Cuban missile crisis boiled up while I was at Harvard. I first got wind of the whole terrifying episode not from radio or television but from a professor of government, Richard Neustadt, another of my Columbia mentors who had moved on to Harvard. He was always professorial-looking—tweed jacket and pipe, very neat. He stood totally erect, as if he were a Roman orator, and all that was important to him lay not just in the Forum but in the heavens. I was walking across campus one day when, as usual, he stopped to chat. This time he seemed distracted. There was no pipe. He told me he had just gotten back from Washington, where he had been meeting with President Kennedy, and that things were not going well there. I asked him what was wrong. He only said that I should stay close to the television for the next few days.

I recall being uneasy following that chance meeting. That night the TV commentators were talking about what might turn out to be the end of the world. There was deep anxiety, even fear of the catastrophic. Yet in the back of most people's minds was the hope, the belief that the president was in control and knew what to do. We had parked our missiles in Turkey, and now the Soviets had theirs in Cuba.

There were otherwise both good and terribly bleak days for us in Cambridge. It is a rare thing to be among brilliant people all the time, to study under them—and I believe even rarer among students to appreciate the privilege as fully as I think I did. And then there were the friendships I made with the people who read to me, many of whom would go on to do great things in their fields.

On the downside was the little money we had, even with the generous support of our parents. Luckily, with fellowships and scholarships, I was soon earning most of what we needed. Of course, I practically had to kill myself to keep up the necessary grades (no mulligans for blind boys). And there was always the interminable work: the hours spent at night—when I ought to have been sleeping—learning all that I could, not only about my coursework but about my thesis topic, which was South Africa. I pored over history books and entire encyclopedias on the country.

The bleakest day of all—among the bleakest in American history—was November 22, 1963. The assassination of President Kennedy affected every one of us profoundly. He had represented everything good about the country. To my mind, he also seemed to be someone I could strive to emulate. Now, that role model, like my vision, was gone. A double loss.

THE DAYS WOULD GO LIKE THIS: wake at six; listen to tapes; prepare for class; see Sue off to school; listen to tapes; go to class; meet with readers (morning, noon, and night); talk to professors or classmates walking to and from class, with or without the help of a guide; eat a light lunch (often enough, a tuna sandwich); more classes; walk across the quad, lugging the tape recorder; nick my shins or elbows or knees; arrive home and listen to tapes; wait for Sue to arrive home; arrange things as tidily as possible; fail at this effort, or succeed only marginally;

keep listening to tapes from the classes; take a few minutes to consider the world and the perils of the future.

When Sue returned in the evening, she would throw down her stuff, let out a long breath, and begin to cook dinner, something simple and filling. We would talk for a bit, then eat. After that, I would continue with my tapes while she looked over her students' work. We were too tired to talk much. Visitors would often come over after dinner to read to me, and Sue would entertain them for a while as well. Sometimes they had dinner with us, and then our awkward silence would temporarily disappear.

Then we slept. In the morning, the same routine began.

Out of my own necessity, I also invented, and later patented, a compressed-speech machine that speeds up the reproduction of words from recordings without distorting any sound so that anyone who needs to absorb large amounts of recorded speech can listen to two to three hundred words or more in a minute. An ordinary tape playback could only reproduce one hundred fifty words per minute.

As Professor Cantor had recommended, I applied for a Marshall Scholarship to study at Oxford University. It was a scholarly thing to do, as well as prestigious, and I needed all the prestige and scholarship I could find in those humbling days. What would become of us after the conclusion of my studies at Harvard was uncertain. My experience and heritage seemed to require that I anticipate misfortune. Any advantage might help, and the Marshall selection committee thankfully obliged.

Sue's and my parents came to the dock to see us off to England. As we walked up the gangway, waving goodbye, Sue wept. But she was still young, and her spirit was too strong to be down for long. She did not know what misery lay ahead in England. Nor did I.

At Oxford, I was to continue working on my doctoral thesis on South Africa, following which I would return to Harvard to complete my work for the degree. Owing to the generosity of one of the professors at Oxford, I was given a gigantic office in the Bodleian Library to accommodate my many readers—an unprecedented gesture. Most faculty members did not have offices that large.

The Bodleian is the second-largest library in England, containing, among many other wonderful things, a complete set of Shakespeare's first folios. The library's holdings of letters and correspondence comprise "the sentences of gods," as a graduate student in Victorian English, one of my readers, expressed it to me. She was openly envious that I had my own workspace in the library. I admitted that I was lucky to be situated among so much of the collected brilliance of the world—as if its brilliance would drip off onto me. It was a bitter-cold brilliance, however. The library was frigid, offering nothing that could be detected in the way of physical heat. Cold makes me sleepy. Every single day I had the urge to flip the hood of my jacket up and lay my head on the table. In fact, what I remember most about England is that cold: Sue and I huddled up in our little rented apartment, the to-and-fro to the library, everywhere. It was the kind of cold you cannot imagine ever being able to shake off. And I grew up in Buffalo!

At one point, we ran out of money entirely and could no longer afford to heat our own little rented rooms. Not long after that we were hit with a triple whammy, part of it weather related. Sue came down with a burning pneumonia. Meanwhile, I found an odd lump emerging from the side of my face. In addition, complications from my previous eye surgeries had to be dealt with. All three problems required medical attention, and so we made an emergency trip home. I went on to Detroit for eye surgery before we returned to the country that sunshine seemed to have forgotten.

Eventually, Oxford wore me down. I had never thought of myself as pampered, but the winter cold was unrelenting, and the omnipresent hard surfaces were a constant threat to a blind graduate student trying to feel his way around an unfamiliar campus. Even so, I would never trade away that experience. Study at Oxford taught me, sometimes with gleeful nastiness, to seek precision in words. That in turn entailed an unrelenting pursuit of precision in thought, which in turn demanded accurately limned perception of the facts and clear, logical reasoning, all of which has been a priceless gift in disparate realms, from government and business to philanthropy and my personal thoughts. Oxford also provided us with a few memories that warm me still: the lovely English spring, mornings and evenings on Christ Church Meadow, rowing and punting on the Thames.

FOLLOWING OUR RETURN FROM ENGLAND, we spent a brief period back in Cambridge so I could finish up my studies and present my thesis. The oral exams for my doctorate were presided over by the world-renowned scholar Carl Friedrich, and they were intellectually violent. The one man among the panel whom I thought would be my advocate, Rupert Emerson, had been a kind, supportive adviser. But that day he treated me as if I were on trial at Nuremberg. It was as if my past three years studying political theory, international affairs, international economics, American government, and constitutional law meant very little.

It was not that I did not know the answers—it was as if the questions were not really being put to me as questions. They were more like accusations.

I finished the orals and went outside. All I remember, for some reason, was my right hand touching my left hand, as if to make sure my limbs were still there. I do not think I had ever experienced such an intellectual assault—and I had experienced many.

Afterward, I felt like a wake would be appropriate, but Sue and I had anticipated an easier time, and we had already agreed to meet good friends for lunch at a restaurant on Brattle Street called the Window Shoppe. The name was appropriate; it had always been a place to look in but never to enter. For us, it represented Yankee gentility. It was not so much that we could not afford to dine there (although we couldn't); it was more that we did not belong there, maybe today most of all. But our friends had insisted on treating us, and so off we went.

Bernard Shapiro, a Canadian who was working on his PhD in education, was one of my readers, and he and his wife, Phyllis, had become fast friends of ours. We would have them over for Passover seders, and they had us over many times as well. Phyllis, an exuberant woman, was always outgoing, always "on." Bernard cared deeply about providing education; he had graduated from McGill and would eventually become its president, or "principal" as that position is officially known. The Shapiros were a few years older than Sue and I, and it was nice to have been taken under their wing.

They greeted us at an outside table. I was still shaken. I felt no anticipated wave of euphoria, just headachy and tired, and I think Sue knew it. She told me to behave, that these were our friends and it was a special occasion. I do not recall what we talked about. They wanted to know how my trial went. I don't remember much about the food, just that I was sitting next to a white trellis, freshly painted, clean. The lunch concluded, and we all hugged. They congratulated me, and Sue and I went home.

I think we straightened up the apartment a bit, although I'm not sure why. Finally, I told her that I was exhausted and was going to sleep. I recall that being the deepest and most rewarding sleep I had ever had. It was like being dead, and being dead was terrific. I was several fathoms down. There was no sense of time or place, no dreams, just the vague comfort of knowing that I was finished, that I was warm, that I was somehow released, at least for the time being, from burden. Time passed. Sue slept next to me. She was warm, and that, as always, felt very good.

At around nine o'clock in the evening the phone in the other room started to ring. It must have been ringing a long time before I heard it. I do not know where Sue was; perhaps she was as deeply asleep as I. I remember being annoyed that she had not gotten up to answer the phone. I got up and ran for it, slamming my head into a projecting corner. Blood came out in spurts, splattering the walls, drenching me. At that, Sue woke up. She must have put a towel or cloth to my head, which did little to stop the bleeding. We knew the drill; we went to the Harvard health center. While we waited, even amid all the blood (it was hard to imagine that the human body could produce so much), I remember thinking that it was actually a pretty nice facility. The walls had a newly painted smell. I was eventually patched up, and we left at around four in the morning.

I didn't know it at the time because I hadn't been able to answer the phone, but I had my PhD. Stitches and all, I was now Dr. Sanford D. Greenberg, the crowning achievement of an educational odyssey that seemed (in my fevered memory) to have endured as many challenges as that famous odyssey chronicled by Homer 2,500 years ago.

Far more important to me, I had also found the opportunity along the way to begin reimbursing Arthur for his endless kindness.

SUE AND I WERE STILL IN OXFORD when I got a call from Arthur, who was now in architecture school. "Sandy, I'm really unhappy. I don't like being in architecture school. I don't like doing this."

"So what is it you want to do?" I asked.

"I really love to sing," he said. "You remember my high-school friend Paul, the guy who plays the guitar? We want to try our hand in the music business, but in order to do that, I have to have $400." This was in 1964—$400 was a lot of money then. In fact, Sue and my entire savings amounted to just over that amount, but I sent the money off to Arthur immediately. What else could I possibly have done?

PART 3

Tikkun
Olam

14

The Start of Something Big

After gaining my doctorate, I set my sights on a law degree. I applied to Harvard and was accepted. This was the path I had wanted to follow all along. It was woven throughout my mentality and had been since I had become aware, from the experience of my family, of where the perversion of law might lead. It also began to dawn on me that if I had gone straight to law school, I would have missed the intellectual excitement of the last several years. I was beginning to see the advantages of my turn in the road.

In the meantime, Arthur had been paying us visits in Cambridge, driving up from New York City on his motorcycle. One time he took off its front wheel to keep it from getting stolen and put it in our apartment bathtub. He thought this was reasonable. When Sue came home, she was not happy about it, and she let him know.

Those demanding years in Cambridge and Oxford may suggest that I was suffering from a kind of compulsion. I was. For what reason did it all have to be done with such urgency? It would have been reasonable in everyone's eyes for me to have taken my time about it, or to have foregone one or two of my degrees.

But I was bitten by some kind of bug. Once someone gets his or her resolve up and running, and gets it focused in a direction, it is hard to put on the brakes. In a word, there is momentum. Also, aggressive work habits form. For us blind people, it is especially hard to hold back because we are always concerned about security. Like those who survived and prospered long after the Great Depression but could never shake the habit of stockpiling food and cash for a rainy day, we never feel comfortable, in our guts, about sitting back and saying, "Okay, that's it. I've done enough."

So there was this hunger, but a hunger for what precisely? Surely not security alone, for even after Columbia I might have gotten decent employment of some sort. I have devoted a lot of thought to this question over the years, and I have come to realize that I had an endless hunger for *ideas*. Living an informed life within the mind, a mind in which thoughts proliferate and assemble, requires a steady diet of thought. The busyness in my mind, in the so-called darkness, is undisturbed by the constant flow of visual sense images. Picture thoughts as stars; during the daytime, sunlight obscures them. But not for me. When I listen to music, for example, my mind is at the ready—ready to be surprised and delighted by every note, every chord. This is one of the compensations for the loss of eyesight.

At Harvard, I had studied political science with Stanley Hoffmann, the author of many books on international politics and American foreign policy and later the founder of Harvard's Center for European Studies. At Oxford, I had the good fortune to come under the spell of Sir Arthur Goodhart. Sir Arthur, an American who had been granted an honorary British knighthood, was investigating how, in the post–World War II era, world leaders might create effective international legal institutions.

Surrounding those two scholars—and there were many, many others—lay a realm of ideas of the very highest importance for mankind. Within the work of these scholars shone, among other things, the nature of the rule of law. That central concept of today's liberal democracies is, on the one hand, a term of art, an abstraction within the scholar's field of study. On the other hand, the rule of law, built on principles of justice, is far from theoretical. It underlay the very real and practical salvation of my family.

After a half century of thought, I've come to the conclusion that the only really worthwhile things in the world are people and ideas. That is why the Western intellectual tradition, the tradition for which the Parthenon stands as a symbol, has meant more to me than merely collecting an array of intellectual concepts. It is the *substance* of that work, the collective force of the content, that has helped save me from slumping on a porch in the western New York hinterlands.

Arthur put his finger directly on this when, during that walk on Saranac Avenue in Buffalo so long ago, he reminded me that the words of the greats we were studying at Columbia were far more than mere words. The libraries at Columbia, the Bodleian at Oxford, the Widener at Harvard, and the main New York

Public Library on 42nd Street: these have all been for me an extension of the great wisdom underlying the Acropolis and the Temple Mount and Jabneh. How I love dropping the names of the great thinkers and innovators of history who made it possible for me to come back from that hospital bed in Detroit. And the names of the teachers who enabled my learning. Why not? This is my account, and I owe so much to them all.

I WAS A GOOD TEACHER MYSELF. I might have made a career out of that, might have become like one of those scholars I so admired throughout all those years. But that was not to be my way. I applied for one of the fellowship posts in the White House. After extensive interviews and other checks, I was offered a slot. The one-year post in the White House was a prestigious, once-in-a-lifetime opportunity for a young person. It would require that I take a leave of absence from Harvard Law School. (I never returned, I should add.)

I also had a wife. That was a major consideration. There are times when life can come before love, but it never did for us. Sue and I were in agreement on the White House fellowship. Late in the summer of 1966, we arrived in Washington—to stay, as it turned out. The Watergate would become our home in spite of the fact that the rent would eat up more than two-thirds of my salary. The spacious lobby seemed to welcome us in such a way as to say, "You are now living a different life."

In retrospect, I think my arrival at the Watergate apartments was a reprise of the swell of excitement I had experienced on the day my family moved to the house on Saranac Avenue in Buffalo. Here at last, in Washington and at the White House, was where I would be able to prove myself. The sacrifice of a hypothetical far better salary at some company or educational institution mattered little to me. That apartment, that location, was to my mind a confirmation of all Sue and I had struggled so hard to achieve, and her decision to stay with me meant everything in the world.

THE WHITE HOUSE, IF YOU SEE IT from a distance, looks like an ordinary mansion. But inside, it is in every way colossal. That was my perception when I was twenty-five years old, beginning my 1966–1967 service as a White House Fellow. There were seventeen of us—sixteen young men and one young woman—all serving in different capacities. We came from all over the country. Some of us were married, some not. When we arrived, all of us were hopeful, all eager—and not a one of us was cynical. It was a sacred place: *the White House.* You may call it the "old-boy network" or the inner circle or whatever, but one is indeed an insider when one works there. One is witness to how decisions are being made—the most important decisions, I would venture to say, anywhere.

Not only was the White House itself colossal, but I, and everyone else there, was working for a colossus. Except that he was the leader of the free world, President Lyndon B. Johnson reminded me of my father Carl—the rough exterior did not reflect the quality of the man inside.

President Johnson had thick arms and hands. But when you shook his hand, you discovered that there was nothing behind it. With all the handshaking they have to do, politicians apparently learn to save their grip. We shook hands with President Johnson many times, my wife and I.

A reception in the White House was arranged for us new Fellows. We were introduced to the president's cabinet officers. We met the First Lady, a warm and gracious woman. I felt right at home but, at the same time, off the planet. I also felt a great deal of ecstasy mixed with a tiny bit of dread. The parquet floors were gleaming. Servers stood around in crisp white uniforms. We could have whatever we wanted. The chandeliers were like diamonds, sparkling in the summer night. Sue wore a white dress. The red carpeting in the rear of the reception room was like a river. We introduced ourselves, trying to be humble and at the same time trying to make clear we were worthy.

We laughed. Oh, how hard we laughed at the jokes President Johnson told. Not that he was particularly funny, but we were young and awestruck. And power will make you do things you might not ordinarily do.

One day the president's secretary called me in my office. The president wanted to see me. I thought I was done for. I tried to think about what I might have said or done wrong. When I went in to see him, he took me by the shoulders and brought me close. He had a way of doing this, like an uncle. He said he was very proud of me. I had been voted something or other, one of the best something, and he had heard about it. He was pleased that I was serving on his staff. To be touched by him, to please him—it was better than pleasing your father.

Sue thought I was becoming unhinged. I told her, no, no, this sort of thing happens all the time. The White House was a strange, haunting, magical place.

We Fellows wanted to stay neck deep in all this—to arrange ourselves near the president. More than that, we also wanted him to *like* to have us near him, to be listened to by him. Access to the president was the point, the purpose. Was the development of our own power part of it? I would be lying if I said it was not. It has been said about people like us Fellows that the common ingredients are pluck and purpose. To which might be added ambition.

I was a Kennedy man walking into a Johnson house—and as was widely known then, there was no love lost between President Johnson and President Kennedy's brother Bobby, then a United States senator from New York. But working for President Johnson was a very big deal. This was the man who created an enduring legacy in civil rights and in Medicare and Medicaid. And yet...there was the war in Vietnam. During my time in the Johnson White House, my head was spinning, but my stomach was churning. It was a dreadful personal conflict for me.

In the White House, I worked with the Departments of Defense, State, Commerce, and others; with NASA; with information systems and biomedical research. I called leaders in various fields and set up meetings with them and then wrote up reports that might prove useful to the White House. I went on trips to Belgium, Luxembourg, Holland, France, Germany, England, and Italy.

I had to muster all the knowledge I had ever acquired. I discussed physics, especially the physics of sound; hospital technology; proprietary technological processes; the Belgian fair-trade agreements; a national software network. I drove with the head of a major American computer interest down the Amalfi Coast at reckless speeds, feeling the sea air on my face. I stayed at the Hotel des Indes, the Hôtel de Crillon, Hotel Königshof, Hotel Europa, and other hotels in which I could not have imagined I would ever find myself.

We Fellows attended formal dinners, informal dinners, and parties. At one party, a man did a burlesque dance; he went on to become Secretary of the Army. Everyone danced bawdily that night. The woman with the wig that flew off while dancing was my wife. She laughed, and everyone thought she was simply the greatest. (She would later work at the White House herself.) The man who was drinking Scotch had called an air raid down on his own position in Vietnam. The man with a gin and tonic is now the managing director of an investment banking house. The man holding a beer was a physicist who would later become a newspaper executive. Several would go on to be lawyers and businessmen. One would run a museum and another, an oil company. We knew how to let off steam, but when we worked, we worked hard. We were responsible, we were fresh, we brought something new to the table. We thought all that, anyway, and perhaps it was true.

When you work in the White House, people are likely to listen to you and want to talk with you, because, again, it is all about access. This was a real life, not a scholarly life, not a theoretical life. I was done with that. If you did not perform in the White House, then all that had come before in your life was worth nothing. You would go home having lost all you might have built yourself up to be.

But you also lose a certain innocence in the White House. You see things you do not want to see. You see people behaving in an untoward manner, such as a staffer rifling through another staffer's desk. If the president says, "Let us sit down and reason together," it means you've already lost.

I had come into the White House believing everything. I left believing half, or three-fourths, which means that I had lost the comfort of uncritical belief. One *needs* to believe in one's country and in one's president. For most young men my age, even back then, loss of belief did not mean so much. But it meant a lot to me. I lost, well, a certain softness. I had knowledge about the war in Vietnam that was not much discussed then, but we Fellows knew that America was into some very bad things. One thing we knew a year before the *New York Times* and others blew it open was that the war was a disaster for the United States. It was hard to accept.

We Fellows also lost interest in life beyond the White House. Nothing seemed so good or important out there. We lost sleep. We lost time to jog or swim or pay bills or pick up our dry cleaning or see the dentist. We lost visits home to our families. We lost the money we might have been making had we not taken the fellowship in the first place—for our salaries were unremarkable. We all wondered whether our posts were leading us to the very subtle shift from faith to cynicism. We knew only that we would not be the same people as when we started. We did not move from the outer prefectures into the heart of the kingdom only to discover that the emperor resembled our old neighbors. But we saw that he was, in fact, just a man.

On December 15, 1966, an unexpected political shock occurred. Bill Moyers, White House press secretary and special assistant to the president, abruptly resigned. At the age of thirty-two, he was widely considered the most powerful figure in the administration after the president, and he was a man I greatly respected and admired. No one except Bill, who was exceptionally close to President Johnson, knows definitely whether the resignation was forced or not. Bill, to his great credit, has so far as I know steadfastly refused to talk or write about the event or about any of his private conversations with the president. But what was known was that Bill opposed escalation of the war, while President Johnson was torn about it. A defensive president was not a pretty sight to those of us inside his house.

ONE INCIDENT DURING MY WHITE HOUSE DAYS stands out in vivid relief. I arranged to meet with Wernher von Braun during the summer of 1967. He was fifty-five years old. Everybody knew about him, but Jewish people knew about him in a special way. Von Braun had worked with the Nazis at the infamous rocketry base at Peenemünde on the Baltic Sea in northern Germany. He was working there when my Aunt Bertha and her family were hiding under a windmill in Holland.

There is debate about whether he, the architect of the Nazi V-2 rocket program, believed in Hitler's cause. He was an officer of the Schutzstaffel, the SS. He worked alongside slaves, though he later said that the whole slave-labor thing repulsed him. The only thing certain is that his true passion in life was space and space travel.

No one told me I had to go see von Braun to report to my boss about the status of NASA and our space efforts. I wanted to meet von Braun for a personal reason. He was then the director of the Marshall Space Flight Center in Huntsville, Alabama. Having become a naturalized citizen of the United States after the war, he had restarted his life in Alabama. I met him at his office there.

It was a bright and humid summer day. Sweat spread like an oil stain around the trench of my back. His handshake was strong, and I could not help thinking *übermensch*. If Hitler had wanted to design an Aryan, it would surely have been in the image of this rocketeer.

Behind his desk were plastic models of different kinds of rockets. Our conversation was terribly banal. He answered all the questions I put to him—about vertical takeoff and landing designs, the moon program, the space program—in a concise engineer's way. Indeed, he had done great things for the advancement of our space program.

Our meeting lasted about an hour. It still seems implausible: a Jewish man meeting on a friendly basis in the American South with a former officer of the SS. Toward the end of the meeting, I asked him about the evolution of rocketry, a veiled attempt to get him to tell me about his own evolution. He did not go into that.

He might have launched into a soliloquy about the terrible decisions he had made, about his being an accomplice to horrors. Then I would have described how my own family had nearly been drawn back into Germany to be eliminated and might very well have wound up in the same concentration camp where he had worked. He might have asked me to forgive him, and of course, I would not have.

When he talked about rocketry, I tried to pay attention, tried to avoid thinking about the Nazis. On his desk were pencils sitting in what resembled a wooden canoe. (Remember, I create mental images of the places and people I encounter.) The desk itself was wood and was polished so sharply that it shone. A white phone. A brown leather calendar and a dark brown desk blotter. Closed manila folders. A white kerchief stuck out of his breast pocket. He spoke with an unmistakable German accent, one I had heard frequently back in Buffalo.

Von Braun would be celebrated as the person primarily responsible for our country's putting a man on the moon. He also worked at Peenemünde, where more slaves died making the V-2 than were killed by the rocket in England, its target. We concluded the meeting. I stood up, and we shook hands. His hand had shaken that of President Kennedy. His hand had grasped the hand of Gestapo chief Heinrich Himmler. His hand had buttoned the tunic of a black SS uniform, had risen to hail Hitler. On his way back to the officers' quarters after dinner, might he have paused one night to look up at the starry sky he loved so much and seen the souls of Jewish people passing into the heavens?

I left and got on a plane back to Washington.

As MY FELLOWSHIP DREW TO A CLOSE, I had multiple offers to continue in the Johnson administration or elsewhere in government, but I had a desire to start my own technology company and was fortunate enough to attract considerable financial support from Wall Street investors for the enterprise. What's more, having established many relationships at Harvard with participants in President Kennedy's New Frontier program and similar connections with figures in Washington, I also had a large pool of extraordinary talent to draw from. Some of those people, including Bill Moyers and various former cabinet officials, would soon join me. Not long afterwards, I also sold (for a handsome sum) the technology behind my compressed-speech machine and thus was blessed with considerable resources of my own that I could direct toward later businesses.

More about those companies in future chapters, but this first one was wonderfully aligned with what had so inspired me back in my college days: President Kennedy's promise to put a man on the moon before the end of the 1960s. Even when I was newly blind, I felt the thrill of that challenge. Now, my company would be helping design the computer system for the initial lunar excursion module.

ALMOST TWO FULL YEARS AFTER that triumphal moment—on June 28, 1971—I happened to be back in Buffalo. My little sister Brenda's high-school graduation ceremony was that week-end. The whole family was going. Then an urgent call was put through to me from Washington to say that someone was trying to reach me. It was my mother, right there in Buffalo. When I spoke with her, she told me to go to the emergency room at Columbus Hospital. My father, Carl, had been in an accident at his shop.

After having lost all his money in the scrap-metal business, Carl had fallen back on selling rags—far less profitable than metal. For months, I had been asking him to retire, and he had finally agreed. I told him that I would take care of him.

It was the day before his retirement. He was driving a forklift around his warehouse, moving bales of rags from one place to another, and he accidentally drove the forklift into a brick wall. The forks pierced the wall, which fell upon Carl and crushed his chest. How long he had lain there, how he had gotten to the hospital, what it had smelled like among the rags and dust and old brick and ammonia and creosote, and how the broken sternum and the punctured lungs must have felt—these were things I would think about later.

The doctor came out and signaled for me to follow. "How is he?" I asked.

Doctors and nurses brushed by, intent on their various duties.

"Your father expired, Mr. Greenberg."

I thought I hadn't heard correctly. Of course, I knew this was a possibility, but it took my breath away. I didn't hear much else of what the doctor said.

Later that day I made the funeral arrangements and contacted family members. The following day, I gave the eulogy at the service. I settled Carl's debts and other financial liabilities, including a payment of $14,000 that needed to be made to the city because of his responsibility for the collapse of the brick wall—he had been operating in a condemned building. People rested their heads on my shoulders in their grief. I grieved, too, although in a way different from the others, I think. As I have explained, after my biological father, Albert, passed away it was as if I had become the leader of the family. I felt comfortable in the role: I was a son but also a father—to my brother and sisters.

So it was that at night, and for brief moments during the day in Buffalo after Carl's passing, I thought about our family's various burdens, but also of our blessings. The hard ride our family had had, but also that we were a family—that my family before, as well as my family now, understood completely what it really meant to be a family. That it meant something to us to have our religion: that, too, we knew very clearly. One cares for one's brethren—one gives, that is all one can do, and one gives even when one has nothing to give. Carl, for example, had cosigned for houses for other people. And as we would discover only after her death, our mother had given to charities at the very times when she herself had almost nothing.

The larger point is this: Business matters, and business success can be greatly rewarding in multiple ways. But family matters infinitely more.

15

The Beauty of Small Things

I had resisted the notion that fatherhood changes everything. During Sue's first pregnancy, everyone wanted to remind me of this fact. Your whole world will be different, they would say. You'll be different. Your priorities will change. Having a child puts everything into perspective. Work is not the same as it was—you don't see it the same. It's not that it becomes less important, but it just becomes another aspect of your life. This is what everyone wanted to tell me.

I rejected, entirely, the idea that I would soften. I never thought that I would be one of those men who cooed, who spoke in ridiculous baby voices, who handled diapers.

My business colleagues wanted to tell me stories about their children. They told delivery stories like they were telling war tales. It was like being part of a club. Where they were when their wife went into labor, what they thought when they heard, how they made it to the hospital. These were simply stories—nothing else.

I was running a company. We were working very hard to make money, and with that came some pushing and shoving. No one wanted us to make money; we had to fight for it. This was the part of the job I hated, but like anyone who is competitive, the prospect of winning appealed to me a great deal.

Besides, Sue was going about her life deftly. We had, in some sense, been through the worst of it, though that is not to say it was any easier. I was averaging four hours of sleep a night. All I could think about was work. I also had become part of various Washington circuits—political, social, charity, opera, theater. This was how we occupied our free time, though to call it "free" would be somewhat of a falsehood. I enjoyed it, but that didn't mean it wasn't work.

When Sue went into labor, we were both calm. The fathers didn't go in the delivery room back then. We waited in the waiting room. I had every reason to be confident. I paced. I made a list of whom I would call and in what order. I thought about how business would be transacted in my absence and when would be an appropriate time to return. I am not ashamed to admit that these things were in my head.

Finally, I was called in to see Sue. We had a boy. We named him Paul after my Grandmother Pauline. Sue held him in swaddling clothes on her chest. I touched his head. It was very soft, as if the plate of bone were not yet bone but just a thick layer of cartilage. This concerned me. The skin on his little hands was smooth.

A few days later, we took Paul home. I was carrying him in a small wooden basket about the size of a picnic basket. It was May and warm. We brought him into his room and placed him on the changing table. Baby powder and Vaseline were administered.

The belly button was inspected. Sue was very good about this, and so was I.

The phone rang.

"Do you want me to get that?" I said to her.

"No, it's probably my mother, anyway. You stay here. Are you okay to stay here?"

"Of course I am," I said.

She left. I stood in front of the changing table so that there was no way for Paul to fall. I put my hands on his chest. He was very warm. The baby uniform, a little blue cotton one-size they'd dressed him in, was terribly soft. I walked my fingers up and down it to make sure all the buttons were fastened. His little legs were chubby. They seemed to move, along with his arms, in no pattern.

I moved my head down to his. He was as red as a radish, this guy. I kissed his temple. It tasted a little salty. I could feel on my lips the thin hair on his head. I did it again. Sweet, sort of. Kind of like baby powder. I did it again. That's strange, I thought. I could feel the tiny veins in his head pulsing through my lips. I did this the way one would taste wine. Then I did it a few more times. I liked kissing his little temples. I think he liked it, too. Though, of course, I can't be sure. I just got a sense of calm from him.

Sue came back in the room. "What are you doing?" she asked.

"Nothing," I said.

"It looked like you were doing something," she said with a sort of sly smile.

"No," I said. "I wasn't doing anything."

PAUL IS ONE WEEK OLD and wearing yellow-and-white pajamas. I am holding him. He is about the length of my forearm. His eyes

are blue. He has hair, flat on his head. There are yellow carna-
tions on the bedside table, which sits in the corner. The bedside
lamp is aqua-colored. He has a receding chin. He sleeps. He
looks like a tiny old man. Sue plays with his hands. Imagine
the heat coming off his little body. I hold him up for a picture
before I leave in the morning for work. He looks at me. I lie with
him on the white bed.

Arthur, who still resembles a college-age boy, holds him.
Paul has a serious expression on his face. He is looking at the
person taking the picture. Arthur is looking at him.

We capture his first haircut. He does pretty well. His shirt is
off. We've saved the hair. It is here: dark brown, hiding behind
the picture. It is his birthday. There are three candles. Sue holds
a white cake in front of him. I hold Paul and his baby brother,
Jimmy, on my lap after work.

Paul's mouth is covered with chocolate icing, from a giant
gingerbread man. His brother, in a high chair, is laughing at
him. In the hallway, he looks like Elton John, in white, circular plastic glasses. He is holding a silver cup with a plastic red
handle and a plastic green lid and a green straw. He is wearing
a brown shirt and brown-and-white striped pants. His hands are
curling against his thigh.

He tries to put a pacifier in his brother's mouth. His brother's neck is on his knee. Both of them look like they could fall
off the bed at any minute. The two boys on the patio, each sitting on one of Sue's knees. Both boys in tank tops. Paul seems
to be squirming. He must think he is too big a boy for this sort
of thing.

Another snapshot: Maine, late afternoon. The boys are tan.
Both are in pajamas. On the table in front of us is a green squirt
gun. Scrabble. A slide projector. A book. Paul rests his head on

my knee. His face is maturing, offering a sense of what he will look like later on. A vision of the boy, the teenager, the man.

In the afternoon, we eat lunch near the beach, on a red picnic bench. I thought I had forever. The boys are both holding bottles of cola with both hands. Paul is wearing red Converse sneakers and blue shorts and a yellow shirt with green numbers that read "51." His brother imitates everything he does. At night, before they go to sleep, they dress up in crazy costumes. They both have blue Tishman hard hats on. They both have necklaces on. For some reason, Paul is wearing a black winter glove on his right hand.

He is in a yellow bathing suit, standing in the water. The tide comes in.

He's smiling. Beyond him are what? Boats? Lobster trawlers? What?

At his grandmother's surprise party, he is twelve or thirteen. His hair is huge and curly. He is wearing a yellow polo shirt and a blue blazer. There are two buttons on the sleeve. A brown belt. His hand is on his grandmother's shoulder in this photo. A nice smile. In the picture with the whole family, the entirety of us, he is again standing next to his grandmother, his hand on her shoulder. Protective? Covetous of her love? In the buffet line, he holds up his plate of food. In the photo of the five of us—with Sue, Jimmy, little Kathryn, and me—Paul is the only one sitting down. He's next to the cake. His sister is looking at it like she can't believe it. My hand is on his shoulder. His smile is quiet. In the last photo, his cousins, my brother's kids, are messing with him. His hands are at his thighs, a little bit curled. A child with this hair cannot be anything but sweet.

His bar mitzvah announcement reads: "Paul Eric Greenberg, son of Sanford D. Greenberg and Susan R. Greenberg, is a seventh grade honor student at St. Albans School in Washington, D.C. He is quarterback for the seventh grade football team and is also a member of the basketball and baseball teams. He is an avid reader and cartoonist and enjoys music."

At the ceremony, it is as if the ark holding the Torah is golden, but not just golden: illuminated. He seems small and thin before it. I wrap his *tallis* around him. They all watch. His mother and I take a photograph afterward. He smiles. His hands are folded.

Another photo with the entire family: Paul stands next to me. He smells like a young man—fresh, clean, a familiar cologne. I don't know what his mornings are like in his dorm room—if he wakes up early before class, has a cup of coffee, looks over his books, or perhaps just reads a novel. Or if he rolls out of bed, throws on a pair of jeans, and walks across the same quad I walked across when I was his age, still sleepy.

We parents place such heavy burdens on our firstborn. We freight them with sacred family names, wrap them in our own impossible dreams, expect them to lead their brothers and sisters when they are still children themselves. Paul, you have been up to the challenge in every way. When I nuzzled you on that changing table not long after you and your mother came home from the hospital, you melted my heart. You still do. And not you alone.

To pack Jimmy's stuff and send it off to college via moving truck, he must have a 1,000-pound minimum. That is the least, but how to get there?

To begin with, there would be the report cards from his middle school—the letter from his Latin teacher who said he wanted to write an extra recommendation for him because he was such a standout kid. So, two letters of recommendation. Plus the letter he writes me from camp—the summer before he leaves for college. He writes on the envelope: Personal and Confidential. This is meant to keep his mother from reading it, though he knows that someone must read it to his father.

Dear Dad:

I want to bring up a subject with you which is going to change drastically in the next year. I feel that the last 10 years you and I have worked extremely hard to build a solid and compassionate relationship. This has not only kept me going but also saved me during difficult times in high school. I want you to know that just because I am leaving does not mean that I do not want to continue to build....

Well, now I have to attend to some business. I will let you know that I've learned a lesson on managing people this summer, and it was a hard lesson to learn. It looks a lot easier than it is.

I love you and again thank you for your letters. I'll be home soon and we can relax at the beach.

Love Jim.

End.

How much does that weigh? And how about the weight of our family story—the ones who survived the Holocaust and the ones who didn't? And the weight on watching your father walk into walls? Your own father, not being able to make it down the hallway or across the street? Or seeing him cut—the blood coming down his forehead or his knees? Blood is scary to a kid—it can be horrifying. The cuts on his face after he's shaved, and his not knowing it was there. Or hearing a thud, a thump, in the middle of the night and thinking this is it, he's gone down this time for sure. He knocked himself out entirely. Worrying that every time he travels alone he's going to step off the curb at the wrong time and that'll be it. The type of worry that not only gives you bad dreams but makes your stomach cramp. Forget about him dropping you off at the school dance, the pep rally, the Saturday afternoon game. Oh, other kids had drivers, too—we were all well off—but this was something different. You want your dad to be able to do these things. You want not to have to worry about it.

Surely, some poundage can be assigned to that and to the memory of an apology from a little boy:

Dear Dad,
I am sorry I did what I did. I made my first mistake. In an office do you ever make major mistakes like that or not? Jimmy.

The total weight of our family: 517 pounds. That is a big step toward our minimum and to the extent that he carries us with him, then it ought to count.

One summer, Jimmy interned for E.F. Hutton. His boss wrote him this recommendation: "At first, we were all too busy to teach Jimmy. To my delight and surprise, he taught himself. Through a combination of careful listening and dogged research, he carved out, in a very brief time, an area of expertise in the complex bond field which proved quite valuable to my colleagues and me. Indeed, he gave a presentation to forty professionals in our office in which he showed exceptional poise and maturity. I have come to have a high regard for Jimmy. He has an unusual blend of pragmatic intelligence, judgment, and great personal charm. He will, I am certain, have great success in life and be a valuable contributor, and leader, throughout his career."

In college, he is indebted, and that has a weight also. We bought him a Volvo Turbo, and he wrote that the car was not a car but an expression of what we've always done for him, which is to support him and love him. All this is true and so perhaps it rebalances; it tares the weight of his having seen what he saw with me and all that came along with it. What is the weight of that car—3,500 lbs.? That puts us way over the limit.

We're headed in the right direction. St. Louis, here we come. Business school, here we come. The women, the beer, the activities—here we come. I wonder if my burden on him will be heavy there. Will it follow him, weigh upon him even these years later? Will he wake in the night, every night, after hearing a thud, a bump, thinking for a second, before waking, thinking it is me, fallen down, hit something sharp, a wound that will bleed out before it can be repaired? No, I forbid it. I will take him and his friends out to dinner. Everything will be great. There's evidence for it.

Then suddenly he's a financier, doing extremely well at a bank, all on his own, arranging deals, aligning projects, structuring, analyzing, investing. Jimmy is investing. James is investing. Jahmes. James is now married, and now he is a daddy. And very quickly, there is not enough time. He's got these kids. All the work. It's work, day and night. It took all this time to understand. How did you do it, Dad? The weight of that he could not have imagined and he calls me at night, not in tears but close to tears, and they taste like the tears I might have once shed had I a father with whom to share them.

ON A SHEET OF LINED NOTEBOOK PAPER Kathryn has made a green globe with gray, brown, blue, orange, pink, and purple flowers. Several purple clouds line the top of the page, with a rainbow.

She writes "Welcome Back Dad" and, below, a purple heart balloon. On another sheet of paper, she writes "Dear Dad, from

Kathryn." That is followed by what looks like pieces of fruit: a banana, a plum, an orange, an apple, and, perhaps, a waffle.

She draws a rainbow-colored ice-cream cone. The ice cream must be bubble-gum ice cream. Below this in neon orange: "to Dad, Happy Birthday."

She draws a girl. I assume this is her. I cannot tell whether she is standing on some kind of blue pyramid, or the pyramid is actually a dress. It looks as if she has four arms. Blonde hair. Green legs.

In blue crayon, she writes: "DEAR DAD THIS IS WHAT I DO AT CAMP I THINK I PLAY ARE TEACHER READS US A STORY BEFORE SWIMMING LUNCH WE GO AND AFTER LUNCH...."

She writes a book about me: *Kathryn's Book About My Dad.*

This is a story about a boy named Sandy. He was born in Buffalo, New York on Friday, December 13. It was a cold and wintry day. He loved his mom and his grandmom and his dad. He wanted to play with Kathryn but she was not born yet! The end.

On a square piece of cardboard, she takes thick string and makes a flag. Blue string crosses orange string. In the upper right-hand corner, yellow string is wound around itself to make a sun. The right side reads: "to Dad, love Kathryn."

She and her friend Lauren make a small envelope out of wrapping paper and in it place two notes. Kathryn's reads: "Dear Daddy, get well soon." The other reads, "Get well from Lauren." Both are written in pink and red, and both have stars and circles on them. They have thoughtfully but oddly included string inside the envelope.

On August 12, 1984, she has written an anniversary card to Sue and me, this time with blue clouds and a rainbow and a pair of lips with a tongue coming out and flowers near the bottom. The sun has a smiley face on it.

For Father's Day she attaches a piece of red paper, folded in half, to a theater program from her class at Sidwell Friends School. The play is called *The Amazing Voyage of the New Orleans*. Kathryn is playing Townsperson One, Mr. Wilson (silent). She begins to include stickers—flashy red hearts—on her letters to me. She begins to sign her name KLG.

For Father's Day she reminds me that I am a great father, even if she gets mad at me. "Your Loving Daughter, Kathryn (Curly Pie)."

A sentimental father? A pushover? Not me! Except I use her fingers to trace her name on my fingers and on my hands and the back of my hands. On my arm with various colored magic markers, she designs flowers and bumblebees and cherry trees and smiling suns. She makes little circles on my elbows. She makes triangles on the insteps of my feet, in the sand. On my face, she writes "I love you Daddy." I wash my face, shave, and it comes off; I have her write it again.

When Kathryn goes off to camp in the summer, I send her long letters that detail our life without her, and then when she comes home, I ask that she write on my chest everything that she has done, and on my shoulders I ask that she spell out that she received my letters. I ask that she chronicle, in case I forget, which I will not—but just in case—all the trips we make, the plays she has been in, the iterations of the images she has of herself: little girl in the clouds, little girl in winter, little girl on the beach, little girl in a helicopter. Write it here and here and here.

"Why?" she wants to know. Answer: "So that I will remember, as I have on every night."

And then the poems, so many of them, so knowing. The one, for example, written in the shadow of Father's Day 1987 when she was only ten:

He is a palm tree, shading people from the sun.
He is a pillow all nice and soft.
He is a racing car, sometimes moving very fast.
He is a turtle, moving very slowly, taking a walk, enjoying every
*   second of life.*
He is a tree, tall and strong.
He is a summer breeze, so kind and gentle.
He is very generous.
He is my dad and I love him to bits.

And the one from a decade later, mailed to me on Father's Day, not handed over in a homemade rococo envelope:

Grow
as a speck of dust would grow.
Let me begin by being a better daughter
Let me begin by understanding
the silence of your life;
by showing you the sounds of sight:
How a peach (your favorite, I know, especially in France)
full in the sun might be the sun,
how a flock of starlings fanning the sky
is like one large wing,
by knowing your gentleness your quiet but deliberate way
of speaking, so easily read by you. Let me begin with patience—
that I need not shout, simply face you when I speak.

There are also the moments she remembers that I would have liked to have protected her from. The big family trip to Florence, say—the one she took with her uncle and his son, and her two grandmothers, and all the rest of us. We all ate together in Sue's and my room—a wonderful time! Afterward, Kathryn went off to sleep in a room with her two grandmothers. There is little else that a child could want in life than to be with her two grandmothers. Combined, they would have known everything about being a woman that she would ever need to know, and they would always be there for her to ask. All the questions about boys, if that came to pass, and questions about how to be a bride, a young lady, and manners, most important. Later there would be questions about her parents when they were young people—what they were like. That might happen when she was a teenager, but at the time I'm remembering, she was too young to know, to even ask.

Except that's not the way this memory turns out. Kathryn thinks she remembers her father's mother talking to her mother's mother in their bedroom but getting no response. She vaguely recalls her father's mother racing out of the room but having to stay put herself. She supposes that she must have known by then that her mother's mother was dead, but what she really remembers, she says, are the bricks under the Ponte Vecchio—it was as if the entire bridge might collapse. And her mother going to pieces. And how her brothers tried to help her even though they, too, were too young for this.

And now Kathryn, like her brothers, is grown: lovely, charming, smart, competent beyond measure. But still the memories go on.

16

Road Tripping

We decide to do a road trip—not Kak, she's still too young for this, just the guys: Paul, Jimmy, me, and Artie, of course.

In Los Angeles, we take the boys on a tour of Universal Studios. We walk on the back lot. The hills are green with round shrubbery and the land is brown. Paul has sprouted up. He is fourteen years old. Jimmy is shorter, twelve. Both boys have quiet ways about them. Arthur follows us around—black jeans and white knit shirt. We might both be their fathers. I have my hand on Jimmy's shoulder. The boys wear cutoff jeans and knee-high socks. They are skinny.

Arthur is skinny. We all look young and vibrant.

We see the home where *Psycho* was filmed. The set of the New England town where *Jaws* was shot.

We take a helicopter tour of Los Angeles. Jimmy sits in front. We see Dodger Stadium. Cars corkscrew around the highway like little toys on a child's racetrack. We fly out toward the ocean. Over the beach. People walk into the waves; they all seem to be tanned.

Thursday, August 19, 1982. I tell the camera that we were just checking out of the Bel-Air Hotel. Jimmy follows me. He is smiling a clever smile. We walk on a path under low tropical-looking trees. There is a pool. We stop. Paul is filming. I tell him to make sure he gets us all in the shot—that is the most important thing. Arthur leads us to the Lincoln Town Car we're renting for the trip. He says, "Step right this way, to the American West."

We pass by the San Bernardino Mountains. Seventies music is on the tape machine. Arthur has planned all the music to correspond to the geography. In a little town, Arthur slows down. He says, "Maybe I can get a quick milk here. That'll tide me over."

The ruddy hills are turning into steeper mountains, and the shrubs are becoming pines. We listen to a Quincy Jones song. Jimmy is discussing the drumming, but Arthur tells him to hold on. This is the prettiest scene yet, he thinks. "We're twenty-six miles out of LA, just passed Big Bear," he announces. He describes a lake. Flat and completely like glass. It is impossible to differentiate the actual terrain from its reflection—the real from the image of the real. "It reminds me," I say, "of the time we were in Israel, and we looked out into Lebanon and Jordan. Just like that." A place where the desert was so wide it all looked like water, like an oasis.

When we listen to the song "The Boxer," Arthur says it reminds him of baseball. "Whenever I get up there to sing it, that's what I think about."

Paul is trying hard to hold the camera steady. All you can see now, near Barstow, are pink, rugged hills. We could be on

Mars. "We are now fully aware that we exist," Arthur says. "It's our earth now."

Now we are on the road. Arthur wants Paul to film just the road, only the road. "Cecilia" comes on. Arthur says this is one of the hardest songs to do. Jimmy asks why. "Oh, it's the groove, the rhythm of it." Arthur sings along to "Bridge Over Troubled Water." He blows it. He wants another take. We laugh at him. "It's not funny, Jimmy," he says sarcastically. Jimmy can't stop laughing. His voice is still like a little kid's.

We are listening to classical music. The sunset is thin and bright. These are the types of skies in which one expects to see celestial events. I explain that the mountains are proud. They rise up like the pyramids. Arthur says we are 229 miles outside of Los Angeles and 100 miles short of Las Vegas. At one point, someone asks me if I can see the mountains. "It's hard for me to say," I reply. "I think I can sense the shadow."

We are in front of Tower Records in Las Vegas. Arthur is inside looking for Brandenburg Concertos, numbers four, five, and six. Paul tells me to sing. I sing "Chantilly Lace." Arthur comes back without the Brandenburgs; instead, he got Crosby, Stills & Nash.

Arthur is lost in Vegas. He cannot find his way out. He says he has never gone this way before. Later, he explains that when we laugh, we put the internal part of ourselves in the proper place. Then we begin to heal ourselves from the core on out.

Arthur explains that straight ahead is a brownish lump, which is a mountain. A little to the left is a grayish lump. He says there is a satiny look to the bottom of it. "You know, I think Teddy Roosevelt is really our president on this trip," Arthur says. "He was a great naturalist. A great traveler."

Jimmy says, "It's an oven outside."

"That's a simile," Arthur says. He explains similes and metaphors. He says metaphors become more important the older one gets. "People who use metaphors well are a joy to listen to. There are not many."

On top of Hoover Dam, Paul makes sure to film me in my nearly invisible white shorts. I stand behind Jimmy. They think this is the funniest thing.

"Clearly, this is the most enormous stretch of concrete you've ever seen," Arthur says. The water is green near the edges and blue in the middle. We're 487 miles outside of Los Angeles when we hit Arizona. We listen to Billy Joel. Arthur sings along. At the Utah state line, I get out with Jimmy and Arthur and stand in front of the mountain daylight time sign. If we go on, we will slip into the past.

A motel room at night. Arthur reads to us from *Independence*, a Hollywood tell-all, in his room. He is sitting up on his bed, his head against a white concrete wall. "That book is delicious," I say. "A very readable book," Arthur agrees.

The following morning, the mountains become giant and steep and orange. The space between them possesses a very specific, very tangible force that wafts up against the car as we make our way along the road cut into the mountains.

In Zion National Park, it begins to rain. I ask what it is like out. "Raining," Arthur says. "When you get to the bottom, you get the earth that's fed by the underwater wetness of the Colorado River." He could be a geologist.

We stop at the visitor's center. We take an indoor tour. We look out on the canyons. There is no drop-off; it feels as if we are suspended above the opening. Clouds are hanging below the mountaintops. The ridgeline looks as if it is made out of paper. The tour guide, a plain-looking blonde woman, discusses glaciers. She explains that contrary to popular belief, glaciers would not have formed the canyons. She says we can throw out the idea of glaciers. It is just a theory, she says. Back in the car, I say that the drive through Zion was the best so far. Well, actually, Arthur says, I missed a great deal of it.

"You were looking only a little bit left. If you were looking all the way to your left, you would have seen an amazing view."

Jimmy says that there is a sign that reads forty-five miles per hour. "Who would want to go forty-five?"

"Chickens," Arthur says. "Old people. Very cautious people. People who are so cautious, they're actually a danger to other people."

It is five o'clock on Arthur's watch. The sky is blue. It is hard to see his face. His lips have the silhouette of a woman's lips. Tender.

Arthur is worried about the air-conditioning. We lost it for nearly three minutes. He was timing, but he didn't say anything until now.

"It could be," he says, "shades of things to come." It's so like Arthur to use a word like shade. "In Salt Lake, we may want to have the car checked," he says, admitting that he has no clue when it comes to things mechanical.

We listen to one of his concerts. He says it sounds fragile. I ask if we can listen to it again. "Do you like it?" he asks, turning to me.

"Beautiful," I say. He looks back at me again to see my expression. He wants to see whether I am telling the truth.

Now we are driving through Salt Lake City. It is eighty-eight degrees. Artie likes it here. Very wide streets. Clean. He thinks the Mormon Tabernacle Choir is great. He complains that it is hard to be driving through the town and looking for the scenic spots and *also* looking for the Safeway. He says it is hard to remember the city as he saw it eleven years ago, the last time he was here. The memory has been replaced by this last half hour. "It's bigger now," he says.

"You know what I'd like to do?" I say. "I'd like to find a Yellow Pages." What I want to do is find a synagogue. It is my father's *yahrtzeit*; I want to say *Kaddish*. There are no synagogues to be found in Salt Lake City. Instead, we stand beside a building, the four of us. We bow our heads. There are miles of grassland in front of us. I put a handkerchief on my head and do the prayer for the dead. It is the closest I can come.

At 1,305 miles outside of Los Angeles, we are listening to the soundtrack from *A Hard Day's Night*. Paul McCartney is singing "And I Love Her." "His voice," Arthur explains, "used to be tenor. It's lower now. It's hard to lock into that pitch."

Somewhere in Idaho we get out at a cemetery in a field. Arthur stands off at the edge of the small square of land, near a sprinkler, his arms crossed. "Shepherd," one tombstone reads. Another says, "Dr. Richard F. Sutton." The boys walk around, inspecting quietly, reverently. This is Arthur's favorite part of the trip. Back in the car, we listen to synthesized music. Arthur says that if the ear tries to contain the pulsing and the breathing of the music, one gets a tremendous combination. Michael McDonald comes on. Arthur pats his hands in time against the steering wheel. I air-drum. Jimmy laughs at me. Arthur listens to a song of his. He says he is embarrassed. "I can sing better than that." He does. He turns down the music and sings live.

Thursday, August 26, 1982—1,497 miles outside of Los Angeles. We are in Teton country. Switchbacks. Rises to our left, rivers on the right, 204 miles driven today. The peaks of the Tetons are covered with snow. One of the youngest mountain ranges, according to Arthur. He climbed them once. The clouds in front of us look like downspouts, like funnels. Arthur says that Paul may have just shot a future album cover on our movie camera. "All you have to do is lift a frame," he says. He opens the window. You can hear the trees whisk by. Later, the slope off the river beside the car is so steep that the tops of the trees rising up from the shore do not even reach the edge of the road.

Yellowstone National Park. We get out to see Old Faithful. It's steaming. Then it goes up. As it calms down, I say, foolishly, that I want to walk closer. "I mean, no one's there. There's nothing blocking us."

"Go for it, Dad," Paul says. Arthur says he is exhausted. He wants to check into our room and take a nap. I take Jimmy and Paul, and we walk around the sulfur pools. They look like the inside of someone's organ—a bile duct or kidney. The liquid in them is flat and clear, and the rock underneath is cream or green or aqua. I can feel heat from them as we walk along the concrete path. The vapor smells.

That evening we eat in a giant lodge. People all around us. We are talking when Jimmy begins to cough. And then nothing. I realize that he is having an asthma attack. It was the vapor from the sulfur pools. If we do not get him a shot of adrenaline, he will die. Sue isn't around to give him a shot. The waiter comes over and wants to know if everything is all right, although it is unclear to me whether he is asking about the food or Jimmy. "Listen," I say. "My son is having an asthma attack. I need to get him a shot of adrenaline. Is there a doctor around here? A nurse?"

"No," he says impassively, "we don't have anything like that here." I remain calm. I do not think Arthur knows enough about Jimmy's situation to act fast enough, and Paul's still a kid. I am on my own.

"Well, is there a park ranger or something? Somebody who can do *something*?"

"Yeah," he says, "we have a ranger. I'll go get him." I follow the waiter about halfway to the middle of the dining room. He takes off running. I am standing there. I cannot find my way to follow him, and I cannot find my way back to the table. Finally, the waiter returns with the park ranger. I explain the situation. Jimmy is hardly breathing.

"There's a station a ways out," he says, "where we can get what you need. But it's going to be tricky getting there."

I gather everyone. We rush into the ranger's truck. The night is black. It is as if the trees and the mountains are conspiring against us. This ranger, he is not joking around. He is skilled in the art of emergencies. His truck bounces violently along trails that were not meant to be driven on. This is a new kind of danger. We make it to the outpost, though as we enter, I feel what I think are tent flaps. "My God," I think. Jimmy is taking the thinnest, most desperate breaths. A shot is administered. His lungs open up like a balloon.

The following day nobody mentions the episode.

I say that in the spring we should take a drive down to see the Kentucky Derby. Arthur says he'll be free; he'll be doing a movie in Paris that starts afterward.

"Who's directing that?" I ask.

"Volker Schlöndorff."

"Schlöndorff? No kidding! Volk's doing that?" I say. Of course, I don't know Volk.

We enter Montana. We are listening to Copland. The hills are softer, lower, browner. Then we listen to a Gregorian chant. Paul is in a dead sleep. He is wearing an orange Baltimore Orioles shirt. "Can you feel the archaic quality to the harmonies?"

Arthur wants to know. Jimmy tells me to sing it. "I don't know this tune," I say. But I do it anyway. Jimmy wants Paul to sing. He wakes him up. Paul gives Jimmy the finger. At the same time, Arthur is saying, "That's what the nature of music is."

Alongside the rise of a mountain, Arthur asks, "Who do we know who's had a peaceful, fulfilling latter part of life? Milton, perhaps."

"You can't really take Milton seriously," I say. "He was blind."

"Well, that's true," Arthur says. "Rousseau was one. Though he became disenchanted. He spent the last ten years of his life on a lake in Switzerland. As a botanist."

Artie is alone in life. He doesn't have a mate, but this is only partly true. When Paul was born, I knew very little about being a father, but what I did know was that I wanted my children to see beauty in this world. Arthur, more than I, more than Sue, would be able to provide that. He became a second father to my children. That evening we enjoy the Sabbath dinner. I want the boys to know that they can do this anywhere—being away from home does not mean the Sabbath does not matter. They still need to separate the secular from the sacred. I cannot find *challah* where we are, so instead I get some rolls and lay napkins over them. I get some wine. We order room service. Jimmy wants to know if Arthur reads dictionaries. "Sometimes," he says. "I take them into the bathroom with me. When your mind is in a place to find a dictionary interesting, you're in a very good place mentally."

At 1,988 miles outside of Los Angeles, I ask if there is a television around here. Arthur says no, not in these places. We are in the corner of America. We might as well be off the map.

Great Falls, Montana. Farther north—Glacier Lake. We listen to Vaughan Williams's "The Lark Ascending" as we ourselves rise. "It only gets prettier," Arthur says. A giant rock formation, like an isosceles triangle, rises up to the west; its peak is flattened out. A washed-out lake appears at the side of the road. Its bed looks like pudding. Blond trees stand before it.

We take a small road down level with the lake. Large old cabins line the small street. "We're here, because we're here, because we're here," Arthur says. We stay at a large inn called the War Bonnet. It looks like a ski lodge, very rustic. In front of the inn, water laps against the rocks on the shore. Then a blunt mountain, its shadow falling over the lake. It is real country.

I take the boys on a hike. We circle half of Glacier Lake and enter the park. A sign reads: "Beware of Bears." We go in anyhow. It is dead quiet. I can hear pine needles falling. Mist crawls between the upper layers of the trees, as if it is watching us. The boys understand the solemnity of the moment. We do not see any bears. But they might have seen us.

We are at Logan Pass. The Continental Divide. Elevation: 2,033 meters. We are up against the mountainside. Clouds come up like out of a steaming pot. We cannot see twenty yards in front of us. Jimmy says it looks as if we are at the edge of the earth. We get out of the car. There is a thin stream curving across the floor of a valley. Arthur and I stand next to each other. We are at Bird Woman Falls. Mist comes out of our mouths.

We stay a few days in Montana and fly to San Francisco. On our descent, we are all glued to the windows. The sun is setting.

In the morning: August 31, 1982, a week and three days since we left Los Angeles. We are atop a hill, the city of San Francisco is below us. A trolley car passes to our left. We are listening to "Bridge Over Troubled Water" again. Arthur has always felt the violins held the last note too long.

We get out of the car to look at the breakers. The water is churning below us. I hold Jimmy in my arms. We go over the Golden Gate Bridge. Its suspension lines look as if it is made not of steel cable but of simple rods of steel, rising up to meet the tip of the slopes. "Look at how the ocean just breathes up and down," Arthur says. The land here is surf and brush and rocks.

And then the trip is over. We have made a circle around the west. I have tried my hardest to show my boys that I am a regular father, they are regular boys, my friend is their friend and will be forever. I felt I needed to show them this sooner rather than later. Later, it might be too late.

KATHRYN GETS A ROAD TRIP ALL HER OWN, except of course for Artie and me. She is wearing a white dress. It's her fifth birthday. She's sitting in the back seat of the car as we drive through New York. She's quiet and doesn't want to say anything. It doesn't matter. This present is for me, not her.

"Don't you love to have a camera pointed at you?" Arthur asks her. "Whatever you do, it's looking at you."

She smiles. She's eating candy the way a little girl eats candy—delicately, with the tips of her fingers. She puts her leg up on the headrest in front of her.

She's wearing white knee-high socks.

Arthur sings, "There's no business, like show business." His arms are crossed. He leans down into her. She smiles. All this is being filmed for posterity. Arthur says, "I'm one of those few people who realize that the camera is by definition an intimidating thing. There's no way to have a real connection with a camera lens. You try to look into it like it's a friend, but sooner or later you realize it's just a piece of machinery. How do you look at a piece of machinery and have any kind of real expression?"

Kathryn goes into a bag for another piece of candy. Arthur says she must be stuffed. She's had one frozen yogurt, two hot dogs, one bag of M&Ms, an orange soda, some Diet Pepsi, a lollipop on the plane, an orange juice. She smiles at Arthur. She holds some bubble gum up to Arthur's nose. He smells it. We discuss candy. Her lips are orange.

"Sometimes," I tell him, "at night I look down into Kathryn's tummy and I can see all that she has eaten."

"Here is one of New York's main hotels," Arthur says. "The Plaza Hotel. It's May 15, 1982. Saturday, 2:15. We are on earth."

"We can all sit in the carriage," Kathryn says. She explains, pointing to a horse-drawn carriage, how it's going to work and where everyone is going to sit. Arthur says that's how we all used to travel. By carriage. On the front bench of the carriage beside us is the driver, who is wearing a white tuxedo. Kathryn sits on my lap. I hold her shoulders. We plan our trip through Central Park.

"Here we are at the carousel," Arthur says. "Is there a place to, as we say, park?" People bike by, hooting. It is a beautiful spring day. Arthur and I are wearing the same thing: blue shirts and khaki pants, our old standard undergraduate uniform. Kathryn walks ahead of us, on the grass. She's not sure she wants to go on the carousel. Arthur wants a picture of the three of us, against a green fence. Kathryn doesn't want to face the camera.

"Artie, c'mon," she says.

While Arthur goes to get the tickets, Kathryn sits on the armrest of a bench. "Since you were born, I wanted to take you here," I say. "Five years ago. Now it's five years later."

Kathryn gets on a white horse on the inside of the carousel. I get on one, too. They rise up and go back down. She watches me intently. I touch her shoulder. She holds onto the reins. She has two gold barrettes in her hair. A bell rings, signaling the ride is over. We dismount and switch horses.

Somewhere in the park, a band is playing "When the Saints Go Marching In." Arthur and I sing along just as we did in college.

Arthur says to Kathryn, "I see you're wearing your Docksides. I see the sides of your Docksides. But where are the docks of your Docksides?" He kisses her. He blames her for this affection. She's the cute one. Irresistible. He can't help it.

The horse leading our carriage towers above the cabs in front of us. Arthur points out the General Motors building, the FAO Schwarz building. Kathryn plays with her hair, as if she were just discovering it. People stare at us from the sidewalk.

Kathryn doesn't want to go to the park zoo. I say we'll go, but not for too long. She eats more candy. This time a Hershey's bar. Her fingers are completely covered with chocolate. Then her face is. She licks her fingers clean. She takes a napkin, licks it, and then smears it on her face. She giggles as she does this.

Arthur talks to the people in the adjacent car. He asks them what language they're speaking. They're from Madagascar. They recognized him.

Because we're going to the zoo, Arthur sings, "At the Zoo." From across the street, some kid says, "There's what's-his-name."

Kathryn wants another hot dog. And a grape soda. We go through the gates of the zoo. Kathryn asks that Artie hold the drink while I push her on the swings. But the swings are too crowded, so we go on the seesaw. Kathryn sits with Arthur. They plant themselves on the ground and loft me into the air. The seesaw bends from the weight of Arthur and me, two adults where no adult should be. But Kathryn, dear Kathryn, is the balance that keeps us even.

17

My Blindness Balance Sheet: Debits

Assuming my blindness was a mistake set in motion by Dr. Mortson's poor management and my own refusal to face facts, I cannot help but look back at the pros and cons of my life ever since. On this cosmic ledger, I'll start with the cons, the torts, some of which I have already hinted at:

> *I have not seen the faces of my children.*
>
> *I have not seen the faces of my grandchildren.*
>
> *I have banged myself up—cut my forehead and all parts of my body—too many times to count. I need serious medical attention about four times a year.*
>
> *I am no longer able to participate effectively in many of the activities I enjoyed while sighted, such as baseball and tennis, not*

to mention those I might have picked up subsequently. Sports were a big part of my life.

I do not know what contemporary styles look like.

I cannot read without the use of all sorts of complex technology, or my beloved human readers. (I never use braille—it's too slow.) That means that I cannot quickly go to written reference material and search easily, although new text-to-speech technology has made some searches easier. At any rate, I must rely heavily on my memory, which, while good, is not perfect.

I have to move too slowly for my taste, although everyone tells me I need to slow down.

Visual artworks have to be described and explained to me.

I am unaware of the expressions on people's faces when we speak, so I cannot read those nonverbal cues so useful in business and social situations. Nor do I always know whether people are paying attention to me.

Being in the company of a blind man often makes people uncomfortable.

Mornings before Sue is awake are often the hardest time for me. I know the topography of my home well because we have lived in the same place for more than four decades. Nevertheless, the most basic things can all too easily go wrong. The housekeeper lays out the soap and shampoo in the shower the day before, but if the soap slips out of my hand, I have to bend down, the pads of my fingers on the rough surface of the shower stall, probing for support while I grope for it. I do not have the luxury of a light grip on the bar of soap; I need to know that it will not fall again.

I am tall. That helps me get ready in the morning because I am able to lean well over the sink when I shave, and that's important. If I cut myself, the blood will spill into the sink. When

I do cut myself, I may or may not be aware of it, but regardless, every day after I have finished shaving, I wash my face with very cold water to seal up any nicks or cuts. I make minor prayers for tiny nicks, hoping to avoid the more serious cuts. My life is full of minor prayers.

I stand in my dressing room knowing that my suits are on one side, my wife's things on the other. On my dresser lies everything I will need for the day—cash, wallet, keys, cell phones. My things are arranged in neat piles—for example, a stack of one-dollar bills, a stack of fives, and so on. I put each stack in a different pocket of my specially tailored Oxford suit, and then I use the bills for tipping doormen or stewards. My wallet is thin and neat, and I know, by touch, where each of my credit cards is.

The wallet still smells like leather because I will not allow the wallet or anything else of mine to appear old or worn. Even my underwear. I am as sharp as a newly minted coin and have been since I went blind. This has become the caliber of my life. I am able to pull everyday personal articles out of places unseen—a magician's trick. Imported goods and all kinds of swank contraband complete my disguise—British shoes and belts, lustrous ties (done in executive-suite half-Windsor knots), custom-made shirts in sharp colors and bespoke suits, linen handkerchiefs. I must stay at the edge and not slip back to that uncertain past—which is what being sloppy signifies for me. The psychological jargon would have it that "Greenberg is compensating." Yes, Greenberg is compensating, and it works fine.

If you were to see me in bright light, you would notice that on my forehead there are tiny lines—scars from my having run into walls, columns, corners. Similarly, there are scars on my elbows, shins, knees, and feet. These things are part of the cost of my decision to not "be blind." Because I can afford it, I am able to have a plastic surgeon who will see me on short notice to stitch me up. (There is a different physician for weekend emergencies.) Small accidents require Band-Aids. In more serious accidents, I may split open a vein or artery. Blood will fall like a curtain, and I will need stitches. The doctor will talk casually with me in his office, and I, blood dried on my face and my lips and shirt, will chat, too, as if I were getting a haircut. These sessions are irritating—not because of the pain, to which I have become somewhat inured—but because I know that if I get stitches, I will have to wait at least a day to exercise, which I find annoying. It is also annoying that I will have to return to the doctor's office to have the stitches removed.

Aside from people in my company, others assist me during my day: my wife, an assistant, a driver, my two sisters, who now live near me.

Since becoming blind, I have been very conscious of the need to be healthy and strong. As a result, I do a great deal of exercising, including aerobic training four days a week and strength training two days a week. In part, this regimen has to do with my insistence on looking sharp. But it all belongs to the determination not to be blind.

If you were to see me in the hallway of the Watergate, you would not know that I am blind. My eyes look fairly normal, in spite of a half-dozen surgeries over the course of sixty years. Seeing me when I am eating, of course, you would know, as my hand searches around for the water glass, the bread basket, and the napkin. If I were to walk fast, you would definitely know. But I walk slowly, for my own safety.

When Jerry Speyer gave the commencement speech at Columbia Business School in 2008, I realized that others had long been onto my game. He mentioned that I had "deftly adjusted" to my new life and then said, "Upon meeting someone for the first time, Sandy would extend his hand quickly, thereby avoiding having to search for the other person's hand. He also wore a watch and glasses to make it easier for the rest of the world to bear the tragedy of *his* blindness." Yes, sparing other people pain and embarrassment has been part of my game.

You would think after all this time that when I take a walk with my wife, and she holds my arm, I wouldn't care what other people think. But I do, a little. I don't like thinking that others are taking pity, imagining the burden of our lives. The insecure part of me worries about that. I'd prefer that a stranger think simply that here is a nice, handsome couple, in the way they would call a 1950s couple handsome.

Over the course of my lifetime, I have traveled alone many times, and it can be awkward. It is always interesting, shall I say, for me to try to use the bathroom on an airplane. The aisles are narrow; I bump into people, into their armrests. If the drink cart is in the aisle, flight attendants will sometimes get annoyed with me. Should I worry about turbulence? I don't know because I can't see other people's faces. Sometimes that's a good thing.

When we land, a flight attendant has to help me off the plane. Then someone has to meet me at the gate, which is nearly impossible these days. I have to coordinate the entire affair ahead of time, which involves paperwork to get my driver through security. If I'm by myself at the hotel, I have to get myself to my room, find my toiletries kit in my suitcase, find my shaving gear, and so forth.

One thing I have to do alone is use public men's rooms. This involves its own set of delicate issues. In fact, going to the men's room gives rise to the generalized apprehension constantly simmering just below my conscious thoughts.

I often have to ask a stranger if he would be so kind as to show me to the men's room, or show me out. When the stranger is silent, I have to wonder if he's unsure what precisely I am asking of him. If I'm in a restaurant, I may turn left to go slowly down the hall, as directed. Am I about to enter the men's or the women's? I will slow down even more and turn up my hearing to a high sensitivity, straining to hear molecules bouncing off a ceramic urinal. I move as slowly as the formation of planets from a gathering of dust. And yet I fail all the time.

People without sight have a special reverence for trust. I must trust people to lead me in places where I have never been. I must trust people to read written materials to me accurately and completely. I must trust accountants and business partners (and there have been betrayals in my life), as well as people who make change for me, especially with paper currency, and so on. Many are people I have encountered by chance, and so they surely cannot yet have earned my trust. It is all too frequently just not practical for me to wait around while someone earns my trust. Hence, that casual everyday term: blind trust. I am something of a Federal Reserve of trust, doling it out—sometimes reluctantly, often under pressure of circumstance—as if there is no end to it. Yet I admit my reliance on trust. The oft-repeated phrase of modern diplomacy "trust but verify" may sound wise at first blush, but it is actually an oxymoron. If you do the one, the other is negated.

Then there are the everyday pleasures of life, or what should be pleasures. Sue and I like to go to movies every so often. A blind person going to a movie might seem to be a silly thing, and yet it is not. Steven Spielberg once said that movies are about music and the story, both of which are accessible to me. An excursion to see a movie is one of the small adventures of a handicapped life, and it means a lot, but the excursions don't always turn out as hoped.

I recall a particular movie Sue and I saw in a suburban Maryland theater. She drove. On the way, we talked about our children, of course—a normal thing for parents. Then we talked about what we had heard of the movie, the reviews and the word of mouth, and what other movies we had seen starring the actors in this movie. It was a big Holocaust movie, *Schindler's List*, directed by none other than Steven Spielberg. He had provided me with valuable assistance at an important time in my life, putting me in touch with players in the movie industry.

Even though we got there early, the place was packed, which was not a surprise. A nervous high-school kid was in charge of things; he obviously had very clear instructions about when to let the ticket-holders standing in line into the theater. There were even police on hand to make sure there were no crowd issues.

Standing in line with other middle-aged people, I heard talk about all the research that went into the production of the movie to try to make it as accurate as possible and about the tours the director took of the concentration camps and the team of scholars he put together. There was a tone of reverence.

Finally, the nervous boy let everyone in. He reminded all of us that we needed to hang on to our ticket stubs because the show was sold out and there were a ton of people who wanted to see it.

Forewarned, we filed into the theater. The lights, according to my wife, were low, a sort of amber color. The place was already crowded, so we had to make our way up to the middle of the theater. I stumbled on some steps and reached out for a banister. At first I hit it with my forearm, then rammed my shin into the step. Sue turned around. "Are you okay?" she asked, even though this kind of thing happens all the time. I said I was fine. I sensed that people saw this and took note.

We usually try to sit somewhere in the back so we do not disturb other people. During a movie, Sue will lean into me, her hands cupped against my ear and say, "The man is wearing a black suit, like out of the forties," or, "Okay, she's wearing a red dress," or, "He's got a gun, you can't really see it, but I bet he's going to use it." One might think that my wife's having to color in the movie would be a burden to her. But I think she secretly likes it, and I sort of like it, too.

On this occasion, as on many, Sue took my hand and led me into the row. Legs were pulled to the side, and some men stood to let us by. We found two seats together, the crowd surrounding us like a wool blanket.

The movie began. There was a dedication: to all the people who died in the Holocaust. Everyone was rapt. You could hear the cells growing on people's fingernails. One must revere the Holocaust, but since we are so far from it these days, the closest thing we can revere is a movie about it.

The first part of the movie was noisy, a lot of black-and-white shots of concentration camps and rustling around and horrified prisoners. There was dialogue in German. My wife began reading the subtitles for me. People around us started growing restless, shifting in their seats. Perhaps they were wondering how we could be so insensitive during a movie like this.

The space about me still felt very thick and warm. We were witnessing history. But "witness" in my case was qualified. Sue kept translating for me. She is tough. She has been in the trenches with me and does not care at all what someone might think of her or me. She was well aware that people were irked by her whispering, but she had no intention of stopping.

Known for his use of contrast between light and dark, Spielberg chose to do this movie in black and white. He had, in the first part of the film, created some compositions that my wife felt were important to mention at the moment. Or perhaps mention because she is irreverent. And so the more restless people became, the more she was determined to share miscellaneous details about the film's composition.

There was a particularly poignant scene, one involving actual gas chambers, and she described the entire terrible moment to me. The people in the theater were dead quiet, unnaturally so. Movies can do this to a crowd; it is the strangest thing.

"It's very interesting," my wife said into my ear. "Really, it's very interesting. Hold on, hold on—they're about to turn on, hold on, wait, yes, I think, okay, they're turning on the gas. They think it's showers." The scene was horrifying, and then it was over. That's when the trouble began.

A man in front of us turned around. "Listen," he said, "I'm sorry, but this is too much." His voice was indignant, filled with conviction. We were staining his movie experience, one of the most important movie experiences of his life. We were disrespecting the audience, the filmmaker, everyone affiliated with the film, not to mention, of course, all the human beings who suffered in the real event being depicted on screen. "Can you please shut up?" he said. My wife began her rejoinder, but he shook his head. "Just shut up," he hissed, and turned back.

My wife and I turned toward each other. I could feel the heat from her face; she was about as angry as I have ever known her to be. I am calm-headed because I must be. We just did not know what to say, so we said nothing. People all around were looking at us, affirming what the man had just said. We were baking. On the screen, Jews were being gassed, but that was no longer of paramount importance to Sue and me, or maybe even to the people around us. I thought, it's just a movie. It's not the real thing. "I can't see, you guys," I wanted to say. But I didn't.

I wish there was an area in theaters where blind people could sit in comfort and have their companions tell them the story. But I don't know of any such theater.

I could not fully grasp that this man told us to shut up. And I could not believe that everyone had gone along with it. After all, this was just a movie, a for-profit endeavor that was going to enrich some people (the actors about to be gassed, for example).

The movie continued, but my spirits were crushed. It was a reminder that the only time you can forget about being blind is during sleep. After about ten minutes of total awkwardness, I felt a cramping in my stomach. I knew that feeling. It is emergent, and I knew that if I did not find a men's room within a few minutes there was going to be a different kind of unpleasantness. I waited, as I have waited my entire life, for a discreet exit, but this night it was not meant to be. I leaned over to Sue and told her I had to go to the bathroom. She was watching the movie, but I could tell that her attention was perfunctory. "Now?" she said. "Oh yes," I said.

We both had to get up, Sue leading me by the hand down the row of furious moviegoers. You are not supposed to say or do anything when something about the Holocaust is being presented. But sometimes you have to go to the bathroom. The pressure was intense, almost painful. We brushed by boney knees and fat knees, everyone making noises of disgust at our rudeness.

We went around the left side of the theater, moved slowly down the stairs, and then we were out the door.

It was very quiet in the lobby. My wife led me to the men's room, and from there I was able to continue on my own. I then went out to where my wife was waiting for me.

"Are you okay?" she asked.

"Yes," I said. "I'm perfectly fine. I'm terrific. Never been better. In fact, I feel like a million bucks."

"Okay," she said. She did not mention the cranky man in the movie theater. We headed back toward the theater, and the nervous young man who had shepherded the line said, "You guys left the movie?"

"Yes," my wife said. "Is there something wrong with that?"

"No. But you guys are the first to leave. Would you believe that? People sit for three hours straight. It's crazy, but they have been doing that since the show opened. I guess it's supposed to be a very important movie."

"Yes," my wife said.

The smell of popcorn was all around us, heavy, as if the air itself were chewable. Candy, too.

"Are you guys going back in?" the boy asked.

I looked at my wife. I did not see her face, but I knew that she was looking at me. Perhaps there was another option.

"No," I said, "we're not going back in."

"We're not?" said Sue.

"I guess not," said the young man, with a smile of empathy.

"Well," I said to him. "Thanks."

"Anytime," he said.

SOMETIMES MY BLINDNESS CAN CRUSH even the people I love most in unexpected ways. There are few people to whom I have been able even to attempt to explain the phenomenon of my fascination with the trumpet, as it necessarily involves something beyond the reach of logical explication. My best friend the artist and singer is one such person. My wife, too. She surprised me on a recent birthday of mine when she flew my brother and sister-in-law in from Rochester, New York, for the occasion. My brother, a couple of years younger than I, is an optometrist—no coincidence. At the birthday party Sue produced a present for me. As I unwrapped it, I felt that it was a piece of luggage, a hard case, its texture rough and durable. We already had nice luggage, but I pretended to be excited. She told me to open the case. I found the two clasps and unhooked them. Inside the case I expected to find some small gift, perhaps a gadget for travel. Instead, what I touched was the bell of a trumpet.

I did not remove the instrument but instead ran my fingers along the tapers of its throat. I lifted it out and handled the mouthpiece. The brass felt cold, and the instrument seemed perfect, as in fact it was. Sue had purchased a Bach Stradivarius, an instrument so finely crafted that for anyone but a master to play it would be almost obscene, the way one would not play catch with a baseball signed by Lou Gehrig or Babe Ruth. It is an instrument so well balanced that only a professional would be able to appreciate it fully. In fact, she had asked the principal trumpeter in the National Symphony Orchestra which instrument was the very best. He told her, and she got one for me.

I removed the trumpet, slowly, from the velvet around it—even the housing in the case was so well made that I could practically hear a pop as I freed the instrument. As I ran my fingers around the rim of the bell, although no one else mentioned hearing it, a light tone began to sound, the way a good crystal wineglass would ring if one were to slide a dampened finger around its rim. I did not say it (I didn't say anything at all, actually), but I thought, and would think later, that this would be sufficient, that I would never need to play it—my running my fingers around the rim, the sound resonating at a pitch that only I seemed able to hear, would be sufficient.

Then I heard the instrument itself singing, without my stroking it, as if in its very existence it was required to make music. Strange. I sensed that the others seated around me were still hearing nothing. I did not know whether I should tell them. Then I thought, no, I had better not. This feeling—the wanting to tell someone something and not being able to—is not uncommon for me. They would have laughed, even though we were in my own home. Company was all around, yet here I was holding an instrument that was making music on its own, as if it were inclined to do so. I withhold these kinds of secrets from people—the secret life of the blind.

I fitted the mouthpiece into the instrument and put my lips to it. I could hear the smiles of the people at the party, lips pulling back against teeth and gums. My wife told me to play something. As I put the instrument to my lips I remembered: embouchure. But my brother, a sweet man, said softly that I had better not try to play the instrument. "It's the pressure," he said. The pressure from playing the instrument could be painful for my eyes. It is an aspect of glaucoma. To play a wind instrument might cause blood vessels in my eyes to pop. My wife left the room; I found out later she was in tears.

Yes, it was sad, very sad. I thanked her nonetheless, deeply, sincerely.

But later that night, when the other guests were gone and she and my brother and sister-in-law were asleep, I found my way to my study, where I had placed the trumpet. Secretly, I worried that I would not be able to find it and would have to ask for help. It was in its case, right on my desk. As I opened it, the clasps snapping back seemed awfully loud. I took out the trumpet, covetously. It was not that I intended to play it, although I did insert the mouthpiece and put the instrument up to my mouth again, like kissing it. Then I just held it against my chest. I liked the heft of it. I liked the way it felt through the fabric of my nightshirt. I ran my finger around the rim of the bell again. And again a sound: not just a tone, but music and, with music, joy—pure joy, the sort of joy that is also a prayer. I think that in writing these remembrances, prayer has been my companion all along.

18

My Blindness Balance Sheet: Assets

Happily, balance sheets feature two opposing sets of figures: debits *and* assets. I'm rich in the latter.

In spite of the abuses I have suffered, both emotional and physical, I am healthy.

Not seeing people's facial expressions can be a good thing. The words spoken to me by the ugliest, most disfigured, most poorly dressed person imaginable may come to me with a weight equal to those from the most splendid face and physique. I do not judge a person on looks because I cannot. For me, the tone of voice and the content of the speech are what matter.

While I can't see, per se, I do have an elevated sense of place, of objects around me—I can feel their distance as clearly as if I could see them. For example, when I play basketball, it is easy for me to dodge a defender, to launch an accurate shot from the top of the key, and slide through big men toward the hoop. I sense the distance of people from me in waves. (I should add this capacity has its limits. Bill Bradley—the one-time Princeton all-American and former New York Knick, All-Pro, NBA champ, and US senator—humors me as he would anyone in our rare games; then when the game gets tight, Bill turns up the heat, clamps down on me, and scores almost at will.)

Because I was blessedly gifted with sight until my junior year in college, I have stored mental images of the world upon which I can still draw: great art and architecture, colors and shapes, and the faces of my old friends, my family, and my wife. My manic prowling among museums and art galleries in New York seems in retrospect like the activity of a squirrel preparing for winter. To this day, I collect art, visiting galleries often with Jerry Speyer, just as we did back in our undergraduate days, or with an art consultant who acts as my eyes. From learning at Columbia how to identify entire drawings from a single line or section, I can in a similar way put together a work of art or an entire room.

Sometimes I even commission work. Some years back, I asked Frank Stella to turn the prototype of the speech-compression machine I had invented into a piece of art. The machine had helped launch my business career, and I wanted to honor it. Frank thought about my request for six months and worked on the project far longer than that before he presented me with a soaring metallic structure with my prototype right at its heart. I can't see the sculpture, of course, but I can feel it, even sense it, and I know exactly what it looks like—although that might not be exactly what it looks like at all.

If not for my blindness, I would never have made deep friendships with many of those who have helped me, from my readers to my close college friends to my business colleagues. Each has been an individual light in my life.

I have been all over the world. What I have experienced of it is, on balance, more good than bad. In all those places, no one has lifted my wallet or kidnapped me for ransom.

I've had to learn how to live with fear and risk.

Sue earned a master's in special education and an MBA in finance. Her White House work during the Clinton years has been a blessing to us both. Would she have done all that if I had not gone blind? Who knows?

I am not aware of recent signs of aging in other people. I know my wife is slightly younger than I am, but I see her ageless and beautiful.

My family is healthy and, I believe, happy.

Having to develop other ways to see the world has benefited me in multiple ways. One I have mentioned often in these pages is the imagination, a twin of scholarly thought. Imagination seems to me more a generalized mental *activity* than a path to a clear-cut end result. I can say only from personal experience that memory and imagination, in my darkened life, percolating within the mind, often blend indistinguishably. For better or worse, I am perforce prone to reflection. I've had to be my own guru on the road to self-knowledge, and to slowness, and maybe ultimately to serenity—which I believe cannot be achieved by force of will alone.

I happily admit that I have a vivid imagination that often takes me into the realm of fantasy. Reality is rich, but fantasy makes life richer and often fosters creativity. I love imagining different scenarios for my own life, and this in turn has made me try to see things from other people's perspectives.

Saint-Exupéry observed, "It is only with the heart that one can see rightly; what is essential is invisible to the eye." And, in Helen Keller's words, "The best and most beautiful things in the world cannot be seen or even touched. They must be felt with the heart." I am told by an old expert on Japan that there is an appreciation in that country for places and things that are off limits to the public, including great national treasures within certain temple precincts. I take that to be a tribute to the special role played by imagination: how much richer those places and objects may become to us when we know *of* them, yet cannot confront them and "check them off."

For sighted people, the consciousness is normally dominated by the constant stream of visual perceptions. Sounds run a distant second to the role of visual distraction. The visual stream is like having the television on all day; the eye is drawn constantly toward the screen. Since I don't have that, you might think that I would be locked within my mind. But that's not the case. My imagination allows for rich engagement, not just in an imaginary world but in the real one.

I'm not sure this counts as an unblemished asset, but an odd side effect of being sightless has to do with confidences. My local community, Washington, is a town full of secrets, or supposed secrets. People tell me their secrets the way you might tell a bartender something that is on your mind. Sometimes very personal secrets, as at a confessional—so perhaps in this way I am like the priest who is unable to see the penitent but is there to grant absolution.

Often, the secrets I hear are silly or trivial. Sometimes, however, they are not. Indeed, you would probably find it hard to believe what I hear in confidence. (Of course, I can't tell you.) Cabinet members, senators, heads of federal agencies, heads of educational institutions, old Hollywood icons, Supreme Court justices, captains of industry and finance—leaning close to me, out of the sides of their mouths, they confess all sorts of things. Mistakes. Transgressions. Bypasses that should not have been taken. Things overlooked that should not have been overlooked. Evidence uncovered that should not have been uncovered. Sometimes they want to get it off their chests, and they know I am discreet. I could have ruined lives. My word, or my ear, it seems, is good—and all the better because I have no eyes. As they say, go figure.

Powerful people have told me secrets about their lives, but sometimes that is nearly all I know about them. The rest of their lives is a mystery, and so there would be no point in revealing the little I know. Sometimes I wonder what is the correct amount of my own life to disclose to people and whether everything would be better if I disclosed a little more. Or would it be better if I disclosed less?

SOMETHING SPECIAL ABOUT US BLIND PEOPLE—and this, I have come to realize is an unqualified asset—is that we do not see horizons. It is a subtle thing, but not insignificant. I can testify that there are no longer any horizons in my own life. Since I left the hospital in Detroit, I have not perceived any of the everyday horizons that sighted people experience. My not seeing topological horizons might seem like something Delphic or metaphorical. It is not. Horizons are essentially a function of spatial perceptions, and only tangentially (pun intended) an aspect of experience.

We blind people cannot go toward a horizon, nor can we feel the limitation of space suggested by a horizon. We do not wonder what is beyond the horizon because we do not *have* horizons. For us, horizons just do not exist. No such thing. Walls and the like do exist for us, for example, when we physically encounter them. But except for echoes when the walls are very near, I do not establish a mental environment hemmed in by walls, either. I have developed a way to approximate the layout of a room, but with a diminished sense of enclosure. It's subtle.

Schopenhauer wrote, "Every man takes the limit of his own field of vision for the limits of the world." With no horizons and no visual sensations to compete with and anchor my thoughts, I don't have the same sense of boundaries shared by people impaired with sight. Sometimes this has to do with the physical world in front of me; sometimes I experience it as a vague border between the dream state and the waking state.

I also lack perspective. Not the sort that is supposed to inform judgment and decision making, I hope, but the kind that concerns visual artists. The sort of perspective that Professor Schnorrenberg once brought up at the university in discussing the innovations of the Renaissance painters: the concept of the vanishing point. Aside from visual memories from before I lost my eyesight—a blessing the magnitude of which I cannot express—I know no vanishing points. My image of the topographical world can cram in distant things without their having to be all squeezed together, as they would in perspective. I am a functional surrealist.

The duality of boundaries for me as a blind person is another element of my bent mentality. As I sit in a room, for instance, my maximum boundary of safety and freedom from fear of movement is…zero. The zone of pure safety stops at my skin. That was the safe zone I faced back in Buffalo after the Detroit operation. But the flip side of having no safe space is that I also see no dangers. That may sound odd, but when I sit in a room that has no boundaries—in other words every room—the only thing out there is the entire universe. It is either completely filled with danger, or it has none at all. It's my existential choice.

Far-fetched? Maybe, but I can assure you that it is a functioning element in my mentality. If you are sighted, spend a week or so blindfolded, and let me know if it still seems far-fetched. After losing the vision of my eyes, I crafted a personal vision for my new life. I had to. In losing horizons, I could feel boundaries beginning to lose much of their hold over me. I began to feel free again, albeit in a new and unexpected way. My boundaries began opening up into a beautiful and widening circle of friends and family.

Maybe that's why the great humanitarian Michael Bloomberg once said, "Sandy has aspiration, hope, a role for all of us." I can't help it: I have no way of limiting what I imagine.

A REPORTER FROM THE GERMAN *Financial Times* once quoted me as having said, "In the dark I am able to think about what kind of enterprises I want to create," while other people are usually preoccupied by the often trivial things they see around themselves.

There is joy to be experienced from working with complex ideas. Joy.

Ideas can be beautiful in and of themselves, as beautiful in their way as the experience of listening to the "Kol Nidre" or a Bach cantata. Physicists find beauty in a mathematical proof or clever experimental validation of some hypothesis. To experience the beauty of an idea is to experience joy.

The years from my first steps through the gates of Columbia, to graduate study, and on to the White House and beyond were my glory days of reveling in ideas. But there is no end to experiencing the joy of discovering and working with new ideas. Learning gives me a sensation of adding light to the darkness.

It's only a metaphor—there are no actual flashes—but I do sometimes have a sense of a burst of light.

But I must once more acknowledge this: Acquiring and using intellectual capital, as I did, required determination, the real-world sort of determination and endurance that I saw in my father Carl's toil in the junkyard. It took many years of driven exercise to narrow and intensify a focus on a life within my mind. It was not something implanted whole in my brain at birth, nor was it a sudden flash of insight. It also had to be nourished constantly. It was a long road I had to take, but I have loved it. That's the reality of my blind life.

So ON BALANCE—debits subtracted from assets because this is, after all, a balance sheet? On balance, I consider myself the luckiest man in the world. I picked up that line from Lou Gehrig's famous farewell speech at Yankee Stadium on July 4, 1939, two years before his death at age thirty-seven of ALS: "For the past two weeks you have been reading about a bad break. Today I consider myself the luckiest man on the face of the earth."

Same here, Lou.

Sandy, as a White House Fellow, visiting with then-Vice President Hubert Humphrey.

To Sandy Greenberg - with warm regards and admiration.

Hubert H Humphrey

For my great friend Sandy Greenberg, with deepest respect and appreciation for all your help, Al Gore

With then-Vice President Al Gore. The inscription reads: "For my great friend Sandy Greenberg, with deepest respect and appreciation for all your help."

As a White House Fellow, Sandy visited South Africa in 1966. He is shown here with anti-apartheid activist Helen Suzman.

Sandy with Bill Moyers. Sandy was a White House Fellow when Moyers was serving as Lyndon Johnson's Press Secretary and Special Assistant.

Lyndon Johnson was thrilled to learn that four of the "Ten Most Outstanding Young Men in America" for 1967 were working for him. From left, they are Les Brown, William Carpenter, Sandy, and future HEW Secretary Joseph Califano. Carpenter was the famous "lonesome end" of the West Point football team.

To Sandy Greenberg
    A valued member of my staff,

Pressing the flesh with Lyndon Johnson as other White House Fellows look on.

Sandy with congressman and former Buffalo Bills quarterback Jack Kemp, at left, and Justice William Brennan, during Sandy's 1986 induction as a fellow at Brandeis University. Justice Brennan was one of Sandy's "wise elders," while Kemp's advice to "throw deep" has played a key role in his life.

A presidential parentheses: Gerald Ford and Jimmy Carter on either side of Sandy.

Is it Elvis? Or is it Sandy? Only daughter Kathryn knows for sure!

With President Bill Clinton, who appointed Sandy to the National Science Board, which oversees the National Science Foundation.

(Right) Kathryn Greenberg, circa age five.

(Below) A mother-daughter reunion: Kathryn and Sue in the early 2000s.

Sue Greenberg hitting the dance floor with Al Gore.

Sue and Sandy at his induction into the American Academy of Arts & Sciences, October 2016.

Sandy and Art Garfunkel retraced Sandy's harrowing 1962 New York City subway ride for a 2016 National Geographic *special issue on blindness.*

Sandy and Sue with grandchildren Helena, Sacha, Eli, and Lorelei.

Sandy with Michael Bloomberg, left, and Columbia roommate Jerry Speyer.

(Left & Below)
Sandy and daughter
Kathryn together in
Sarasota, Florida,
in 2018.

With his Watergate neighbor and dear friend Justice Ruth Bader Ginsburg.

Sandy with the celebrated blind tenor Andrea Bocelli at the World Economic Forum in Davos, Switzerland, 2015.

With Booker Prize winning novelist Margaret Atwood. As a Harvard graduate student, Atwood volunteered to read to blind fellow-students.

Sandy and Art Garfunkel on the Columbia University campus in a photo taken for a 2018 Readers Digest *article.*

Sue and Sandy at Davos, Switzerland, in 2007.

19

Speak, Memory

Just as high blood pressure can cause the human heart to enlarge, blindness did the same to my memory. I have a very good one. My mind became an archive, and I live my days, for the most part, somewhere in the stacks. That said, I wasn't certain if the central role of memory in the life of the blind qualifies as an asset or a debit—bad old times as well as the good are ever with me—so I opted to give the subject a short chapter of its own. The title, by the way, is borrowed from Vladimir Nabokov's elegant autobiography of the same name. My memory speaks all the time.

A few years ago Sue and I decided to take a trip to Buffalo to revisit our roots. Our motives for going back after so many years of living in Washington were different, I suspect, but I did not say so. Sue had left the night before to catch up with some twenty of her old girlfriends from Bennett High School; I met up with her in the city the following day.

I asked our hosts, old neighborhood friends, if we could visit my old home on Butler Avenue. They were a little hesitant. It wasn't a nice area when I'd grown up there, they said, and it had gotten worse. It would look strange, four people, driving around in an expensive car in what had become an impoverished community. But it was daytime.

When we got on Humboldt Parkway, I started to point out where everyone had lived. I had a very clear image in my head of what everything looked like. I knew where our synagogue was, where Dr. Mortson's office had been. I wanted it all to be very clean and neat and orderly and not to think about those visits with Dr. Mortson.

We stopped at 163 Butler. The houses along here were a hundred years old, and in front of them were cement blocks holding up the front stairs. It was a beautiful day, warm and dry. Sue was chatting with our friends.

I put my hand on one of the cement blocks. It was rough. It had been some time since I'd felt something so hard and grainy, so raw. I tried to make my way up to the threshold of the door, but I realized someone would have to help me. I ended up just standing there, Sue and the others still talking.

I pictured playing football on summer evenings with Joel. I thought of the bugs floating up to the lampposts. I thought of my mother and grandmother cooking, speaking in Yiddish. What did they *kibitz* about when we weren't around? I could see blind old Will Ludwig looming in front of his house, watching the kids play in the street. I thought of my father, Albert. This is where his coffin had lain—inside, a few feet from where I was standing. I could feel the smoothness of the coffin, the coolness of it. And the wood of the floor, and its smell, something homey and warm.

Several of the neighborhood people were gathering around us. We must have seemed like aliens to them. A little girl went up to Sue, who explained that I had once lived in this house.

"He did?" she said, her voice rising, not believing that this man had lived in her home.

"Do you want to meet him?" Sue asked.

The little girl came over to me. She couldn't have been any older than ten. I put my hand out for her to shake. I told her my name and she told me hers. Her hand, though tiny, was not a young child's hand. It was dry and remarkably coarse.

THE FOLLOWING DAY WE DECIDED to go back to Crystal Beach, a place that was as close to paradise as I could imagine when I was a little boy. Much of what I recalled had changed or been shut down. The amusement park, for example, which we'd never been able to afford, had closed years ago. The property was covered with condos.

Still, I felt like I was no longer in the present but back in the forties. I had a very clear image of a dance hall that had stood on the rise of the beach, off to the side, where only adults were allowed to go. It was a mysterious place, wonderful. At night, my mother and father would go there, and although I was too young to really consider romance, I did think of my parents dancing. Maybe they would kiss, maybe not—I didn't know, but we'd look over at the hall, always in the dark, the doorway and the windows glowing gold in the night.

The reinvention of the place in my head was different, of course, than what had actually happened. At times, in my memory, I was set apart from my family. I was standing on the wide cement pier, the water turbulent, sloshing against the pilings. My mother and Joel were walking past me, and then they would stop and look at me. They appeared, in my memory, like any regular mother and son. Only I wasn't with them. And when they stopped to look at me, this little boy, standing by the pier, they wouldn't necessarily say anything. It was as if they were sort of asking me if I wanted to join them.

I think some of the nostalgia of being there rubbed off on Sue, who said she wanted to visit the old cottage that her parents had rented in the summers. It didn't really matter to us that much of the beach was now a gated community, that things were not precisely as we remembered them.

Near the end of the trip, we visited the cemetery where my family is buried. The weather had darkened a bit. We found the spot, and I rested my hand on my mother's gravestone. It was weathered, but there was still a grit to it, a toughness, something enduring about it, which I felt was appropriate. The grass was soft, and so was the air. I thought about what these people, who had had hard lives, would think about me and the kind of life I had led. Their judgment was massively important to me. I felt that they would have been proud of me. But I sensed no response. But (of course!) the response would have to come from inside myself. I lingered a little while, and then we left.

Ultimately, on that weekend of memory and retrospection, there were a few accompanying feelings of sadness. But there were also rich images of the times Sue and I spent together. I thought about Sue, sixteen years old, coming up out of the water, me watching her from the sand. I thought about how curvy she was, and beautiful, her hair wet as she tucked it behind her neck. She was young and lacking self-consciousness. This beautiful girl was mine and I was hers, and there was the possibility that she would remain so. That is something to which I still cling, an innocent amazement that she is mine.

ONE LAST MEMORY: of standing alone on a dock on the shore of Lake Erie decades ago, near my boyhood home. I throw a stone into the water, and as I watch the ripples extending outward from the point of impact, I become aware of an older me standing nearby, watching. Not just that, but my mother and brother, too. A 3-D memory, as it were—a little bend in the time-space continuum.

I should be too old to engage in such fantasy. Yet I shamelessly admit that I do—all the time. Fantasy will save you if you let it. You are always encouraged to be a proper grown-up, but if you succumb to that pressure (I *never* did, occasional appearances aside), you will miss something important, the magic of daily living. You will miss the magnificent, gargantuan essence— the beauty and the joy—that can be uncovered within all the things we encounter on any day. A day when one steps out into fresh air after a week in the hospital; a day one might be walking with his wife on vacation, dancing at a party amongst friends and relatives—some alive, some from the past; or a day at the edge of a dock, idly throwing a stone, waiting for something extraordinary to happen.

20

No Man Is an Island

When I was growing up in Buffalo, someone told me that "the longest way around is the shortest way home." That bit of folk wisdom has turned out to reflect much of my life. It took me a long time to realize that many of the answers about how I came back to life after I lost my sight lie outside myself. Despite my seeming bravado in facing down the social worker and other well-meaning people, I am *not* independent. I cannot be. It's not all about me, and it never was.

My story is largely one of *dependence*. Like many of us, I have been a taker. When I needed to, I took and took. And I'm not ashamed to admit it. In a larger sense, I was what the Internal Revenue Service refers to as a dependent. That status has helped me realize something. No one is a self-made man.

Yes, I have shown determination throughout my life as a blind person, but here is my secret formula:

Without the support and love from so many people in my life, above all my wife and my family...without the close friendships with which I have been blessed...without the kindness so many people have spontaneously shown...without the oxygen of freedom and rule of law that the United States gave my family...without the education that in my darkness gave me material to help sustain my mind...without the example of great men and women in my life and in history... I am convinced that I would have lain where I fell.

Time and again, in this long journey up from that Detroit hospital bed I have depended on the sheer *example* of many people, both living and not. Selecting superior people and following the examples they set may (and probably will) change your life for the better. The choice comes at absolutely no charge to you, so there is no reason to choose any but from the top shelf—the best. If others of mankind—individuals or entire communities—have attained grace and produced lasting achievements, why not take guidance from their paths? It is a question of what we want ourselves to grow to be.

One example I have followed (or tried to) goes back to my days at Columbia University, not only as an undergraduate but later as an MBA candidate. Benjamin Graham, author of *The Intelligent Investor* (1949) and a fabulously successful investor himself, was a professor at Columbia and an inspiration for Warren Buffett, who studied under him as a graduate business student and then went to work for his investment firm.

Graham was an adherent of "value" investing, as contrasted with harried speculation and quick-as-a-flick profit taking. I believe this approach (which has also been Buffett's) was a cultural inheritance of the Great Depression, but Graham's principles were also consonant with the general tenor of

Eisenhower's America—which was a big part of my own cultural inheritance. Sensitivity to society at large and its needs, not just a monomaniacal drive for profits at any cost, was reflected in the stance of many of the immediate postwar business leaders—and continued to prevail in the lecture halls of Columbia's business school for years after Graham departed the faculty in 1955. That is where I learned about value and finance, but finance of a character that fit me well. Its influence has enabled me to build my career in business unaccompanied by any lingering shame about exploitation.

To my surprise, then, what I subsequently encountered through friends and associates in Washington in 1966 and 1967 was quite a different kettle of fish. Unorthodox approaches to business were in the air. I made new acquaintances who were innovative business doers of a mind-set quite different from the supposedly ideal corporate leaders of the business-school world.

Tom Watson, for example—not the splendid golfer but the entrepreneurial-minded head of IBM. Tom gave me many ideas about what it really meant to be in business and finance and to build a company. He was especially emphatic on the importance of investing in research and development. Bill Hewlett of Hewlett-Packard fame, a member of the President's Science Advisory Committee with which I was associated as a White House Fellow, also became a friend and contributed even more to my understanding of the emerging entrepreneurial ways of American business. Tellingly, all these friends and guides were avid devotees of technology. And yet the business school had been teaching *none* of what I was now learning in Washington!

I HAVE BEEN BLESSED AND SUSTAINED by so many friends across such a broad field of endeavor that I find it hard to sort through them in any way accessible to readers. But David Rockefeller deserves a pedestal of his own. David was a member of the board of overseers at Harvard when I first came somewhat within his orbit. He was always interested in the young scholars at the university. He had been asked by President Johnson to provide private-sector funding for a new "White House Fellows" program, which he did. David was appointed chairman of the first Commission on White House Fellowships. Former secretary of the Treasury Douglas Dillon mentored me in the program and for many years thereafter, as did John Gardner, Secretary of Health, Education, and Welfare.

But David continued to have a large place in my life. Ever since meeting him, he provided me with informal, un-self-conscious tutorials in politics, finance (the two of us acting in concert at times), art, and philanthropy. And he showed an openness of spirit you might not expect in such an Olympian figure in finance and society, generously widening his friendship with me to embrace others in my circle, such as Jerry Speyer.

David was also instrumental in my becoming a member of the Council on Foreign Relations and a member of the board of the National Committee on US-China Relations. In the 1970s, during the early days when Communist China "opened up" to ordinary diplomatic contact with the United States, I was asked to host some of the first wave of Chinese diplomats in our Watergate home. This was an important period of broadening boundaries for the Chinese government and for us. I learned from my experience with those men how talking with each other across borders can lessen ignorance and fear of the unknown.

I also saw in David, to mention one more quality, an amazing grace under pressure. Despite his great wealth and influence, David had experienced severe pressure as well as reverses, yet had not hesitated to turn to others simply and unpretentiously for help and support. He had a highly developed sense of honor, which I have found worth emulating, and he respected all manner of people, high and not so high. I have tried to absorb his ability to carry himself with dignity but at the same time modestly. And here is a man who could throw his weight around almost without limit. (I'll add here that David was one of the people who urged me to share my experiences, in the belief that to do so might help others.)

One further note here. For many years, David was said to be the richest man in the world. For me, he was richest of all in wisdom, a substitute father for the two I had lost along the way. David was already 101 years old when I visited him in late 2016 at his home at Pocantico Hills. We had taken some years earlier to hugging when I left. This time, he asked me to kiss him on his cheek. When I did, he offered me the other cheek, too. I'm sure now this was his way of saying a final goodbye.

ANOTHER PERSON WHO BECAME both an example to me and a friend was former justice William Brennan of the United States Supreme Court. He came onto the bench in 1956 as a recess appointment made by President Eisenhower and would in time stand out as one of the most humane justices to sit on the modern Supreme Court. Our friendship grew into one of the great treasures of my life. He would invite me to his office, where we would order in lunch and discuss issues of jurisprudence and other abstract ideas, as well as the law school we had both attended. Which was the best legal document ever written? The Bible? The United States Constitution? The Talmud? There was always something valuable in his comments, but of even greater value was the guidance that flowed from his personality and from his outlook on life and how it should be lived.

I have often speculated on why these supporters at all levels showed such generosity toward me. Has it often been just sympathy for a blind guy? Could be. But perhaps, I sometimes think, it is because I myself am open with others—as I so often must be. As noted earlier, I need a lot of extra help in living my life. In the process, I necessarily offer my trust to people, which may trigger a correspondingly generous response, especially from good people who happen to be imbued with the spirit of helping others. In other words, I suspect that a reciprocity is established. Whether that is so or not, the fact is that my reliance on so many people has greatly enriched my life. Yet another compensatory balance, perhaps.

A FEW PEOPLE IN ONE'S LIFE stand apart from, and in some way above, one's community, and even one's friends. In my life, those people have been my late mother and grandmother and now, after the half century or so we have been together, my wife. In this account of my life, Sue stands alone—not just for the usual sentimental reasons, although I harbor a lot of those, but in ways practical and rational.

There were a multitude of things Sue did not have to do. She did not have to wait for me or worry about me when I was in college, not feeling well, my prospects extremely doubtful. She worried so much that it made *her* sick. She lost twenty pounds, this from an already slender young woman. I had diminished her, and it seemed unfair. And then she married me, another thing she did not have to do.

She was still young and might have had a number of suitors. I might have seemed like a catch at one point, but when I returned from college and then Detroit, my eyes shot, I more likely resembled a man without much of a future. She waited out that period, read to me, and stayed with me. What does that say about her? It says she is persistent, she is hopeful, she has faith—even though she is not especially religious. She has faith in the human spirit.

She definitely did not have to stick around with me during the horrid graduate-school years when, as clear as day to anyone, I was headed nowhere but straight into professional student-dom and perpetual debt. Her father would say to me, "When are you going to get a W-2?" and I would tell him, weakly, that the longest way around was the shortest way home.

As powerful as that old bromide was to me, Sue's father found it less explanatory of our immediate circumstances, and Sue almost certainly would have agreed. She did not *want* to give me care after I graduated from college, but she did it anyway. She did not want to make my dinner; she did not want to stay up when I had to, reading to me in our shabby graduate-student apartments; and she did not want to record tape after tape after tape for me. She wanted none of that, but she did it.

They say there is no truly selfless act, but I believe that Sue has lived an essentially selfless life, doing for others, not for herself. I cannot account for any aspect of Sue's commitment. Oh, I could say I was a kind man, an excellent lover, and a terrific companion in those hard years, and even if all that was true, it still would not have made sense for her to choose to endure the difficulties of being with me the way she did.

I do not know why Sue stayed with me—is love an answer? Does that mean she believes in love? I don't know, but Sue is the center of gravity of the story I am struggling to tell here. She is the love of my life, and not just because she stuck with me and was my support.

RESPECTABILITY ALWAYS CATCHES ME by surprise. At one level of self-perception, I'm a blind guy, the kid from Buffalo. What's the big deal? At another level, honors accrue, and I honor them.

One of the sweetest moments for me was the letter I received in 2016 inviting me to join the American Academy of Arts and Sciences. Launched by John Adams and James Bowdoin way back in 1780, the Academy is among America's oldest learned societies. Its members range from Benjamin Franklin to Alexander Hamilton, Thomas Jefferson, Thomas Edison, Ralph Waldo Emerson, and (to jump way forward) me. Talk about asymmetry! But I was incredibly flattered to be tapped—there have been fewer than five thousand fellows inducted in the nearly 240 years of the Academy—and I join in whenever I can in the rich array of symposia available to its members. Apart from the intellectual stimulation, I feel almost duty-bound to do so, given all the opportunities America has afforded me and my family. But whatever takes me to Academy events—my own induction, talks by others, presentations in which I take part—I always know that I am there by the grace and upon the shoulders of those I have mentioned in this chapter and so many others.

21

A Promise That Cannot Be Broken

I withheld the names of two other friends and mentors from the previous chapter, not because they are less important but because they propelled me so powerfully into the future that they seemed to deserve a special mention.

One of those wise counselors, Ron Wyden, the senior senator from Oregon, put much of this book, and my life, into perspective when he told me how important it is "to be in the *tikkun olam* business," evoking a solemn commandment of the Jewish religion literally to repair the world.

"Perfecting the world, the opportunity—both for our country and for our world—to make them a better place for those who come after us is a very important Jewish value," Ron continued, "and I happen to believe that Jewish values are American values."

I agree, and would say the same thing of fundamental Muslim values, and Buddhist ones, and Christian ones, and Shinto ones, and agnostic and atheistic ones, and on and on. At heart, just about all of us want to make the world a better place for those who come after us. But Ron's words had a special resonance for me because as he spoke, I was remembering my own *tikkun olam* moment: that dismal winter day in 1961 when, lying in my Detroit hospital bed, I answered a Call from a higher power and made a promise to help end blindness forever.

Have I been absolutely steadfast in delivering on my promise? No, not really. Education, marriage, children, the White House Fellows program, launching my first companies, the Council on Foreign Relations, the National Committee on US-China Relations—they all intervened. Success in school and in business is rarely time-neutral. But the Call was always there, waiting to be served, and I seized what opportunities I could to push it forward.

When I was asked to join the boards of Johns Hopkins University and Johns Hopkins Medicine, with its school of medicine and hospital and its acclaimed Wilmer Eye Institute for advanced research and treatment in ophthalmology, I eagerly accepted. Later, I became chairman of the board of governors of the Wilmer Eye Institute—a position uncannily appropriate for a blind person who has dedicated himself to ending all forms of blindness.

I was equally happy to serve as chairman of the Rural Health Care Corporation, created by Congress to bring the benefits of telemedicine to rural America. This work was particularly meaningful to me since rural areas are obviously underserved medically and often impoverished. It reminded me how important that service would have been to the people I knew in my childhood. It might even have prevented a young boy from going blind.

In that same spirit, I gladly accepted President Clinton's invitation to serve on the National Science Board, which operates the National Science Foundation. That, in turn, gave me the standing to push hard for funding for further research on a retinal prosthesis being developed by Dr. Mark Humayun, a gifted young clinician-scientist then on the Wilmer faculty. Our first two attempts to secure funding came up short, but I'm nothing if not persistent, in business and in life, and our third try in 1998 proved the charm. Mark went on to invent and commercialize a retinal implant designed to help patients with genetic retinitis pigmentosa, but he didn't stop there.

In the two decades since, Mark has done further breathtaking work on electronic visual prosthetics. I'll let him describe his most recent breakthrough:

"Currently, the focus is primarily on developing a visual cortical implant that bypasses the eye and optic nerve completely. So far, six subjects have been implanted with good results."

Six subjects is far from clinical confirmation, but the very real possibility that the blind can "see" essentially without working eyes and a functioning optic nerve suggests just how bold and daring the thinking has become in a field that once offered only alternatives to sight instead of hope for its recovery.

Along with my public service, many of the companies I founded were involved with medical technology. My first interest as a businessperson had to be the viability of each—I don't shy from profit—but I also focused on whether each new company might provide value for the common good.

One of the companies I founded was a marriage of the biological sciences with information technology. We tracked how antibiotics work against various diseases. Hospitals would use antibiotic X or Y and report on that use and its outcomes into a database. My company would then aggregate and maintain the data from a number of hospitals and share the information with drug companies or whoever else wanted to pay to receive it. The information was used, in turn, in whatever research, development, or initiative the customers were undertaking. We also classified and catalogued patients' reactions to certain antibiotics. It was not a flashy business, certainly, but it was an endeavor that—down the road—would improve medical care and health outcomes for many people. In a way, we were librarians, archivists of disease.

I cite this company as an example of the kind of business that has attracted me. It was an opportunity to do something for my larger community. As Tom Stoppard wrote, "Information is light." That this and other companies I founded did very well gave me the means to indulge my Call in ways unavailable to most Americans.

Two early examples stand out in this regard. The first, in 1984, came about with the personal help of Dr. Torsten Wiesel, winner of a Nobel Prize for mapping the visual cortex. At my request, Dr. Wiesel organized a symposium of outstanding scientists, held privately in Washington, to assess the work going on in the field. Further colloquies were later held through the good offices of Dr. Elias Zerhouni, then director of the National Institutes of Health.

These gatherings were rich with leading experts and invariably intellectually exciting, but none of them gave me confidence that the relevant science was far enough along to yield feasible clinical results anytime soon, or perhaps even within my lifetime. In the end, much as I enjoyed them, they left me more anxious than satisfied.

YES, ALL THESE OUTREACHES were "proof" that I had made a good-faith effort to fulfill my promise—I was actually *trying* to find a way so that youngsters like I had been would never again go blind. But if I lacked faith that these efforts would produce anything close to the desired outcome, was I just making a devil's compromise with my own ambition?

I imagined that if I went back in time and explained to my newly blind self that I had tried "really hard" to accomplish what I had promised, that stern young man would reply, "Not good enough! You think it is okay just to try? Columbia doesn't grade on effort expended, on hard work. It grades on results. Just trying is insufficient."

At least, I comforted myself, my promise to end blindness was closely held. My mother and my lifelong friend Sandy Hoffman had been in the hospital when I made the vow. Later, I told my college roommates Art and Jerry, and Sue, of course. But that was it. I had wisely spared myself the public embarrassment of shouting it from the rooftops, then coming up short.

"Wisely"? The more I thought about it, the more that adverb caught in my throat. Maybe, I finally acknowledged, the problem lay right there. I hadn't dared enough. I had talked big in a small circle. I had even thought big along a narrow track. Perhaps the time had come to reach out to a wider world.

As I pondered this, I found my thoughts returning more and more to my close friend Sol Linowitz. Sol had won early fame by turning a company called Haloid (soon to be rechristened Xerox) around, but he had subsequently emerged as a highly successful diplomat and a leading Washington lawyer and powerbroker. If I was going to take the Call beyond my immediate circle and broaden its ambition, I couldn't think of a better person to include, and so I did. Sometime later Sol called me and said that he would like me to meet Dr. Jonas Salk of polio vaccine fame.

And that, as Robert Frost once wrote, "has made all the difference."

The three of us duly convened in Sol's office for the better part of an afternoon. When the meeting was over, I walked outside and asked my driver to take me to a peaceful open space so I could be alone. At first, I only listened to the chatter of birds, but then my excitement grew. For the first time, I felt there was realistic hope for the promise I had made to God. The reason: Dr. Salk had urged upon me a focus beyond the treatment of a disease's symptoms or its individual physiological effects. After all, he had made his own objective nothing less than to *end* a disease…and he succeeded! In my mind, I repeated, "End it! End it! End it!" I have never forgotten that.

THAT WAS THE FIRST STEP not only to regaining confidence that I could deliver on my vow but also to thinking in a larger, far bolder arc. To date, at least in my own mind, I had been defining *success* as developing techniques to regenerate the optic nerve. (That would hold the potential for allowing me to see again, for example.) But blindness takes multiple forms, just as polio does, and Jonas Salk's genius, I now realized from sitting with him for an afternoon, was twofold: to attack the entire range of the disease and to start at the finish line—not with incremental progress but with routing the disease itself.

Just as John F. Kennedy had with his vow to land a man on the moon before the end of the 1960s, so Dr. Salk had raised a signpost for others to see and follow. Both men provided an organizing principle that broke down narrow interest groups— the MBA term is "silos"—and turned isolated, helter-skelter research to common purpose. And, of course, in both instances, the results were giant steps forward for mankind.

If outer space and polio, I began to think, why not blindness, too? If Jack Kennedy and Jonas Salk, why not—of all people—a blind Buffalo guy named Sandy Greenberg? And if blindness, why not the whole range of other conditions that would bene-fit from the capacity to regenerate and otherwise repair tissue across the entire central nervous system? Isn't that the essence of a *tikkun olam*—something so large, so ambitious, so crazy, really, that it almost scares? It was time to jump into the deep end.

Accordingly, on October 18, 2012, Sue and I announced the establishment of the End Blindness by 2020 Prize, accompanied by a substantial award—$3 million—to be bestowed Decem-ber 14, 2020, upon the person, group, or institution deemed to have made the greatest scientific and medical contribution toward advancing vision science for human patients. The award ceremony—to take place in the chambers of the United States Supreme Court, thanks to the kindness of Justice Ruth Bader Ginsburg—will be a celebration, of course. How could it be otherwise? Darkness shall become light! The blind shall see! But we also intend to frame the moment as a judgment, the righting of an ancient wrong. And thus, to borrow from Virgil's *Aeneid,* which did so much to rally my spirits and lead me to the book you are now reading: "Even this we will be pleased to remember."

(More about the prize, the accompanying campaign, and the governing council and scientific advisory board can be found in the epilogue. I urge readers to take a look.)

I MOST DEFINITELY DO NOT WISH to inflate my importance in all this. I am not a player in the world of science. I am not even a coach or a team owner although I have had a financial interest in various professional teams and once owned a sports venue: the venerable Cleveland Coliseum. The players in this far more important arena are the researchers, their professional leaders—their coaches, as it were—and their colleagues around the world who produce knowledge in ancillary but possibly quite relevant areas. I am a businessman, but I do tinker with ideas, and many of them run toward technology and science. Most important, I am a dreamer who, because of my limitations, knows no horizons.

That is precisely why I dared to raise this new signpost and why I dare to look beyond blindness to where our prize and all this effort might ultimately lead.

From the intricate knowledge of every ocular-system cell might we not reasonably anticipate that important new medical diagnostics and dispositive treatments would subsequently flow? What if instead of laboriously drilling down toward the mysteries of the most basic platform of human life and struggling to connect the parts, we were able to understand and follow the processes of life from that base upward, change by physiological change, interaction by interaction? Imagine, then, the enhanced predictability of diagnoses and treatments for disease, and even prevention. And go further: imagine how this approach might spread to aid Parkinson's and Alzheimer's victims, para- and quadriplegics, and so many more who find themselves at the mercy of failed nerve clusters.

Not reasonable? Unrealistic? Yes, and no. "Yes," perhaps, when all the well-informed ifs, ands, and buts of today are tallied, exclusive of dreams. But saying instead "no, not unrealistic" to boundaries and limitations—that is the direction I have learned to take in my life. "No" to the idea that I should just accept being blind and learn to make screwdrivers back home in Buffalo. "No" to all the warnings that I should not return to Columbia, and in any case should not try to graduate with my class. "No" to the well-meaning admonition that I would be wise not to apply to big-time grad schools. "No" now to the injustice of blindness in the largest sense—that it needs to exist at all. Humans weren't meant to live in darkness. We were made to see the light.

MAYBE I WILL BE PROVEN WRONG. Perhaps blindness is endemic to the human condition, a burden resistant to the wonders of science, to be randomly distributed across all of time. But given my own life experiences, given all the good fortune that has come my way, given the resources at my disposal, not to attempt to end blindness would be the biggest injustice of all. That, too, is of the essence of the *tikkun olam*, to pursue perfection even if it should prove unattainable. But here's my deepest secret: I absolutely believe that blindness can be ended, that justice for those of us forced to go through life in the dark half-light of the unsighted is well within our reach. Sue's and my End Blindness by 2020 Prize isn't meant to conjure up a miracle cure. We're merely hoping to nudge the clock forward to a time when all God's children can not only feel the sun shining on their faces but also witness with their own eyes its rising and its setting.

I've never forgotten the wisdom of Congressman Jack Kemp, the former Buffalo Bills quarterback: "throw deep"—a bit of advice I have often followed, both in my business life and in my quest to satisfy my promise to my ghostly monitor to help make blindness a thing of the past. More wisdom underlies "throw deep" than may at first be apparent. Why? Because it is a default bit of human nature to give careful consideration to negative aspects of a contemplated action—essentially, negotiating with oneself. Too often, that ends with the action compromised or even avoided.

But throwing deep is not the same as acting rashly or, in the case of a Hail Mary pass, from desperation. Throwing deep is acting toward that which one truly desires, after having considered—and rejected or countered—the limitations. (In the case of Jack Kemp and other NFL quarterbacks, these considerations must be run through in scant seconds, with Everest-sized linemen bearing down on them!) All this differs greatly from the sorts of internal compromises and toxic regrets that negotiating with oneself tends to produce. But to me, the choice between the two has long been clear.

To throw deep is to honor one's highest beliefs and aspirations. It is to answer the Call, to fulfill our *tikkun olam*, whatever that solemn vow might be. For an adventure such as pushing toward an end to blindness, throwing deep is hardly hyperbole and not necessarily the end of the story, either. It might be only the beginning.

22

Old Friends Sat on the Park Bench Like Bookends

As readers of the epilogue will learn, our End Blindness Prize has not been a stealth campaign. One of my many appearances brought the prize and my backstory to the attention of Susan Goldberg, editor in chief of *National Geographic* magazine, and at her urging, on March 18, 2016, Arthur and I reprised our 1962 subway odyssey for a lead-in to an issue devoted to blindness viewed globally.

Once again, we started out in Midtown Manhattan, but this time I knew Arthur was with me and the *Geographic* was photographing as we went. I didn't bump into people and smash myself up. Nor did I have to grope my way hand over hand from the 116th Street station to the gates of Columbia. Still, when we made it back to the Columbia University campus and I went to sit down on a bench, my leg slammed into it—almost predictably. I soon realized that this was the same stone bench on which I'd sat in 1961 with classics professor Moses Hadas while he told me, without beating around the bush, that I was "finished," that Columbia was over for me because of my blindness.

I had long remembered that pronouncement as a thunderclap of doom. What was now flashing through my mind as I sat in that same spot more than a half century later was something entirely opposite. With this reenactment, my life as a blind person had come full circle in an unimaginably beautiful way. Thoughts and memories just kept flooding my brain, pouring in from somewhere. I've never experienced anything like it.

What was it? Relief? That old sense of being fortunate beyond any reckoning, maybe even undeservedly so? Both, I'm sure, were a part of the moment. But really, at the heart of what overwhelmed me was something I have seldom allowed myself to feel: pride. Pride that a junk dealer's son, a blind kid from Buffalo, had done all this. Pride of accomplishment. Pride that I'd managed the impossible despite Moses Hadas's malevolent benediction—finished at Columbia and with my own class, won fellowships and advanced degrees at Harvard and Columbia, attended Oxford and Harvard Law School, been a White House Fellow, served on important boards, founded highly successful businesses, made much more than a good living for my wife and children, even helped launch a substantial prize that my wife and I believe will help end blindness forever.

Richard Axel, the 2004 Nobel laureate in Physiology or Medicine and (appropriately) a long-time Columbia professor, would later say that in my story he recognized, "perhaps for the first time, a true triumph of the human spirit…. Sandy showed me that it is possible not only to endure, but to prevail." I'm still deeply touched by those words, and by their echo of William Faulkner's unforgettable Nobel Prize acceptance speech in the early, often terrifying days of the Cold War. Sitting on that stone bench after Arthur's and my reprisal of what seems in memory almost a primal event, I had something of the same thought: Dammit, Sandy, you did do it! But the thing is, I had no idea how I had managed it—and still don't.

It's no exaggeration to say that the psychic aftermath of that reenacted subway ride has changed the architecture of the life in my mind. My old feeling that every day was a dawn-to-dusk marathon, of having to constantly prove myself to others (and myself most of all), was finally gone. The race was over; the jury, in. I'd won. It's a strange thing to admit, but for the first time since becoming an adult, I felt fully human.

A famous prayer in the Jewish religion has taken on new meaning for me. It is the Shehecheyanu: "Blessed art thou, Lord our God, King of the universe, who has kept us in life, sustained us and enabled us to reach this glorious moment." For me, that glorious moment arrived as I sat on that stone bench on the Columbia campus, my journey finally over.

Just then, I heard the strangest thing: music coming from I knew not where. Not from Arthur, although he is apt to break out in song at any moment. Not from any external source that I could discern. And then I realized the music was coming from inside me—my own internal celebration in music and song of the life I've led, the challenges I've overcome, and the many friends who have helped me along the way; a symphonic and choral arrangement orchestrated by me and performed solely for the enjoyment of the luckiest man in the world.

23

My Big Party

While I'm on the subject of music, there's a lot of it coming from the ballroom. Trumpets mostly—I've paid for them to go all night long. What with the bright lights, the musicians almost seem to be holding champagne flutes to their mouths.

This is a party, a really big party—my big party, spun entirely out of my imagination. But remember, for the blind, the imagined and the real are often a hair's breadth apart. Even dead people get to attend. In fact, they are the ones who do the most dancing, along with me, on the wide parquet dance floor.

The smokers are smoking. The silverware is cool and comfortable to the touch, and all the drinks go down smoothly, disintegrating worry. You can eat the food—every kind you could want—and never get full, only satisfied. Clocks keep on going, but at this party we are making a big fool of time, and space, too.

Arthur and I take over playing and singing together for a time, he on the guitar, me on the drums but coming in occasionally on the trumpet—switching back and forth from the instrument Sarah and Carl had given me back in Buffalo to the one Sue gave me much later. Sue's gift is magnificent, shiny and new, while the one from my Buffalo days is a bit dull, scratched and dented. Yet to everyone's amazement, each produces a brilliant, rounded tone. We swing into one of our college favorites: the Gospel hymn and jazz-band classic "When the Saints Go Marching In." Unless I'm mistaken—and I'm not—that's Bill Clinton wailing away beside us on the sax. Party on, Mr. President!

Even better than back at Columbia, a parade of actual saints now begins streaming by, almost three thousand of them—you really cannot fail to invite even one saint—from the early martyrs Peter and Paul and Stephen, referred to as "the Jew," thought to be the first Christian martyr, beating out Paul; to better-knowns including Teresa of Ávila, Thomas Becket of Canterbury, and Joan of Arc; to the more obscure, ranging from the virgin Bega, patron of bracelets; Guy of Anderlecht, patron of bad business deals; and Nicholas Owen, patron of basements; followed by the last saint to strut in, the virgin Lutgardis, who rejoiced in losing her sight as a God-given means of detaching her from the distractions of the visible world. (I'm not sure that was such a great idea.) For this party, she strides by confidently, without aid. The parade would normally have lasted a full day, but time for now is elastic—the clocks calibrated not by hours but in units of serenity.

There's no need for speeches on multiculturalism or political correctness at this affair because everyone was invited, and why not? The invitees have all meant something to me, even if I am not always aware of just what it is. In fact, in most cases I am definitely unaware, but the way I see it, that may be irrelevant to their meaning for my life. Which is probably the significance of the thousands of holy *bodhisattvas* and *pratyekabuddhas* who file in after the saints. They are followed by the quite extensive cast of the Bhagavad Gita, by the Jewish sages and assorted *rebbes* (disputing so loudly with each other that you can hardly hear the music), by crowds of *bō-san* from medieval Japan holding beggars' bowls, by the many spirit gods of old Egypt (a really motley crew), by a huge crowd of gods of the hearth from ancient Rome and gods from pretty much everywhere else in the ancient world (there is even a squirrel spirit from Scandinavia, Loki), and by all manner of other religious luminaries from around the world and across time.

The whole Mount Olympus gang is here. An ancient Greek Chorus has popped up, in full throat—somewhat to the annoyance of many of the guests. Joshua and Moses are among the many eminences who have chosen to participate as well.

Four Sues are here: the one from sixth grade, still ignoring me; the one from high school who finally acknowledged me; the one at our wedding; and, of course, the Sue of today. All the old friends from the Buffalo block have come, too, as well as many other dear friends from my life. Barack Obama, a young revolutionary in his own way, chats with another one, Alexander Hamilton, as they pose with Arthur, Jerry and me—Columbia alums all—for a photograph by Edward Steichen. And while I'm on the subject of Columbia alums, that pinstripe uniform I see across the ballroom with number 3 on the back could be only Lou Gehrig.

Also here: Michael Bloomberg, as gifted at governance and business as he is magnanimous in philanthropy; Justice William

Brennan, in so many ways wisdom personified; David Rockefeller, who showed me how to carry myself; President Lyndon
Johnson, my former boss in the White House, who bobbled a
war but otherwise changed America for the better in many ways;
my cherished friend and neighbor, Marty Ginsburg; Herman
Wouk, who generously partook of our Jewish heritage with
me and who refused to autograph his book *Winds of War* for
six provincial governors from the People's Republic of China
at a dinner in my home because it was the Sabbath; both Paul
Simons, the senator and the singer; a zany Rhodes Scholar
friend from our Oxford days; Mike, a reader of mine at Harvard
Law School, who personified the nation's terrible tensions of
the bottom half of the twentieth century.

I see Supreme Court justice Ruth Bader Ginsburg, who
administered the marriage oath at the wedding of my Kathryn: "By the authority vested in me by the Constitution and
laws of the United States…" Her beautiful human qualities, her
intellect and greatness of spirit, are shared by another guest
who has honored us by coming, Vice President Al Gore—the
two also sharing more than their just due of heartbreaks. And
there's President George Washington himself, complimenting
Justice Ginsburg on her omission of the usual word "respect-
fully" from her historic "I dissent" in *Bush v. Gore*, and praising
Vice President Gore, too, for honorably declining to press his
case after the decision went against him.

President Clinton, who appointed Justice Ginsburg to the
Supreme Court and convinced Vice President Gore to be his
running mate, is hurrying this way as well, beaming with pride.

Now that I have moved on to towering presences, there's
Ford's Theatre itself, dark and empty just as it was on that memorable day when I stood in the fatal box where Abraham Lincoln

had been shot and felt down to my soul a strong connection with him, truly a mystic chord.

The Wizard of Oz original cast and L. Frank Baum are here (Tik-Tok is buzzing around), along with Jimmy Stewart, Bambi, Boris Karloff, Bette Davis, E.T., Marlon Brando, Beyoncé, all the Lassies, Billy Wilder, Edward G. Robinson, Ella Fitzgerald, George Gershwin, and W. C. Fields twisting the ear of a sniffling Baby LeRoy.

Julius Caesar, his ribs covered with bandages, is going over some maps with Alexander the Great. Others I spot: Cyrus the (yet another) Great; Booker T. Washington; Maurice Ravel (a special invite for him in honor of his Mother Goose Suite); James Taylor and John Coltrane; Hamlet's father, in his ghostly phase, while Polonius explains something or other to Walter Lippmann; Moctezuma, keeping an eye out for Cortés; Bugs Bunny; Otto von Bismarck; William Wordsworth; Peter Pan; Benito Mussolini (upside down, as in what he complains is a prejudicial photograph); Siddhartha Gautama; Rosa Parks; Paul Revere; Al Capone; Immanuel Kant (he arrived most promptly at the party); Rainer Maria Rilke holding a panther on a leash; and Ray Dalio transcendentally meditating amidst the hubbub.

Merlin and Steve Jobs have arrived with Muhammad Ali, Marilyn Monroe, and Og Mandino in tow. Did they share a cab? Possibly with Jeff Bezos? There's the man at the Giza Pyramids who wanted to buy my daughter! The city of Florence is here, too, I guess to apologize to Sue and me for its lack of hospitality to us, unintended or not.

Over there I see P. H. Viswanathan, the young man from Gujarat, India, who read an article about my blindness and wrote to offer the transplant of one of his eyes as a gift. (With deepest gratitude, I declined his offer.) Standing nearby is the man with whom I sat in meetings who subsequently jumped off the roof of a building. Just over his shoulder, far away in the smoking lounge, Albert Einstein is arranging three balls on a billiards table. An agitated Leo Tolstoy is waving a copy of his *What Is Art?* in Kazimir Malevich's face. There are Ed and Jane Muskie with the Brennans, Michael Jordan, and Bill Bradley. Just to test me, Bill fakes left and goes right, but I'm onto him. Now Senator Muskie has gone to stand arm in arm with Yitzhak Rabin, who was Israeli ambassador to the United States, a reminder of a different time in the modern world. My father-in-law, Marty Roseno, is next to the senator, poking him with a golf club to get back to the game that the three of us were enjoying with Tiger Woods. My lifelong friend and business associate, Washington's Abe Pollin, is playing night basketball with LeBron James and me on the court Abe built at my home; Thomas Edison is presenting his beta version of a light bulb for the blind. Marshall McLuhan, fascinated by the compressed-speech machine I invented, is here, trying (unsuccessfully, it would seem) to explain the principle to Johannes Gutenberg.

Mohandas Gandhi is standing nearby, all by himself, which I take to be a symbolic statement: how much more one man may be able to accomplish than entire armies and powerful empires. He won't be alone for long, though. Dr. Martin Luther King Jr. is headed his way to talk about their common experiences. I wish I were closer.

As Pericles listens, Mustafa Kemal Atatürk recites his famous 1934 letter to the Australian people, who lost so many sons (ultimately pointlessly, as usual) battling his Turkish troops on his country's Gallipoli Peninsula during the First World War: "Those Australian heroes who shed their blood and lost their lives—you are now lying in the soil of a friendly country. Therefore rest in peace. There is no difference between the Johnnies and the Mehmets; to us they lie side by side, here in this country of ours. You, the mothers who sent their sons from far-away countries, wipe away your tears; your sons are now lying in our bosom and are at peace. After having lost their lives on this land they have become our sons as well."

Other party guests nearby, among whom are Kaiser Wilhelm II, generals Douglas Haig and Curtis Lemay, and Robert McNamara, nod solemnly in agreement—unfortunately, agreement that comes too late. Winston Churchill is looking down at the floor, I suppose so that none of the Gallipoli dead might catch his eye. The Chorus now speaks of the unreasonableness of life—its unfathomable direction...the caprice that so delights the gods. Oh, yes...caprice.

I see that the *Australopithecus afarensis* "Lucy" is here, late of the Cradle of Mankind in South Africa, although that was not her name for it. She is really old—some three million years old and change—and there are much older creatures here from the broad human family. (In her day, by the way, she was addressed as Ma-ba within her circle; they tell me she finds the "Lucy" tag annoying—and unfortunately we did use it on the invitation.) Jack Benny is giving tips on the violin to Emperor Nero, while the Pony Express is represented by Ichabod Crane, attired in his finest green, who left the Van Tassel party to attend this one.

Wynton Marsalis and Raphael Mendez have asked me to join them in a rare trio for the trumpet while Andrea Bocelli and Stevie Wonder sing a dulcet duet. Elizabeth and Bob Dole seem to enjoy the performance, although not nearly as much as I enjoy their company. Bob's heroism in battle and Elizabeth's tireless attention to the caregivers of wounded warriors have made America a better place. So has Tom Hanks's support for

Elizabeth's foundation. Must explain why he's beaming nearby. Oh, and did I mention that I can see all this? My eyesight has returned. (Talk about chutzpah!)

Robert Rauschenberg, who once spoke to me as "Berg to Berg," has sidled over to complain that I offered a commission for a piece of sculpture to Frank Stella instead of to him. As Frank is standing right here, I should be a little embarrassed, but happily, he is locked in conversation with his fellow Princetonian Michelle Obama.

Speaking of embarrassing encounters, Dr. Sugar, the eye surgeon who thankfully resolved (if that's the right word) my advanced glaucoma, showed up, but accompanied by Dr. Mortson, the maladroit Buffalo ophthalmologist who ruined my eyes—much being forgiven at a party like this one, or no longer being of true importance. Hermann von Helmholtz is waving at me, probably to say something about my vision problem. A termagant landlady from Oxford is here, and an unpleasant blind Oxford professor, arguing with the unpleasant blind rabbi from the hospital in Detroit. (Some people never change.)

All the folks who read to me in my schools after I became blind are in attendance as honored guests—after all, I would not have been able to swing the party without their help. Even the dean from the law school who told me that as a blind student I ought not to attempt the law right off the bat was invited, and of course has come, hitting the hors d'oeuvres trays pretty hard, I notice. Nobel prizewinners Robert Hofstadter, Leon Lederman, Dan Nathans, Robert Solow, and Torsten Wiesel have come up to invite me for a nightcap.

Lawgivers are thick on the ground at the party. I see Thomas Jefferson talking with Jerry Brown, as Clarence Darrow listens in. Aristotle is pacing back and forth nearby, in conversation about the rule of law with Thurgood Marshall, Amal Clooney, Robert Mueller, and John Lewis.

Edmund Burke is grasping his head in his hands as he listens to two Williams: Buckley and Kristol. Although they have been asked to keep it down, the Greek Chorus is back, now intoning about the error of arrogance and attempts to disavow the past, and the sure retribution of the gods. This time it is Mao Tse-tung who stomps out, beckoning to Chou En-lai, who however does not budge from his conversation with Sun Yat-sen and George Kennan.

Sir Isaac Newton and Stephen Hawking are poking their fingers in each other's chest in some dispute. Sir Isaac is carrying some papers of his that he won't let anyone see. Stan Lee is here, as are Charles Darwin, Jonas Salk, Ralph Bunche, Ellen DeGeneres, Jack Ma, and Mark Zuckerberg, sharing a laugh. Also a VC whose name I did not catch in all the hubbub (an early investor in Uber and Spotify, natch).

All Johns Hopkins trustees for the past century and a half are gathered around an antique-looking man in a starched collar. I veer closer for a look and discover that the object of their attention is none other than Johns Hopkins himself. Despite the general din, I can hear him saying how proud he is that his bequests to the school have mushroomed into such a wonderful university, with its world-class medical school, famous hospital, and the preeminent Wilmer Eye Institute. And then he adds, "I'm also so thankful to all of you for your stewardship." More than a few eyes seem to be moistening up as I turn away.

Nearby—this must be the Mediterranean Wing—whom should I spot but Jimmy Carter, Menachem Begin, and Anwar Sadat. Mazel tov to them all for the 1978 Camp David Accords. John Lennon must agree because somewhere far across the room he has begun to sing, *a cappella*, "All we are saying is give peace a chance." Unless I'm mistaken, Johns Hopkins—Quaker that he was—is humming along with fellow abolitionist Harriet Tubman.

I excuse myself to greet Benjamin Franklin and Ralph Waldo Emerson—fellow members of the American Academy of Arts and Sciences, and far more deserving of the honor than I. I could stand here all night long, absorbing knowledge out of the air around me, the way I did at Columbia. But the band is back from its break, and my Moroccan friends Ahmed and his mother, Ilham, want to show me how well Ahmed has done since the brain operation that American medical genius had provided them.

Now I see Jay-Z; Melinda Gates; Avicii; Mr. Clean; Mindy Kaling; Bill Hewlett; Dave Grohl; Henry Ford; Kate Spade; General Ulysses Grant; Leonardo da Vinci; Robin Williams; H. R. Haldeman, standing by himself, nervously searching the crowd, probably to avoid running into Judge Sirica (John Ehrlichman flatly refused to attend); Stephen Colbert (making silly jokes to try to make Grohl and Eddie Murphy laugh).

Homer is here. He, John Milton, Maya Angelou, and Jorge Luis Borges are discussing whether music preceded poetry or evolved from it, while Henry Thoreau is trying to sell them pencils. (We sent invitations to any and all of the ancient Greek Homers, on the advice of some scholarly authorities, but only the one responded and came, so it may be that the theories that there were two Homers, or no actual Homer at all, are off base.)

Another bard, this one of Avon, has just wandered gloomily by, muttering something about life being a tale "told by an idiot, full of sound and fury, signifying …," but I miss the last word when Søren Kierkegaard shouts in my ear (in Danish no less),

"Faith sees best in dark!" I know, believe me, but tonight I'm seeing *everything*!

Others I have run into so far, some of whom I knew already, most of whom I did not, are Alexander Fleming, José Orozco, Friedrich Nietzsche (who came with Arthur Schopenhauer, but they have begun quarreling), John Keats, a guillotine, Bill Gates, Chuck Yeager, Grandmother Pauline's Singer sewing machine, Prince Peter Kropotkin, Frank Sinatra (Sue insisted that his invitation go out in the first batch), and Chuang-tzu. The Ramak—Moses Cordovero of Galilee—Yosef Caro, and the Ari, Isaac ben Solomon Luria, are debating about some complicated old book. Moses Maimonides cocks his head as he listens. Why, it's just like old times.

Harvard's Samuel P. Huntington and Columbia's William T. R. Fox have come up to me, still trying to convince me to go into a career in academe—as they had around the time I was a graduate student in Cambridge. Oprah is here, devising plans for arts centers in every town in America; Andrew Carnegie is feeding her tips on how he did it for libraries, while J. K. Rowling is asking Toni Morrison if she knows a good editor.

Brad Pitt, Denzel Washington, and Robert Downey Jr. wander by in a kind of moving rugby scrum. I hear either "prequel" or "sequel" as they shuffle by, but I am too transfixed by Paul Klee's *Vocal Fabric of the Singer Rosa Silber* to inquire further. Now, my siblings—Joel, Ruth, and Brenda—are approaching with the four sons from the Passover seder. They are explaining the basis for trust to the simple, wicked, and immature sons (the wise son already knows).

Rembrandt van Rijn says he will teach me some techniques of portraiture later in the party. Meanwhile, Babe Ruth offers pitching tips, and Jackie Robinson is squaring off to show me how to bunt. Not to be outdone, Gene Kelly promises a quick lesson in some nifty dance steps. Well, this is my party, after all. Elvis Presley, in rapt attention watching all the Christian saints, is asking me to sing "When the Saints" with him. Sue, getting into the spirit of the occasion, is asking the Everly Brothers to sing "Wake Up Little Susie" for herself and me.

Why, there's President Franklin Roosevelt sitting by the fire, deep in discussion with George Marshall, for whom my Oxford scholarship was named. Standing next to them is Eleanor Roosevelt, accompanied by the entire Upper West Side of Manhattan, including her understated statue at the southern end of Riverside Park. Honoré de Balzac and Margaret Atwood (attended by a bevy of adoring handmaidens) are offering writing advice to Gustave Flaubert, who can't be bothered, focused as he is on pacing and speaking his own words aloud. Then there's Hippocrates and Thornton Wilder and, standing next to him, President John F. Kennedy.

I notice that President Johnson—who even in this crowd is hard to miss—is now speaking warmly with Bobby Kennedy. It seems that, after all, people of good will can and do leave their old differences at the door when they come to a party like this, although the practice is unfortunately not universal. I see tears on the face of Frederick Douglass. It may be that some of the people he sees at the party—such as Napoleon Bonaparte, Tojo Hideki, Attila, and Hernán Cortés in a little huddle over there—remind him of all the misery that has been launched on humankind by monomaniacal adventurers.

The women in my immediate family are dressed in the finest haute couture, the men in white tie and tails. The entire generation above me and the generations above them are here: my mother, Sarah, and my beloved grandmother Pauline; my fathers, Albert and Carl—Carl with his big hands. My in-laws, Helma and Marty. How did they get here? They don't care; all they know is that they are dancing, and they do not have to work tomorrow. In fact, they do not have to work ever again. They are truly serene at last, able to rest in peace.

My children and their children Sacha, Lorelei, Eli, and Helena, standing near Sue, are watching all this. They do not quite recognize their ancestors twirling around them, but they do know that they are their ancestors. Having decked myself out in an Elvis outfit (including an outrageous Presleyan hairpiece), I am exhausted from having just done a turn on the dance floor with Kathryn. Her dogs Kady, Penny, and Hope, eyes agape, look on in amazement. My dear sisters Brenda and Ruth; their spouses, Jim Schmand and Richard Chaifetz; and my brother Joel and his wife, Marilyn, are here of course, along with their children—Josh and Whitney, Carly and Danny; Peshie, Rebekah, and Evan, Carl and Melissa; Cary and Stacy, Scott and Audrey, now with their own children as well. But, in fact, all the people and things mentioned in this book are here, and almost all from my life who are not mentioned have shown up as well.

The final cost for the party has not yet been determined. Fortunately, the party planner, my friend Art Linkletter, agrees with my principle: the more guests the merrier. I hope that Art will be fair, but as is usual in billing (and in life, too, for that matter), one never really knows until afterward.

I sense it is that time in the course of a party when I, as the host, ought to give a little speech, and perhaps propose a toast. I decide on both.

"LADIES AND GENTLEMEN, please allow me to say a few words," I begin. "The few words that I feel need saying to you all to honor your presence at this party are about…the future. In life, the future is scary for some, exhilarating for others. What can we, or rather, what can I, make of it?

"Permit me first to speak about biological heritage—our genes. Genes spread by force or by persuasion (all too often force). What a mishmash it all is! Virtually unpredictable at the moment of conception, like a deck of cards being shuffled.

"The genetic mix is followed by a cultural mix. After all, someone raises us, right?

"I wonder, my honored friends and things, does our genetic cocktail and its cultural garnish, its heritage, somehow lie behind our own loudly trumpeted exceptionalism in the United States?

"While we are undeniably different, are we truly exceptional…yet? And perhaps a more basic question: Will the genes and cultures from the West and East—in a grand pincer movement of all sorts of peoples—meld to produce a new, distinctive, and homogeneous people sometime in the future? Might we develop a profoundly exceptional new way forward on the path of the progress of humanity? We hope so. And as I often say, with aspiration, hope has to be the first step.

"I have a great responsibility standing here before you. What can I say to you all that informs you, affirms you, makes you feel like laughing and crying both, something unique in which you all share, in spite of the dizzying size of the invitation list?

"Hard to think of things. All the words of the world, at least the ones I know, are sitting on my tongue like pins, waiting to be unleashed. One wants to inform, please, delight, and surprise one's listeners, particularly if they have traveled forward or struggled against the arrow of time to arrive at this singular point."

(By the way, dear reader, did I mention to you that this ballroom is in something like a houseboat? Outside, there is water—a river or lake, perhaps an ocean—dappled with sunlight. It is evidently spring, or early summer. As I glance at my notes, I see that the writing is becoming smaller and smaller. Reading a talk for an audience is something I have often done in the past, although I am told I am blind.)

"Well, it's a helluva day—it sure is. The water is breaking yellow and blue and white. I notice that as the sun presses down on the dark blue water, for a moment it is as if the color from the sun, the color caught on the water, remains suspended, like ink or paint being spilled from a brush, and then the droplets separate and are dispersed. In much the same way, the color in the little crests of waves that rise up and break, which is white, seems to remain poised in slow motion, appearing as tiny bursts of light spreading briefly in the air, like starbursts. Light is so precious…"

(Pause for breath.)

At that, toward the end of this sunny day, the light begins to dim, almost imperceptibly at first. The guests sense it. So it is with every party like this: with the falling light, an ending, or rather endings, seem imminent. The party starts to wind down, and the water and the shore and the dozens of family members and ancient friends are beginning slowly to disperse like the spray from the water lapping the concrete pier and the sides of the boat. What remains undiminished, oddly, are the images of the young faces and unformed personalities of the babies— our children and their children, and one can even begin to see the faces, albeit vague at this point, of their children, and their children, and on and on, the smooth faces and little bodies of all babies. The youngsters are beginning to file out from the ballroom into the spring air out on the deck of the craft, which means that it is time for the rest of us to leave and go our separate ways.

"I COULD NOT HAVE EXPECTED all of you to stay here at my party forever," I conclude, "but we do remain, we know, in whatever etchings we have made in the character of those still living and yet to live, and on the earth that is home to all of us. So it is with great pride and comfort that we leave the children, clear-eyed and strong as we ever were and even more so, to raise anchor and move off into the waters on their own."

Here I pause. I am choked up and cannot speak. How proud I am to see my children and their children leaving for... for what, I do not know. I can only have hopes for them, and for all children. Will my grandmother's standards, which have so enriched my life, survive and bear fruit beyond me? Let it be so. In so many ways, do we not create the future we desire by honoring the past?

But then there is the cruel irony, the darker side of those admonitions and expectations: everything we old-timers at the party have achieved or hoped for seems about to be wrenched from us and vested in our young ones. That makes me feel a deeper sadness than I have ever before experienced, despite its being tempered by my pride in the children's Possibles. Yes, there is my hope for them wherever they venture, but a hope tinged with a terrible concern. Oh, how I do want to go with them, to guide them, but also to participate with them along the surely immense journey. Yet I know I must be content with having left them with some shards of what passes for wisdom and guidance. Still, it is such a saddening realization. Loss has been a hallmark of my life. Will I now be losing my children? A foolish thought…something of me, of my soul, of my wife's goodness and sense, and of my mother's and grandmother's strength and righteousness, will always be with them. That is not a loss for me, is it? No, I think you will agree that it is surely a gift.

The crowd is waiting for me to continue, but the children are showing some impatience, waiting to get the boat launch underway and move on to their own games and adventures. There's Sue, with Arthur's wife, Kim, and their sons, James and Beau, holding each other's hands. From somewhere I summon up a modicum of focus and clear my throat.

"Therefore, a toast, if you will: to those who continue…"

As I LOOK OUT OVER THE CROWD, perhaps it is from exhaustion that I feel my heart fill almost to bursting. It is a moment of immeasurable, inexpressible wonder and joy. I am no longer myself. I feel as if my skin has opened and I am nowhere and everywhere, and everyone and everywhere and everything are part of me. Suddenly there are tears running down my cheeks. Why? Why the tears? Why the joy? I do not understand. All that comes to mind is the blessing that is life. Some may call it a mixed blessing, but for me—and you may well think of me as blind to reality—it is simply an uncountable succession of blessings. But how can there be such a thing as only blessings?

You know that my luck has come on an oscillating curve: bad, good, bad, good—on the verge of beginning the life I wanted, losing my eyesight and then becoming, as in my exuberant exaggeration, the luckiest man in the world. Yet this joy that I feel now is unadulterated by pain and suffering. I have no sense of a calculation of the bad measured against the good. I consider: That I have chosen life and embraced it. That I have a golden place in life, with family and friends.

And I see something else, a scene that is so mystical, so beautiful—but so implausible, really, even at a no-holds-barred party like this one—that I unthinkingly rub my eyes (which I am not supposed to do). I see my own soul joined with Arthur's soul, just as it was written in 1 Samuel some three millennia ago: "The soul of Jonathan was knit with the soul of David, and Jonathan loved him as his own soul." How can we see souls, even here at this party? It may be my imagination; I am just about running on empty by now. Samuel goes on to say that "the Lord be between thee and me, and between my seed and thy seed, forever."

Well, I am feeling tired. It has been a long, demanding day, one very likely to fatigue anyone's senses. Just as I am not given vision, I am not much given to visions. This vision before me, coming so late in the party, is surely being offered to me not as something real, like a table or a trumpet or a galaxy, but as a benediction—that the promise Arthur and I made to each other long ago will be honored through future generations. I am not just one soul. Nor, would I suppose, are you.

Now, this is splendid—the sun itself has come to the party. The one in our own solar system, that is, to the evident excitement and joy of the Egyptian priests and also, I see, of other religious figures whose doctrines I cannot place. (I think I see Mani, although that makes me think specifically of light, and I cannot suppress a twinge of regret.) I am happy to see the sun at my party because, after all, without it we would have no heritage, and there would be no party. There would be none of us at all. So many guests are paying respects to the sun—I see even a dripping-wet Icarus, a good loser, among the knot of admirers—that I wonder whether all religions, including my own, do not somehow spring in spirit from the ancient human awe and respect for such a stupendous life-giving entity.

Standing behind the sun are all the stars and clouds of matter and forces of all sorts, giving our own petite sun an unaccustomed pride of place in honor of the occasion. The other guests passing near stare at them all in utter awe, becoming silent for a moment. Even the irritating Greek Chorus. The stars—are some of them in fact the souls of good, innocent men, women, and especially children, as well as animals, who have perished?

I think, too, of lines from the first love poem I ever wrote to Sue: "...And, my beloved, when our day is done, / Let us together hide amid a crowd of stars / Until the sun shines no more."

WHAT A GAS! And how rewarding. I've been planning this party my entire life—a blow-out thank-you gala for the myriad people living and dead, things, forces, concepts, even creatures that have helped shape my life and led me to where I am at this very moment, sitting at my desk, dictating the end of these remembrances. That's humbling enough. Why bother with Sandy Greenberg?

But another thought came to me just now, too. All these guests, even those I couldn't have met or barely know of, have been planning this party just for me at the same time. That's how the world really works, I've come to realize. We're connected across time and space—sometimes minute, sometimes infinite—with the entire history of our species, the whole of this fragile and wonderful earth. The past sets the table for the present; the present must take care to set the table for the future. That single insight, so hard-won and to me so precious, might well serve as a coda.

Epilogue

To End Blindness Forever

I often wonder if John F. Kennedy, had he lived, would have been surprised when Neil Armstrong took that first step on the lunar surface on July 20, 1969. Yes, the president had established the goal of landing a man on the moon before the end of the decade in his May 25, 1961, address to a joint session of Congress. But did he really think that something so far beyond the boundaries of existing technology was achievable in less than ten years? Or was he simply trying to wake up a slow-moving space program before the Soviets topped it again?

Apollo 11 was much on my mind when Sue and I established our End Blindness by 2020 prize. By intent, the duration between our 2012 announcement of the prize and its presentation on December 14, 2020—2,978 days—is exactly the same as the space between Jack Kennedy's address to Congress and Armstrong's first "giant leap for mankind."

I also had some of the same questions about my own motives when I announced our blindness quest. Was it really possible to end the ancient scourge of blindness within less than a decade? Or was our prize—initially $2 million, now grown to $3 million—more aspirational in nature, a signpost meant to pull together researchers worldwide to the common benefit of humanity? Now, eight years after we first made the prize public, I can say with confidence that both those are true and that the two goals have worked together in remarkable harmony.

BECAUSE BLINDNESS IS MANY DISCRETE DISEASES that arrive ultimately at the same place—the loss of sight—a more measured approach to fulfilling my *tikkun olam* might seem to have been in order. Perhaps an End Glaucoma prize, followed by an End Retinitis Pigmentosa campaign, and so on down the gamut of conditions that threaten vision. But I believed that the sheer audacity and sweeping nature of our goal—to end *all* blindness, *forever*—would demand the attention that a lesser goal might have failed to garner. And in that assumption I was quickly proved correct.

On December 12, 2012, only two months after Sue and I first announced the prize, Senators Chris Coons of Delaware and Rand Paul of Kentucky (himself an ophthalmologist) held a colloquy on the floor of the United States Senate to advocate the value of the End Blindness Prize.

As Senator Coons said: "Is this outrageous? Is this audacious? Maybe. But that is what experts said when President Kennedy stood before this Congress—in the same year, 1961, that Sandy lost his sight—and challenged our nation to put a man on the moon by the end of that decade. The best and brightest minds, the top scientists and researchers of [President] Kennedy's generation rose to that challenge and achieved his impossible dream. Now, for this generation, Sandy and his wife, Sue, have once again raised our sights and challenged the best scientific and medical researchers in the world to rise to an enormous challenge—a challenge that has been with us from the beginning of mankind.

"In the Bible itself we hear of blindness, of people who could not see with their eyes but only their hearts. For millennia, humanity has struggled to understand and overcome blindness. Yet today we have the scientific tools necessary to reach for a cure—to restore the physical sight so many of us take for granted to those who otherwise live in darkness…"

(Art Garfunkel might have put it even better when he wrote of our Call: "We are searching for nothing less than *light*.")

The following year, at the 2013 World Economic Forum in Davos, Switzerland, I attended a dinner celebrating eleven winners of the Nobel Prize. Inspired by a sudden rash impulse—and given courage, I'm sure, by our blindness prize—I approached the host, *Nature* editor Philip Campbell, and poured out to him the rationale for ending blindness. To my amazement, after a brief silence that hung in the air, he generously allowed me to give an unscheduled after-dinner talk on our concept, what amounted to an extemporaneous mission statement.

Afterward, several people came over and introduced themselves, among them the great neuroscientist Dr. Eric Kandel. He later recommended me to be on the panel of the 2014 Charlie Rose television program about blindness (*The Brain Series*), on which I described our campaign, as well as my harrowing adventure on the New York subway system. The panel discussed the technological advances in the treatment of eye disease made by guest researchers on several fronts, who themselves explained developments in such areas as gene therapy, retinal prosthesis, and stem-cell therapy, such as for nerve regeneration.

Aware of my efforts concerning blindness, Professor Klaus Schwab, founder and head of the Davos Forum, elevated the End Blindness by 2020 campaign by making it a topic for its own dedicated panel session in 2014. That session featured Dr. Joshua Sanes and Dr. Alfred Sommer, two of the world's leading medical scientists who are members of the scientific advisory board for the End Blindness by 2020 Prize. In one stroke, this raised the campaign to the level of international awareness among leaders in government, business, and technology. Momentum was building.

For the following year Professor Schwab expanded the structure of the panel, asking Susan Goldberg, editor in chief of *National Geographic* magazine, to serve as moderator, so as to give it even more weight at the forum. Researchers in the physiology of the eye at the very top of their fields participated in both forums. At that session, Susan asked me to present the objective of the End Blindness Prize. Later, Susan teamed Arthur and me up with a photographer to reenact our subway odyssey of fifty-five years earlier, as described in chapter 22. The resulting September 2016 *National Geographic* cover story, "The End of Blindness," brought widespread attention to our cause. To further highlight the campaign, the famous—and blind—operatic tenor Andrea Bocelli performed at the 2015 plenary session.

The BBC World Service's *Outlook* also devoted two programs to End Blindness by 2020. In 2018, the Public Broadcasting System of the Netherlands produced a television documentary describing the progress the End Blindness by 2020 campaign has made.

OUR SIGNPOST, IN SHORT, HAS BEEN SEEN. Our Call to end blindness forever has taken root in the public's imagination, just as landing on the moon did a half century ago. Meanwhile, the well-publicized "bigness" of our ambition has helped immensely in recruiting the necessary infrastructure for our prize.

From the outset, my intent was to establish both a national governing council for the End Blindness Prize and a scientific advisory board to help determine the winners. I had hoped to people both with America's leading lights of civic virtue and scientific and medical accomplishment, but I never dared dream that so many of those I asked to serve would agree so willingly. I truly am the luckiest man in the world to have the support of such as these.

Governing Council

· The Honorable Michael Bloomberg, founder and CEO, Bloomberg LP; philanthropist; three-term mayor of New York City
· Dr. William Brody, president emeritus, the Salk Institute and Johns Hopkins University
· The Honorable Bob Dole, statesman, United States Senator, Congressman
· The Honorable Elizabeth Dole, United States Senator, cabinet secretary, founder of the Elizabeth Dole Foundation
· Mr. Art Garfunkel, singer, poet, and actor; winner of eight Grammy Awards, including a Lifetime Achievement Award
· Dr. Morton Goldberg, chairman of the board, Foundation Fighting Blindness Clinical Research Institute
· Mrs. Susan Greenberg, educator, the White House, 1993–2001
· Mr. John McCarter, chairman emeritus of the Board of Regents, the Smithsonian Institution
· Dr. Peter McDonnell, William Holland Wilmer Professor of Ophthalmology; director, the Johns Hopkins Wilmer Eye Institute
· The Honorable Michael Mukasey, eighty-first attorney general of the United States

- Mr. Jerry Speyer, founder, chairman, Tishman Speyer Properties
- *In memoriam*, David Rockefeller

Scientific Advisory Board

- Dr. Richard Axel, university professor, Department of Neuroscience, Columbia University; Nobel Prize in Physiology or Medicine
- Dr. Constance Cepko, professor of genetics and ophthalmology, Harvard University
- Dr. John Dowling, professor of ophthalmology (neuroscience), Harvard University
- Dr. Carol Greider, Daniel Nathans Professor; director, Department of Molecular Biology and Genetics; Bloomberg Distinguished Professor, Johns Hopkins University; Nobel Prize in Physiology or Medicine
- Dr. Julia Haller, professor and chair, ophthalmology; ophthalmologist-in-chief, Wills Eye Hospital
- Dr. Eric Kandel, university professor, Department of Neuroscience; director, Kavli Institute for Brain Science, Columbia University; Nobel Prize in Physiology or Medicine
- Dr. Joan Miller, chair, Department of Ophthalmology, Harvard University
- Dr. Jeremy Nathans, professor of molecular biology and genetics, neuroscience, and ophthalmology, Johns Hopkins University
- Dr. Joshua Sanes, professor of molecular and cellular biology; director, Center for Brain Science, Harvard University
- Dr. Carla Shatz, professor of biology and neurobiology, Stanford University
- Dr. Alfred Sommer, professor of epidemiology, ophthalmology, and international health; dean emeritus, School of Public Health, Johns Hopkins University; Albert Lasker Clinical Medical Research Award
- Dr. James Tsai, president, New York Eye and Ear Infirmary of Mount Sinai

Finally comes the end point of all this effort by so many immensely talented people: galvanizing the attention and focusing the efforts of those who can actually *answer* my Call. And here again, thinking big, going deep, and daring to risk the unknown has served the End Blindness campaign more than well.

In 2017, almost five years after we had first announced the prize, I was invited to speak to 4,000 members of the International Society for Stem Cell Research gathered at the Boston Convention Center—heady territory for a guy with no degrees in the sciences. But the first time I knew for certain that this critical part of the larger plan was working came three years earlier when I delivered the keynote address at the March 2014 plenary session of the Lasker/IRRF (International Retinal Research Foundation) Initiative for Innovation in Vision Science, led by John Dowling, professor of neuroscience at Harvard University and a member of our scientific advisory board.

Leading vision scientists from around the world, representing a variety of specializations, had gathered in a single room at the Janelia Research Campus of the Howard Hughes Medical Institute. To me, this was the chance of a lifetime to further my long-held belief that a cooperative approach among investigators "across all disciplines" will best get us to the ultimate goal. And I wasn't going to waste it.

As with any great human endeavor, I told those gathered, our ultimate objective was transformative, not transactional. Our Call was for a complete and unified physiology of vision and neural function—one that recognized that individual investigations were the *sine qua non* of medical and scientific research, but not its finish line.

To end blindness, I said, we have to dream big first—we have to imagine a world in which we know *everything* about how vision works. The role of every muscle, every fluid, every tissue and cell type and construction, every gene, every protein, every inhibitory function, every neuron grouping, every chemical and electrical interaction along the neural pathway, every interaction among elements along the cascade of vision, every mechanism of natural repair, and every structural gap in natural repair. How nerve tissue grows and assumes its function. What mechanism—or *lack* of mechanism—inhibits damaged nerve tissue from regenerating, contrasted with what routinely happens beneficially when tissue in, say, the skin is damaged. Critically, we also have to know *how all these elements function together*. And then we have to make it all happen. We have to make the dream come true. Then and only then will I have truly fulfilled my Call.

I told the audience that I knew this is not the usual model applied to this sort of scientific inquiry. Physics models tend to start big and then bore down—think of Einstein's Theory of Relativity or Heisenberg's Uncertainty Principle—while medicine traditionally builds breakthroughs from the bottom up. But, I asked, can anyone here dispute the potential high clinical value that lies within a model such as I was proposing? Or the value of unlocking such answers? The value for prevention, the value for diagnoses, the value for treatments—the value most of all for those who might be able to *do* something they never rationally believed they would do again: see, be *unblind*.

I admit to holding my breath somewhat as I ended. At one level, I wondered if JFK's call for a moon landing within the decade had left jaws agape at Cape Canaveral and elsewhere: What is this nutcase president thinking? At a deeper level, though, I knew that if my holistic, top-down iteration of the Call fell flat before an audience of all-star researchers, I was most likely headed back to the drawing board with no idea where to turn next. Happily—make that joyfully—that didn't happen. My concept was very positively, even enthusiastically received at Janelia that evening.

One of the investigators in the audience did voice skepticism about the wisdom of substituting a physics-style model for the medical approach to vision. In response, I offered an analogy with automotive care. No sensible person would rely on a car mechanic who said, "I can locate and fix any problem—so long as it doesn't involve the electrical system or the computer module." A master mechanic can assess and repair across the entire system, just as particle physicists can model the existence of unseen particles or the influence of unknown forces.

I have no idea whether that was sufficient to turn the skeptic around, but if there is some insurmountable barrier standing between us and the *complete and integrated* array of whatever knowledge we might glean and gather, no one has yet shown that such an ultimate wall exists, theoretically or otherwise. Indeed, I would argue exactly the opposite: the wall is there only because we let it be. And that, as I wrote earlier, is maybe the greatest advantage of being blind: we recognize neither walls nor horizons. Our expectation is infinite.

I do know for certain that we are ever closer to the finish line of ending blindness. Whether we cross by or before December 14, 2020, or at some later date, is almost immaterial, especially now that Johns Hopkins University has matched Sue's and my audacity with an audacious act of its own: the creation of the Sanford and Susan Greenberg Center to End Blindness, to carry on my *tikkun olam* even should the prize itself disappear from memory. Between the two—our prize and the new Johns Hopkins center—blindness doesn't have a chance.

I may not be around to witness it, but before this century is out, blindness *will* disappear from the long roster of human injustices. And this, too, will be a giant leap for mankind.

The Final Word

I first met Sanford Greenberg many years ago. It was a cold and stormy night. We, however, were inside, at a party in honour of something or other, and we began talking. The subject of blindness came up, as it does with Sandy. We recalled the days before advanced reading technologies for the blind existed and how difficult it was then to be a student: Although you could have a braille typewriter, you had to rely on the kindness of strangers to read to you. And you certainly had to have an astonishing memory.

As it turned out, we'd overlapped as graduate students at Harvard in the 1960s. Sandy was still negotiating the sudden onset of blindness a few years earlier, and I had been a "reader," someone who'd answered the call for volunteers to read to blind students. I don't know why I did this—maybe the stories of my blind great-aunt had stuck in my head, or maybe it was payback for the pleasures of having been read to as a child—but there I'd been, reading away, though not to Sanford. He decided that because of this action I must be a Good Person, at least in a limited way, and we became Instafriends.

There followed the story of my mother, who had glaucoma and finally became mostly blind at the age of ninety; and the story of my father, who had macular degeneration. Thus I had two potential blindness time-bomb scenarios lurking in my genes. (So far so good, I hasten to add.)

Then followed many stories from Sanford, which by now you will have read, and which you will have been as impressed by as I was. How devastating it would have been to be told at such a young age that you would never see again. How easy it would have been to give up. What willpower and hard work it would have taken to paddle upstream against such a strong current. And how encouraging it is to others to hear that it can be done, because Sanford Greenberg did it—with a little help from his friends, but we all need that.

However, this is a life that has not been merely a dogged trudge up the hill. Hard work, yes, but also a list of stellar accomplishments and a great deal of curiosity and joy, and an enormous desire to give back to the world some of the bounty that Sandy feels he has received from it. His challenge contest, End Blindness by 2020, may not have ended blindness completely, but it's brought that goal closer. To quote Churchill, it is "not the end; it is not even the beginning of the end; but it is, perhaps, the end of the beginning."

Memoirs are what they say they are—accounts of what their writers find good to remember—but there is an implicit hope that the reader will discover something that is good to remember, too. In the case of Sandy Greenberg's memoirs, the takeaway is surely inspirational. Here is a life well lived, despite a major obstacle that would have stopped a lot of people. It's not always true that what doesn't kill you makes you stronger, but it can sometimes be true, and in Sandy's case it has been.

Thanks for the memories, Sandy. And for the numerous contributions to the well-being of the human world. Your many friends, and now your many readers, salute you.

—*Margaret Atwood*

Acknowledgments

No memoir is a solo performance, no matter the teller. We are born out of family histories. We come into a world of cultural influences and are nurtured—or sadly sometimes not—by specific individuals whose influence is inescapable. Teachers leave their imprint on us, as do rabbis, pastors, priests, coaches, mentors, lovers, the entire gestalt of our time and place and the long reach of our traditions. Even if we walk down a road alone, someone else trailblazed the space we travel through.

The blind, though, have a special need for helpers, and for those who have helped me through this life's journey, the word "acknowledgment" seems far too cold and insufficient to the cause. I prefer "gratitude" because I feel it so frequently and in such abundance—gratitude to those who opened up the world to me while I could still see, gratitude to those who led me back to full personhood once my vision had deserted me, gratitude to those who helped me build an adult life not as a person who could not see but as someone who saw in certain ways even more clearly once his sight was gone, gratitude even to strangers on a train like the compassionate orthopedist who insisted I have a bite of his cookie on that dismal train ride I described in the prologue to this book.

All of which is another way of saying that many hands have been holding the metaphorical pen as I have written this memoir and that my gratitude and reverence are boundless for every one of them: for my grandmother Pauline; my mother, Sarah, and fathers, Albert and Carl; for Sue and Paul, Jimmy, and Kathryn; for Joel, Ruth, and Brenda; for my family past, present, and future; for my college roommates, Art Garfunkel and Jerry Speyer; for my friends, my religious heritage, my community, my education, my readers and teachers and all those indispensable others who have made this accounting possible. You are my sacred litany of blessings.

Perhaps this gratitude is repeated throughout my narrative to a degree that seems excessive to you. If so, I apologize, but it is not excessive to my own heart. However my reflections twist and turn, it is central to the story of my transition as a human being. I return to these people again and again for a simple, unassailable reason: This is a book—and a life—that would not exist without them. I am on every page, true, but no matter what direction I take in thinking about my life, each track invariably circles back to one or more of those who have helped me along the way.

They, that collective assembly, have all earned my trust in them. I can only hope that I have equally earned their trust in me.

Finally, special thanks to those who have helped turn this heartfelt narrative into the book in front of you. Publisher Anthony Ziccardi, managing editor Madeline Sturgeon, and the entire team at Post Hill Press and Simon & Schuster, and my agent Steve Ross have been accommodating in the extreme and a joy to work with.

Sanford D. Greenberg
Washington, DC